POLITICAL
POWER
IN
POOR
NEIGHBORHOODS

POLITICAL POWER IN POOR NEIGHBORHOODS

Curt Lamb

SCHENKMAN PUBLISHING COMPANY

HALSTED PRESS DIVISION
JOHN WILEY & SONS
New York—London—Sydney—Toronto

Copyright © 1975 by Schenkman Publishing Company
3 Mount Auburn Place, Cambridge, Mass. 02138

Distributed solely by Halsted Press, a Division
of John Wiley & Sons, Inc., New York

Library of Congress Cataloging in Publication Data

Lamb, Curt.
    Political power in poor neighborhoods.

    Bibliography: p.
    1. Local government—United States.   2. Poor—
United States.   3. Community power.   I. Title.
JS341.L34   301.5'92'0973   75-19435
ISBN 0-470-51196-6
ISBN 0-470-51197-4 pbk.

DEDICATED TO THOSE STRUGGLING AGAINST POVERTY
AND OPPRESSION IN AMERICA WHOSE CONTRIBUTION
TO A BETTER SOCIETY IS DOCUMENTED HERE.

Acknowledgments

I gladly take this opportunity to thank many friends for their contribution to my work. As my values shift toward those emphasizing the integration of work and life, however, I find it difficult to differentiate between generosity to my "personal" and "professional" self. Individuals I once respected as teachers I now see affected me more by how they lived than what they knew. Others I approached on a personal level have greatly influenced my professional values—what is real, what is just, what is true.

I would like to acknowledge, then, in no particular order, a few of those whose gifts to me are reflected in my work. It would have fewer shortcomings if I had been more attentive to what they feel and think: Deborah Pierce, Peter Powell, Robert Dahl, Phil Brown, colleagues at Arrowstreet and the Environmental Design Group, James Barber, John Turner, Mandira Sen, Paul Smith, Janice Perlman, Casper Morsello, Neil Kleinman, Leigh Wessel, Bruce Palmer, Ann Taylor, Hayward Alker, Nancy Phillips, James Magee, Ken Schiff, Harvey Brown, Steve Atlas, Susan Mayer, New Morning Farm, Mike Lerner, Deslonde and Ron Alexander, William Foltz, Jack Spence, Phyllis Brown, Dick and Kate Clark, Gabrielle Yablonsky, Louis Bakanowsky, John Mollenkopf, Masaka Nakagawa, Roberta Hatch.

Several institutions deserve mention for material support of the work reported on here. Original data (and some derived indicators) were made available through Barss Reitzel and

vii

Associates, Cambridge, Massachusetts. Stanley Greenberg, Project Director for the Five City Analysis; Larry Barss, President, Barss Reitzel and Associates; and Bruce Jacobs, Project Director of the data analysis for the Office of Economic Opportunity, were especially helpful.

A grant from the Urban Studies Program, Yale University, under the auspices of Joel Fleishman, Associate Provost for Urban Studies and Programs, was a great help in meeting research expenses. Computer time was made available at several points through the Political Science Department, Yale University. Helpful in the arrangements were David Mahew, Bruce Russett, Charles Taylor, Jeffrey Milstein, and Robin Nadel.

Finally, an impossibly few words to my parents, whose generosity has provided the strongest foundation for my self-actualization, and whose intelligent concern for the human situation is my strongest prompting to give others my best.

Contents

List of Tables

List of Figures

Introduction

The lively era of government support for political militance in poor neighborhoods is over. Headstart positions no longer serve as employment blinds for penniless organizers. Maximum feasible participation and its associates—model cities, community mental health, poverty law—have fallen on hard times. Presidential closedown of the War on Poverty has been so hasty that federal judges label it a breach of executive power.

The benign neglect of government seems to reflect a quiescent mood in poor neighborhoods themselves. Black Panthers no longer monopolize headlines or court dockets. Americans have stopped anticipating summers filled with rebellious citizens, police actions, and large scale moves on the national capital. Bobby Seale is running for elective office.

There is a curious convergence of opinion on these events. Both far right and far left—those most sympathetic and those most opposed to neighborhood militance—agree on important points. Both feel, for example, that for all the protest over the last decade, no measurable change has been accomplished.[1] Both hold that government support of local militance was a faulty approach from the start.

Is this picture of events correct? Was the era of political militance on the part of poor and blacks a false start? Have we now regained an earlier status quo in which new political dynamics can begin to operate—the invisible hand of the right, or the raised fist of the left? Those concerned with social and political change

throughout society should not accept this interpretation unques-
tioningly, for it deeply compromises the rationale for political
militance on the part of other social groups.

Poor and blacks have experienced the broadest movement
toward political revitalization of recent years. Many others,
however, are now coming to the conclusion that oppression is a
matter of degree, that all of us, in some aspect of our lives, are as
under-represented and manipulated as the poor are in central
aspects of theirs; the scholarship student, wondering what
financial independence means when it buys dependence on a
college administration; the Republican housewife, under a Republican President, wondering how politics relates to her sur-
render of a job when only men were promoted; a prisoner pondering
rehabilitation by an institution locking him into a life of crime.

Can these persons learn from the experience of poor and blacks?
The wisdom of far right and left argues no. The analysis to be presented here finds otherwise. Our evidence supports a perspective
that has been overshadowed by the kind of thinking described
above. This perspective holds that militant political action *is*
effective, whether or not supported by government. It does not see
overall change in the situation of the poor as great, but cites as
reasons: first, that too few neighborhoods have been organized,
and second, that government has repeatedly failed to back programs that would capitalize on the energy generated by earlier
mobilization efforts.

The following chapters document the political situation in
poor neighborhoods during the early years of their awakening. It
is not a universally bright picture. Many neighborhoods were
passed by entirely. None affected its poverty in a profound way.
Some progress was registered, however, and this study presents
compelling proof that it was achieved primarily by those neighborhoods most militantly organized for their own interest.

The individual neighborhoods of this study (100 communities
nationwide were involved) are no longer at the particular stage
of development reported on here. Evidence concerns change
over a five year period, 1964-1969. Some neighborhoods have
undoubtedly grown more active with time, others less. Their
experience in the early stages of political development is particularly relevant now, however, because it speaks directly to
the situation of those only recently organized for political change
in other areas.

If others are to learn from the experience of the poor, the dialogue concerning that experience must move from a rhetorical to a factual plane. Political revitalization—mobilization for effective political action—is a complex phenomenon. Empirical analysis has rarely addressed issues involving, at the same time, cultural values, political action, and changes effected by action. We enter this realm through evidence generated by an unusual project, the Local Change Study, in which a broad series of questions were posed to a dozen kinds of persons (over 8,000 in all) in 100 poor neighborhoods nationwide.

The nominal purpose of the Local Change Study was to advise the Office of Economic Opportunity (OEO) on the effectiveness of its Community Action Program (CAP). Data gathering and analysis for the report took several years and cost the government upwards of one million dollars.[2] In conjunction with the project, the following groups of individuals were interviewed between August, 1968 and January, 1969.*

General Residents

In 100 neighborhoods (chosen from CAP "target areas" in cities over 50,000 in population), 40 residents per neighborhood were interviewed concerning persons they considered to be local leaders (Appendix B lists the 100 locations). These residents were also asked a brief series of questions concerning their perception of local problems, group activities and socio-economic status. In neighborhoods of five cities chosen for intensive analysis, 1,114 residents were asked an extended series of questions concerning their socio-economic status, community involvement, political values and activities, racial attitudes, and the like.

Leaders of the Poor

A total of 630 leaders, nominated as such by general residents, were interviewed in the 100 communities. In sessions averaging an hour and a half, each was asked the extended series of questions described above.

*Those interested in the methodology of the study, sampling and reliability considerations, interviewer training, instrument construction, working definitions, analytic framework, and so on, are referred to Appendix A, "Survey Methodology."

Organization Heads

In each of the 100 communities, heads of 3 local organizations were interviewed. The questionnaire for this group, designed by National Opinion Research Center, treated respondents as "expert informants" concerning levels of political mobilization in their communities.

Institutional Leaders

In each neighborhood, 3 PTA presidents, 3 private welfare agency heads and 3 company employment directors were interviewed. Extensive questionnaires were written for each particular representative to acquire reliable information about change in his institutional sector over the period, 1964-1969.

Middle Class Control Group

Occasional reference will be made to a sample of 125 persons from a lower middle-class suburb of Detroit, useful because it allows item by item comparisons of the poor with those somewhat more affluent.*

The Local Change data are unusual in several regards. Most polls dealing with similar issues have taken black America as their sampling population, when not all blacks are poor.[3] Turning to samples of black Americans at large shifts the focus away from areas of greatest political distinctiveness and need: local communities of poor people. A few surveys have dealt with poor populations.[4] They have never sampled a great number of *communities*, however, and analysis of results is generally limited to the presentation of marginals and a few cross-tabulations. The fact that the Local Change Study covers 100 communities is of the greatest importance because it allows analysis to move, with statistical rigor, to the neighborhood level. Studies of political culture, even at the grandest scale, rarely move to the collective

---

*Readers should be aware that certain names appear in the following pages with very precise meanings. These sample names, "general residents," "leaders of the poor," etc. are an example. Names of types of individuals and communities, "pragmatic militants," "neighborhood radicals," etc. are another. Some attribute names, "race pride," "political action potential," etc. fall into this category as well. See Appendix B for the precise definition of the samples and scales of the study.

units whose activities ultimately determine the fate of individual persons.[5] Neighborhoods, viewed by some as ". . . the last remaining unit, . . . of public confidence in our cities," are an increasingly important focus of policy concern.[6] It has been argued that neighborhoods are too ephemeral to be studied as social units.[7] We did not find this so. Clear-cut differences were discovered between neighborhoods, in values, tactics and accomplishments.

Survey analysts, intrigued by the black revolution, have tended to leave poor whites out of consideration. The challenge to study poor white communities has often been given, but rarely accepted.[8] About half of the persons interviewed for the present study were white. The Local Change Survey is unusual as well in its specification of leaders to be studied. Past polls have dealt primarily with *national* leaders and their popularity.[9] The result is good intellectual history but bad social history. Studies of local leadership have generally located those with influence by asking "experts" (academics, journalists, politicians) who they feel has the most power in the community being studied.[10] The limitations of this strategy are manifest. The Local Change Survey asked poor persons themselves who they considered to be their leaders. This procedure will enable us to examine in detail a true cross section of leaders in poor neighborhoods.

Finally, the Local Change Survey is unique in its attempt to measure change in the institutional environment of poor neighborhoods. As those familiar with survey research will know, measurement of "output" variables of this sort, and their integration into an analytic framework, is exceedingly difficult.* This approach is critical for our purposes, however, for it allows us to evaluate political revitalization as it provokes change in social institutions, not just in personal values. It is important not to mistake even change in neighborhood institutions for change in poverty levels. Nevertheless, this concrete evidence concerning progress will help us avoid fallacies of the left (that aggressive protest is good in itself), and the right (that disruption stalls progress), in favor of a perspective truer to the interests of the poor—that what effects meaningful change must be valued.

Survey analysis has many shortcomings as a technique of understanding. It does not lead to the most empathetic forms of

---

*Those interested in the approach chosen by the Local Change Study are referred to Appendix A.

knowledge, for example. The vibrant phenomenal world of personalities and situational reality rarely survives quantitative
transformation. Autobiographies of ghetto residents, organizer's
memoires, or films, are better generators of empathetic understanding. None, of course, can substitute for personal involvement.

It is equally beyond the capacity of survey research to guide
on-the-spot political decisions. Research of the present sort in
fact counts on purely local contingencies cancelling out. Personal
grudges, special opportunities for political initiatives, unexpected
issue tradeoffs can not be comprehended in analysis pitched at
the present level of abstraction.

Survey research is, however, a powerful tool for broadening
understanding in the collective and historical dimension. The
best devices for engaging phenomenal appreciation are often the
worst for fostering a wider understanding of events. Much knowledge is simply unascertainable through personal experience alone.
How can one find out whether poor women are more or less liberated than others? Will talking to one, or two, or a dozen individuals bring one closer to the answer? How concerned should one
be about violence in poor neighborhoods? Will a newspaper
feature on a sniping incident bring one closer to the truth, or perhaps more distant from it? What, finally, are the dynamics of
political revitalization in America? Can one trust mayors on this
question? Community organizers? the media? personal experience? There is no substitute for facts.

An attempt has been made to present data in a fashion which
invites interpretation. The major statistics on which conclusions
have been based are presented in the tables. Readers are urged
not to place interpretations of facts on the same plane as facts
themselves. All will be sure to find some point of disagreement
with interpretations given here. Every attempt has been made to
avoid the easy defenses of empirical science, obscure data and
obscure terminology.

Special ethical problems accompany survey research because
of its costs in time and money, both to researchers and the community itself. Questionnaire reliability, sample size, and precision
in data processing are all related to expense. The longer and
more precise an interview session becomes, the more bothersome
it is to the respondent. Selecting the most active local leaders for
special questioning represents an even greater imposition.

The Local Change Survey, on which the present analysis is

based, was indeed expensive. Over its history, the project cumu-
lated costs of $1,000,000 to its sponsor, OEO. It was not a
reasonable investment of government funds. Policy impact was
infinitesimal. The study was commissioned by an administration
sympathetic to the expansion of anti-poverty programs and was
presented, three years later, to hostile bureaucrats in an administration already committed to dismantling those programs. Sole
media coverage occurred halfway through the project when a few
statistics from the survey were quoted in a *Washington Post* feature on poverty programs. The strongest indictment of the Local
Change Study is not, however, that it was a misplaced priority.
That judgment would be appropriate if the study were part of a
serious commitment to eradicate poverty. It was not. It is, rather,
a perverse priority which gives research professionals a million
dollars to investigate a policy itself starving for funds. The Local
Change Survey was commissioned by a government increasingly
fearful that poverty programs would indeed bring the poor to a
keener consciousness of their situation. The study dutifully concluded that yes, this was a likely result of anti-poverty programs,
and tended its bill for a million dollars. The result—political
knowledge purchased at the expense of political consciousness.

The Local Change Survey, as so much of the War on Poverty,
was long on promises and short on results. Yet the information it
generated represents an unusual potential for insight into the
political situation of the poor. If this information can be reinter-
preted in a way that is useful to those seeking change in other
political situations, perhaps some part of the original promise
can be reclaimed.[12]

There are many ways in which personal values affect survey
analysis.[13] Perhaps most important, they set the agenda of research questions (those without values tend simply to ask dull
questions). Inevitably, as well, values affect the theoretical framework through which empirical results will be evaluated (again,
value free theorizing is generally dispirited theorizing). For all
their importance in setting research priorities, however, values
fall short of determining the conclusions of honest empirical
analysis. Not creative value synthesis, but the testing of value
frameworks against reality is the goal of empirical analysis. While
the philosopher or activist can prefer one idea to another on its
quality as idea, the empirical analyst must constantly turn to
his evidence for judgment. One might *want* poor persons to be

highly mobilized, or black women to be politically conscious, or confrontation to be more effective than accommodation. Once an empirical framework for evaluating these matters has been set up, however, only the evidence can provide answers. The present analysis is offered in the belief that concrete knowledge in the collective and historical dimension can be useful to those concerned with change—in the belief that, in Lenin's words, the truth is always revolutionary.

Work will be presented in three parts. Part I examines levels of political mobilization and institutional change to see precisely which strategies are the most effective in achieving change. Part II turns to a deeper analysis of the dynamics of political mobilization, focusing on popular values, neighborhood leadership, roles played by membership organizations, and the political status of poor women. In Part III we will return to the central question of the study: What lessons does the experience of poor and blacks suggest for those seeking political revitalization in other areas of society?

Part I
Political Revitalization and
Institutional Change

1 A Report on Neighborhood Protest and its Accomplishments

An analysis of political revitalization must begin on the aggregate level because it is groups, not individuals, that achieve political breakthroughs against poverty. If one child in a ghetto neighborhood attends a better school, all do. If one welfare recipient receives a larger clothes allowance, all those in the same category will. If the tenant is protected by legislation against exorbitant rent increases, so are his neighbors. The astute community organizer is constantly scheming to channel energies normally dedicated to personal improvement into activities which can bring collective gains.[1]

COMMUNITY MILITANCE

How politically active are America's poor? Is the typical poor neighborhood highly mobilized, or will we be hard pressed to find even the smallest signs of political revitalization? We put a series of questions concerning levels of local activity to the directors of three large membership organizations in each of the 100 communities studied. Questions concerned activities in their neighborhoods at the time of the study, August, 1968 to January, 1969, and trends that had occurred over the five preceeding years.

Table 1.1 summarizes the judgments of these organization heads. The display deals in attributes of *communities* and can be read simply as the percentage of communities having a given attribute.

3

TABLE 1.1 LEVEL OF POLITICAL MOBILIZATION IN POOR NEIGHBORHOODS*

Percent of Communities Possessing Attribute	Attribute
	A. *Level of Direct Action*
42%	1) Residents are "involved in" over half of following areas: welfare rights organizations, civil rights groups, nationality organizations, tenants unions, PTA.
34%	2) Typical community political organization has conducted one or more sit-in, boycott, demonstration or mass march 1964-1969.
33%	3) Community has experienced "public expressions of demands by residents" in two of the following three areas: welfare rights, community control of schools, tenants' rights.
32%	4) Turnout for "public expressions of demands" averages more than 121 people.
	B. *Level of Conventional Political Activity*
29%	5) Leaders of typical community political organization often go to see city officials about issues in the neighborhood.
39%	6) "Groups of people have made presentations before" half of the following bodies: city council committees, Urban Renewal Board, Board of Education, Community Action Agency board, Neighborhood Center Advisory Board.
28%	7) Average turnout for presentations, (see 6), is over 60 persons.
	C. *Co-ordination of Community Political Efforts*
28%	8) Typical community political organization has "worked on some issue" with half of 12 possible allies, e.g. good government groups, business groups, the mayor, the neighborhood center.
38%	9) Over two-thirds of community political organizations "work with the (CAP) neighborhood center".
40%	10) Typical community political organization and local neighborhood center have some "overlap in membership and some overlapping projects which involve some exchange of information or mutual planning."

Informants are the 287 Organization Heads in 100 communities. See Appendix C-1 for definitions and exact cutoffs.

The first entry states, for example, that in 42 percent of communities, residents are involved in over half of a series of activities. Because all percentages are roughly a third, the table can also be read as a description of the most active third of poor neighborhoods on a given attribute. On most indicators, something less than a third of poor communities show marked political vitality, strong organizations, inventive leadership, active citizenry, and close attention to the coordination of efforts toward common goals.

One of the important new forms of protest is that undertaken by the poor as consumers of government services: housing, welfare, education, etc. Such services are often considered by lawmakers and administrators to be a kind of temporary relief for those too weak to survive the rigors of the competitive struggle for well-being. Control over services, it is thus assumed, should reside exclusively with those who finance them, able-bodied taxpayers, and by proxy, their government. In some poor neighborhoods, yet a minority, this assumption is being aggressively challenged. Organization heads in one-third of the communities surveyed told us that their communities had experienced public expressions of demands in two of the following three areas: welfare rights, community control of schools, or tenant rights. Events marking these demands were attended on the average by over 150 people, a sizeable number, considering the typical neighborhood studied had about 7,000 residents. In another question, organization heads were asked whether local people were involved in civil rights, nationality, tenants, welfare rights or parent-teacher groups. In 42 percent of communities there was some participation in all, or all but one, of these concerns.

The second indicator reported in Table 1.1, "Militant Acts," is especially important and will be prominent in the following analysis (See Appendix B for scale construction). Mollenkopf, who analyzed and reported on the data from organization heads for OEO, holds this and the "Intergroup Alliances" measure to be key underlying dimensions of community militance.[2]

In only one-third of neighborhoods have the largest and most active neighborhood organizations engaged in one or more militant act (sit-ins, boycotts, etc) since 1964. It does not seem a large figure. There are few large cities without several organizations that can boast of more than one such act in five years. We must remember, however, that the figure applies to *neighborhoods,* not cities, and to *typical* not just "peak" organizations. It is hardly a picture of total mobilization that emerges from the Local Change data. Yet in a significant minority of communities there is clear evidence of militant political action.

In about a third of the 100 communities we investigated, participation in more conventional political activities was quite high. In 29 percent of the communities, for example, leaders of important local groups often "go to see city officials about issues in the neighborhood." In almost 40 percent, local persons have made presentations before three or four of the following agencies: city council committees, boards of education, urban renewal agencies, CAA and NC Boards. Of equal importance to the frequency of such visits is the number of persons participating. A small turnout can leave an official wary that he is responding to private interests masquerading as the will of the community. A large turnout, on the other hand, is likely to be taken as evidence of community-wide dissatisfaction backed by a determination to take action.

Communities vary widely in their ability to mount large scale presentations. In 37 percent, for example, the average turnout was desultory indeed, between one and fifteen. In something over a quarter, however, participation was substantial, from 60 persons upward.

Initial stages of community mobilization are often characterized by the formation of small, isolated groups with little inclination or capacity to work together. In the personalized atmosphere of neighborhood politics, inter-group frictions can be particularly destructive. Unfortunately, the multi-purpose nature of many local groups (to be discussed in Chapter 5) makes it especially likely that their interests will, in fact, collide. The Local Change Study provides evidence that in about a quarter of communities, significant actions have been taken to harmonize inter-group relations. We asked organization heads whether major local groups had "worked on some issue" with any of twelve different allies: good government groups, business, labor, private welfare, or religious groups, local foundations, the press, the mayor or city manager, other government and political leaders, the neighborhood center or its advisory board. In 28 percent of communities, the typical organization could count 5 or more of these 12 as allies in one of their activities. The extent to which local groups were coordinating plans with Community Action agencies was of special interest to the OEO sponsors of the Local

Change Study. Founding legislation of the War on Poverty explicitly mandates CAP's to foster co-ordination among local groups. In many communities it is succeeding. About four neighborhoods in ten report that most local groups work with the Neighborhood Center, have members in common with it, and participate in projects involving exchange of information or coordinated planning.

As surely as some poor communities have begun to organize in earnest, others, however, have hardly stepped onto that path. On any of the indicators we have been discussing, roughly a third of the communities investigated showed no protest activity or inter-group co-ordination worthy of the name. In 29 percent, for example, major community organizations have conducted *no* sit-ins, boycotts, or demonstrations. A third have witnessed expressions of demand in none or only one of three areas: welfare rights, community control of schools, and tenants' rights. While the most organized third counts over 120 persons at the typical demonstration, the lowest third musters no more than 50. For every community whose typical organization visits city officials often, another does so only seldom. In 31 percent of communities, groups work with less than a third of the allies noted above. In one out of five there is no contact whatsoever between the neighborhood center and important local groups.

The discovery of such strong variation between communities has important ramifications for our analysis. It is fair warning, for example, that aggregate statistics are apt to mislead. Just as strongly, however, we are warned against studies based on a small number of cases. With such variation in community militance, any single study can hope to account for only a small portion of reality. Finally, the differentials are a compelling invitation to analyze the importance of mobilization to the accomplishment of change. It is important to stop and ask how much change there is to explain in the first place. This question occupies the remainder of this chapter.

CHANGE IN NEIGHBORHOOD INSTITUTIONS

Private Welfare

The contemporary critique of private welfare has roots in a professional's revolt against programs insensitive to the political dimensions of personal improvement. Its locus has moved firmly to the local level now, however, as welfare recipients in neighborhood after neighborhood have begun to examine closely the hand that feeds them.

The most glaring problem, of course, is the patent inadequacy of resources behind private services. In Martin Rein's words, "The services themselves are as impoverished as those who use them." Until it takes its task seriously, this critique argues, private welfare must not be allowed to divert energies from solutions with real potential: a minimum income, universal free medical care, guaranteed jobs.

Private welfare agencies are seen by many as serving the wrong persons, their dedication to the needy being subtly overcome by a tendency to serve only "sympathetic" clients. Rough-housing children and independent-minded adults thus lose, respectful children and deferential adults win. Ethnic minority groups often get short-changed in programs designed and run by White Anglo-Saxon Protestants.

An entrenched paternalism can be found behind many agency practices—an attitude more easily excused if it did not go to the heart of program design. It is paternalism, however, that often keeps private welfare from the insight that lack of power, not simply lack of services, drives the poverty cycle. The fact that private welfare is in the community to give, not take, is little solace if it operates on the pattern of more exploitative local institutions whose rules are set and enforced by outsiders. Services which do not contribute to a person's confidence in problem-solving are sometimes worse than nothing, given the impossibility of private welfare ever meeting the full spectrum of its clients' needs. Until a few years ago, the housing activities of Central Newark's major settlement house consisted of classes in orange crate furnishing.

In each of the 100 neighborhoods of the Local Change Study, directors of the three largest private welfare agencies were interviewed. Many kinds of agencies are found in the sample: in Birmingham, a community center, a day nursery and a YMCA; in Detroit, a YMCA, a family service center and a senior citizens group; in Houston, a visiting nurse association, a YMCA, and a family service center; in Newark, a Jewish community center, a family service bureau, and a Boy's Club, and so on. Table 1.2 indicates how institutions such as these have responded to pressures for change over the five years prior to 1969.

TABLE 1.2 CHANGES IN LOCAL PRIVATE WELFARE AGENCIES*

Percent of Communities Having No Agency Possessing Attribute	Agency Attribute	Percent of Agencies Nation-wide Not Possessing Attribute
	A. Improvements in Amount of Service	
27%	1) Agency had 15% increase in staff and 30% increase in budget in 5 years, 1964-1969.	52%
31%	2) Agency served 15% more people in 5 year period.	38%
33%	3) Agency budget increased 55% over 5 years.	n.a.
	B. Improvements Favoring the Poor	
21%	4) Publicity Methods. Agency instituted one of the following and broadened another over 5 years: press releases, canvasses, public meetings, community announcements, radio, T.V. announcements.	32%
24%	5) Inter-Agency Co-operation. Agency increased referrals by 15% or helped set up new city-wide council of agencies.	57%
28%	6) Participation of the Poor. Agency includes 15% more poor or target area residents on board than 5 years earlier.	60%
52%	7) Services. Agency has changed kind of services it offers to fit needs of the poor over 5 year period.	77%
52%	8) Staff. Agency increased either subprofessionals, employees, or staff drawn from target area or volunteer workers by 15% over 5 years.	70%
54%	9) Poor Served. Agency increased either poor or welfare clientele by 15% over 5 years.	74%

*Informants are Private Welfare Agency Heads in 100 communities. See Appendix C-2 for N's and cutoffs. Data taken in part from Emily Starr, "CAP Impact on Institutions," Barss Reitzel and Associates, *National Evaluation of Community Action Programs*, Report No. 2, (May, 1970), pp. 28-30.

The kinds of change that a community could have experienced are listed down the center. In the left column are the percentages of *neighborhoods* in which *none* of the three agencies questioned changed in the way described in the center. The percentages thus indicate the proportion of communities found at the bottom of the heap—without any major agency changing according to a given criteria. The right column approaches the data from a new perspective, asking how many *agencies,* of the 287 surveyed, have *not* changed according to the criteria. The right column is thus an indicator of resistance to change among agencies.

As Table 1.2 makes painfully clear, in about a third of all neighborhoods there is not a single agency which has changed on any given criteria. In 31 percent of neighborhoods, for example, not a single major agency increased the number of people it served by 15 percent in the five years prior to 1968-69. In the same proportion, no agency increased its budget by 10 percent a year during this period. Only about half of agencies serving poor neighborhoods show some growth in staff (15 percent increase over 5 years) or budget (30 percent increase). For the remainder, program change, when it occurred at all, was a zero-sum game, new programs being added only when old ones could be closed down. In these latter organizations, the self interest of administrators of existing programs must be added to the conservative influences of establishment funding, middle-class parochialism, and white domination.

There is a rough hierarchy in the kind of changes that have occurred in private welfare. Many agencies have changed in ways which are not based on new values and do not require extensive commitment of funds. Two-thirds, for example, show some innovativeness in the use of publicity methods: canvasses, T.V. spots, public meetings, and so on. However, less than half have taken any steps to share power with their clientele.

The hiring of target area residents and poor persons as paid staff members has been a major goal of service reform. The presence of such persons, it is argued, insures greater sensitivity to the true needs of clients, reduces the impersonality of services, and turns agency staff into models for self-improvement, not just agents of self-adjustment.[3]

Some agencies have responded to these demands for inclusion, but not many. One quarter of poor persons live in neighborhoods where no agency has moved to involve the poor in decision-making roles; half live in neighborhoods where no one has taken steps to hire poor persons as staff members.

Equally low in the hierarchy of change is program innovation. A dozen kinds of change are included in the "services" indicator of Table 1.2 which gives prominence to the adoption of legal and consumer services and innovation in the scheduling and use of physical facilities, but also include signs of innovation in job, psychiatric, and educational services and intentions to continue government delegated projects beyond the period of indirect funding. Only one agency in four showed innovativeness according to our criteria. Some half of poor Americans live in neighborhoods where no agency has moved to change its services to meet their needs. The record concerning clientele solicitation is equally desultory. Only one agency in four has increased the proportion of poor persons or welfare recipients among its clientele by as much as 15 percent in the last 5 years.

Scores on our measure summarizing 7 areas of service change give some indication of the overall situation from the neighborhood viewpoint.[4] In one-third of communities the typical service agency has changed in only one of seven possible areas. By any standards this is grudging, half hearted progress. In another third, the typical agency changed in two or three areas, evidencing what might be labelled "subsistence change"—enough to survive in an ever-changing world, but not enough to affect program impact. In the final third, a typical agency marked change in four or more of the seven areas. Here we can begin to speak of a responsiveness to community needs. In an even smaller minority, private agencies have actually led in fostering community development and self assertion.[5]

Schools

Evaluation of education is a difficult task. Some diehard behaviorists argue that before-after tests of student performance are the only reliable way to evaluate an educational system. Others maintain, just as strongly, that this "SAT mentality" is precisely what is wrong with education. Until recently, everyone would have agreed on student-teacher ratios and expenditures per pupil as reliable indicators of school quality. Now, the Coleman report calls even these into question.[6] The Local Change Study evaluated schools by asking three local PTA presidents in each community a great variety of questions about the performance of schools as institutions.[7]

The contemporary movement for educational reform has three major currents. Although in practice their values often overlap, each has a characteristic institutional goal: open schools, freedom schools, or community schools.

The open school movement is a wholesale critique of contemporary public education—its personnel, educational materials, architecture, and philosophy. Public education, it argues, insults the curiosity of the young, saps spontaneous learning, and prepares students to succeed only in the worst of society's institutions—those based on competition, hierarchy, and the precedence of institutional over personal development. The "open school" proposed as an alternative is one where a creative chaos of learning prevails. Students instruct each other, and themselves, in an environment supportive of spontaneous search. Teachers oversee these efforts, provide resources for learning, and insure that basic skills are acquired.

The open school approach has begun to make some headway in American schools, mostly in the lowest grades where students are not expected to be fully disciplined members of society. In Britain, where half of all primary school students are in open classrooms, the approach has taken much stronger root.[8] In many American communities proponents of open schools have given up working through public education bureaucracies. Their ideas simply go further than can be accepted by educational bureaucracies pressured by parents, school boards, and legislators to maintain the status quo.[9]

The "freedom schools" movement grew from the political education program of early civil rights activists in the South. The kind of learning relevant to that situation had little in common with traditional schooling. Long sessions, in which people spoke from their experience, to each other, were found more effective than direct instruction, for example. The integration of action and reflection, in Paulo Freire's terminology, had the highest priority.[10]

Freedom schools are sought, then, by minorities who want to opt out of the "great melting pot" conception of education, and learn of their contemporary situation in preparation for taking action on their own behalf.[11]

Present-day teachers in ghetto-schools are not hostile to race awakening, but they do support the educational version of the culture of poverty hypothesis—that "cultural deprivation" is the major stumbling block to better education in poor areas. Teachers in black areas are relatively "liberal" on race matters, as their race (half black, half white), education (70 percent with some graduate training) and party preference (90 percent Democrat or Independent) suggest.[12]

They recognize the special situation of the black schoolchild. Only 30 percent feel that black children are as well off as white in getting an education. Schools themselves are generally exempted from criticism, however. Over 80 percent rank the quality of teaching staff, textbooks, and the adequacy of supplies of their schools as average or above.[13] The major problem as far as teachers are concerned is the students and their cultural background.[14] Fifty-six percent agree that "many communities provide such a terrible environment for the pupils that education doesn't do much good in the end." Even more popular is the idea that although parents are generally of good will, "far too many other influences distract the pupils." Eighty percent of teachers support this position, so inimical to ethnic nationalists. It is exactly to engage "other influences" in the community that freedom schools are proposed in the first place.[15]

A third approach to educational reform is the "community schools" movement. Advocates of community schools feel that, by design or chance, public schools are now bureaucratized to suffocation. Educational innovations are slowly reduced to a lowest common denominator through layer after layer of authority. David Rogers said of the New York school bureaucracy that ". . . a part of the system could have stopped functioning and headquarters might not even know about it for several months, so slowly does information pass through the institution."[16] Most importantly, bureaucratization leads directly to the alienation of school from community. Education suffers from the resulting segregation of life and learning. Schooling is formalized, reduced to its regulations: laboratory procedures, writing conventions, library rules, color-in handouts, unison singing, etc. The community suffers as well when one more potentially public-spirited facility stays beyond reach. Behind a school's chainlink fences, argue community school advocates, lie neighborhood basketball courts, local cinemas, community clinics, exhibition space, evening craft workshops, adult-student seminars, dining rooms for senior citizens, meeting halls for tenant groups, and above all, a staff paid by *local* revenues, which should support community development.[17] The decentralization utopia is a society serviced by an exciting confusion of schools, each responsive to a particular local community: union, church, ethnic group, commune, university.[18] We can summarize our data on change in local schools in the following manner: nowhere, in any of the hundred poor communities investigated, have schools undergone changes which would be required to turn public schools into open schools, freedom schools or community schools. Optimists might take heart from the evidence of some incremental changes in these directions. Pessimists will view the evidence as strong prompting to give up on public education entirely. Neither should overlook how low we had to define our criteria to capture any progress at all.

Table 1.3 presents data from the Local Change Study on school politics and educational innovation in poor neighborhoods. The center column describes kinds of changes a school could have experienced; the left column lists the percent of *communities* in which *no* school changed in this way, the right, the percent of *schools* (286 in all) that have not yet changed in this way. Criteria for change are slightly more stringent in the left hand column than in the right.[19]

The evidence of extensive citizen involvement with school issues in poor neighborhoods is the most striking development brought out in Table 1.3. Most large cities have by now experienced sustained conflict over school issues, frequently violent at the high school level. As early as 1966, a well-organized boycott of Detroit's Northern High School by 2,300 students ousted a local principal and led to the formation of a commission to investigate school conditions.[20] In Boston, a boycott by black students spread to a dozen schools over a period of months during 1970-71. A few situations—Ocean Hill-Brownsville, the San Francisco bus boycott—became national events.

Our data confirm how widespread citizen activity is at the neighborhood and elementary school level. In 84 percent of communities, 2 out of 3 local schools report an increase in parent

TABLE 1.3 CHANGE IN LOCAL SCHOOLS*

Percent of Communities in Which No Schools Possess Attributes	School Attribute	Percent of Schools Nation-wide Not Possessing Attribute
	A. *Improvement in Overall Resources*	
10%	1) Competency. In 5 years (1964-1969), school has experienced improved "teacher understanding of children," stronger leadership by principal, improved "quality of teaching" or has added a college counselling program.	35%
23%	2) Resources. Over 5 years, school increased physical space per student or number of black or male teachers; reduced students or student-teacher ratio by 25%; or reduced reliance on double shifts or temporary classrooms.	25%
39%	3) Personnel. School added one of following over 5 years: school-community representative, librarian, social worker, counselor, nurse, teacher aide, lunchroom supervisor, music teacher or remedial reading teacher.	46%
	B. *Adjustment to Needs of the Poor*	
32%	4) School has adopted one of following over 5 years: non-graded instruction, kindergarten, team teaching, Afro-American history, texts with integrated pictures.	33%
	C. *Increased Parent Action*	
53%	5) Responsiveness. School has responded to parental demands over 5 years in any 1 of 9 ways, e.g. given school facilities to the PTA, made school phone number more available, sought out parental ideas.	43%
3%	6) Parent Action. School has experienced a general increase in parent activity over 5 years.	23%
53%	7) PTA Change. Over 5 years PTA has increased attendance or membership by 25%, is being led by more persons with experience in community or has placed some men in leadership positions.	53%

*Informants are 286 PTA Presidents in 100 communities. See Appendix C-3 for N's and cutoffs. Data drawn in part from Emily Starr, "CAP Impact on Institutions," Barss Reitzel and Associates, *National Evaluation of Community Action Programs* Report No. 2 (May, 1970), pp. 20-23.

activity (See Table 1.3 for scale). Education was reported the center of a "moderate" or "great deal" of controversy by 80 percent of the local organization heads we interviewed. A quarter of leaders of the poor indicated that the race of local school principals had been an issue in their neighborhoods; a third, that the race of local teachers had been contested.[21] It is important to note that in poor neighborhoods, PTA's do not seem to be the primary locus of new activity. In over half of the neighborhoods we investigated, no PTA had stepped up its activity according to our criteria (a 25 percent increase in attendance or membership, more persons with community experience or more men in leadership positions). We will return later to the importance of PTA's and other community groups in effecting change in local schools.

This upsurge of community activity comes at a time when school districts are in mounting financial distress. Complaints that compensatory education favors inner-city schools notwithstanding, the education of poor children is still under-financed. A 1962 report on Chicago schools by the U.S. Commission on Civil Rights concluded that spending per pupil in predominantly white schools was 27 percent higher than in predominantly black schools, and that the average number of children per classroom in the two situations differed by 52 percent (31 vs. 47).[22]

Disparities in expenditure per pupil within a state are often extraordinary. According to Office of Education figures, in 17 states the highest expenditure per pupil is four times the lowest.[23] A crisis is emerging in the quality of school facilities as well. Graves points out that there are "approximately 1,300 elementary schools and more than 200 junior and senior high schools—more than 1,500 separate buildings—still in use that were constructed before the advent of commercial air travel, television, and sound motion pictures, many of them before the invention of the electric light bulb or the automobile. In 15 major cities in this country, 12.5 percent of all public school buildings were constructed before 1900, and more than 36 percent before 1920."[24]

Financial problems are compounded by several factors; firstly, it "costs more per child to give the educationally deprived pupil a chance to develop his full potential. . . ."[25] Secondly, in inner cities where the poor are concentrated, the tax base has shrunk just as surely as the demands on it have risen. The special competition for the inner-city tax dollar can easily be seen from

the fact that cities spend an average of 65 percent of their tax
dollar on non-school services while suburban communities
reverse the proportion with 65 percent going to education.[26]
The Local Change Study developed several indicators of
change in resources available to schools. Even on a loose measure
of general improvement (See Table 1.3 "competency") only 65
percent of all schools qualify as improving over the 5 years
prior to 1969.[27] Another indicator gave a school credit for
changing if it had improved facilities in any of eight ways: by
reducing temporary classroom use, double shifts, student-
teacher ratio or enrollment, or by increasing physical space per
student or the number of male or black teachers. Fewer changed
by this standard. In one community out of four, not a single
school changed in two or more of these eight ways. In only 11
percent did all schools show some signs of progress. In 39 percent
of neighborhoods none of the schools we investigated added
three or more of the following to their staffs in the five years
prior to 1969: school-community representative, librarian, social
worker, counselor, nurse, teacher-aides, lunchroom supervisor,
music teacher, or remedial reading teacher.

Some educational innovations, such as a changeover to open
schools, take more courage than money. Others, such as personalized attention, field trips, and community aides, are expensive.
For whatever reason, whether want of resources or disinclination to
change, an extraordinary lack of responsiveness to demands for
change is documented in Table 1.3. We have indicated certain
preliminary steps which could be taken to move schools toward
the open or freedom school pattern: adoption of nongraded
instruction, kindergarten, team teaching, Afro-American
history, and texts with integrated pictures. In a third of neighborhoods, not a single school has adopted more than one of these
innovations. In only a quarter are there signs of even subsistence
change (two schools out of three changing on at least two of the
five measures). Progress in reorienting schools toward community needs was measured as well. Included were nine signs of
responsiveness to parental activity, from making the school's
phone number more available, to opening school facilities to the
community.[28] In an extraordinary 53 percent of poor neighborhoods, not a single school was credited by the president of its
own PTA with responsiveness on three or more of these indicators. In only 17 percent was responsiveness characteristic of two

schools out of three. The vast majority of poor communities, then, are presently served by unimaginative, slow-moving educational institutions.

Employment

One of the defining characteristics of poverty is an inability to obtain fulfilling, remunerative employment. It is a problem with ramifications throughout an individual's social and interpersonal life. A classic study of workers in an Austrian village whose only factory closed down revealed that for many of those affected, sense of time grew vague as minor tasks gained salience by default, the waking day shortened by three or four hours, and rational budget planning was abandoned altogether when essentials could not be paid for on a regular basis.[29] Studies in this country show that although welfare can stave off ill effects for a while, unemployment soon takes its toll as a person cuts back his circle of friends, adjusts family relationships defensively, and extends the tentativeness of his employment status to the rest of his life.

In America, racial discrimination plays an important part in an individual's position regarding under-employment and unemployment. The statistics are incontrovertible. Although by 1951, the black median wage was approaching 57 percent of that for whites, Hill reports that since that time, "the gap between the income of white and negro workers has been growing steadily greater."[30] One-third of black men in cities report having been refused work because of their race.[31] Black youth have found their situation getting worse, not better, in recent years. As President Johnson reported in his Howard University address, "In 1948 the eight percent unemployment rate for negro teenage boys was actually less than that of whites. By last year (1964) it had grown to 23 percent as against 13 percent for whites.[32]

Under-employment can be as defeating as unemployment. In 1966 "twenty-five percent of all non-white *full time, year around* male workers earned less than $3,300."[33] Construction work, often the most readily available employment for poor males, is hard, machine-paced work, often inconveniently located. Most importantly, it is highly irregular; layoffs frequently come by the seasons and at the end of each job. As Liebow's perceptive study of a Washington, D.C. slum points out, the "don't work, don't want to work" mentality is indeed characteristic of the streetcorner world, for a simple reason: "the streetcorner man puts no lower value on the job than does the larger society around him."[34] Studies investigating the conditions which led to the Watts riot of 1965 revealed that two percent of local electrical trade workers were black, as were three percent of carpenters, four percent of auto repair personnel, three percent of printers and no boilermakers or telephone home installation men.[35]

More than race is involved. Poor inner-city residents of all colors face bleak employment prospects. A 1966 Department of Labor study found that ". . . unemployment—or subemployment—in the city slums is so much worse than it is in the country as a whole that the national measures of unemployment are utterly irrelevant." In the slums, the study continued, unemployment is typically three times the national figures, leaving one slum person in three with a serious employment problem.[36]

Many strategies for relieving employment problems are being used by the government (although the most obvious, job creation, is rarely given serious consideration). One aimed at the situation of minority workers is simply to ban discriminatory practices in employment. In July, 1965, Title VII of the Civil Rights Act of 1964 went into effect making it illegal to discriminate on the basis of race, color, religion, sex or national origin in any phase of employment. The enforcement mechanisms specified in the legislation, Equal Employment Opportunity Commissions, have proven slow and cumbersome. These have been swamped with personal complaints, few of which have been used as levers for broad scale change.

The major employment strategy of the government has been to prepare individuals for competition in the job market through training and education. Programs have been mounted through the War on Poverty (Job Corps, Neighborhood Youth Corps), the Department of Health, Education and Welfare, and the Labor Department (Manpower Development and Training). "The underlying assumption of training and remedial education programs" Garth Magnum has pointed out, "was that the fault lay in the unemployed, who needed only to be processed in order to have their employability enhanced." Unfortunately, he continues, "Experience has revealed a series of more complex phenomena. The people were deficient, but so was the system."[37] The Local Change Study focuses on one aspect of the "system," local employment practices.

The only study of comparable scope, a Riot Commission survey of 340 personnel officers of firms in poor areas, revealed much about attitudes in the business community that employs the poor.[38] Respondents were uniformly white (100 percent), well to do (66 percent earned over $15,000), well educated (40 percent have graduate training), and Protestant (58 percent). As a group they evidence the syndrome of "white racism" which the Riot Commission found so important in understanding urban violence. Most accept the proposition that they have a "social responsibility to make strong efforts to provide employment to negroes and other minority groups," but their public conscience is occupied exclusively by the problems of middle America. Two-thirds rank "control of crime" a "very serious" problem in their cities, followed by preventing violence and other civil disorder (50 percent), and race relations (46 percent). Far down the list, behind traffic (31 percent) and pollution (26 percent) comes the poverty problem they deal with every day—unemployment. They hide behind a defensive optimism concerning employment problems. Only 35 percent (seven percent *less* than the public at large) feel that blacks are treated worse than other people of similar income groups. More than the public at large, they feel that blacks have as many employment opportunities as others of similar education and income. When asked what criteria they use to select successful applicants for white collar and unskilled positions, the businessmen rank "previous experience" and "recommendations," over "performance on tests of ability" for both. These businessmen, therefore, forge one of the links in the vicious circle of poverty, by their predisposition to make offers of employment depend on past employment records. Powerful persons, *less* sensitive than the public at large to roadblocks their procedures pose for the disadvantaged, contribute to institutional oppression.

Table 1.4 summarizes Local Change data collected from 245 firms that employ heavily in poor neighborhoods. As in previous tables, employer attributes are listed down the middle, percentages of all firms not yet possessing the attribute to the right, and percentages of communities in which *no* firm possesses the attribute to the left. The data substantiates the important conclusion reached by other studies: that businessmen *acknowledge* the responsibility a non-interventionist economy places on their shoulders, but they do little.[39] Three quarters of personnel officers answered affirmatively when asked "Has your company

TABLE 1.4 CHANGE IN EMPLOYERS*

Percent of Communities With no Employers Possessing Attribute	Employer Attribute	Percent of Employers Nation-wide Not Possessing Attribute
9%	1) Recruiting Poor. Company has taken some "special steps (1964-1969) to recruit the . . . hard core unemployed."	25%
30%	2) Meetings. Company participates once a month in meetings with other businessmen "where the need to hire and upgrade the poor is a major topic."	n.a.
38%	3) On-The-Job Training. Company has been in touch with a representative of a Federal or State program about participation in a government sponsored on-the-job training project.	68%
39%	4) Summer Programs. Company has had some special summer employment program for low income youth since 1964.	64%
44%	5) Promoting Blacks. Company shows any increase in percentage of black foremen.	64%
71%	6) Hiring Blacks. Company has changed policy toward hiring blacks and increased blacks employed by 3%.	79%
73%	7) CAP Referrals. Company has called job openings to CAP agency once a month over last year and got referrals "almost every time."	87%

*Informants are 245 personnel directors in 100 communities. For N's and scales see Appendix C-4 Data drawn from Emily Starr, "CAP Impact on Institutions," Barss Reitzel and Associates, *National Evaluation of Community Action Programs*, Report No. 2 (May, 1970), pp. 9-13.

taken any steps since 1964 to recruit the type of person you would describe as "hard-core unemployed?" Only a third have provided special training opportunities for the disadvantaged, however, (36 percent have summer programs of some sort, 32 percent have contacted government officials about job training programs). In the five years prior to 1969, only one third of firms showed any increase at all in the percentage of blacks they employed as foremen. In the same period only one firm in five increased the proportion of blacks on its payroll by three percent. The average increase in percent of black employees

was a miniscule 1.3 percent (representing movement from 15.3 to
16.6 percent). These figures might be more encouraging if they
represented national averages. We are dealing, however, with
major employers of poor persons—firms operating in districts
that average 50 percent black.[40]

From the community perspective this means that most poor
persons live in neighborhoods with concerned employers but
few in neighborhoods where much improvement in employer
practices has been registered. In 70 percent of communities, at
least one of the three firms we interviewed participates in meetings "where the need to hire and upgrade the poor is a major
topic." Yet in 61 percent, not a single firm has increased the
number of blacks on its payroll by three percent in the five years
prior to 1969.

THE POOR LOOK AT LOCAL INSTITUTIONS

We turn now to the attitudes of poor persons themselves
toward this situation. Table 1.5 presents opinions concerning
local institutions of general residents and leaders of the poor.
The data reveal a deep alienation. Almost 60 percent of poor
persons feel, for example, that "police rough up people un-
necessarily when they are arresting them or afterwards . . . in
this neighborhood." Just a little under half say that children in
the local schools do *not* get a good education and that the community has no voice in decisions about the schools. We asked
those who had heard of the private welfare agencies we studied
in each neighborhood if they felt local persons had a hand in
planning and running agency programs. Forty percent said no.
On a composite scale, 56 percent of the residents at large ranked
local institutions "low."

Leaders, as Table 1.5 indicates, are even less generous in
evaluating local schools than residents at large. Nine percent
more leaders than residents feel local children do not get a good
education, 18 percent more that schools in the neighborhood
are worse than those elsewhere in the city. Concerning private
welfare and police, there is little difference between leaders and
followers, however, and on our indicator, "overall evaluation of
local institutions," both are equally pessimistic.

Both residents and leaders are somewhat more positive concerning recent progress in institutions than they are concerning
their present state. About a third of residents and leaders feel

TABLE 1.5 EVALUATION OF LOCAL INSTITUTIONS BY LEADERS AND GENERAL RESIDENTS*

Percent of Leaders Holding Opinion	Percent of Residents Holding Opinion	Opinion
		A. *Evaluation of Present State of Local Institutions*
59%	57%	1) Feel "the police rough up people unnecessarily when they are arresting them or afterwards . . . in this neighborhood."
56%	47%	2) Do not "think that children in the schools around here get a good education."
55%	44%	3) Do not feel "the community has a voice in decisions about the schools."
48%	30%	4) Feel that "schools around here are worse compared to other schools in the city."
36%	41%	5) Say "people from this neighborhood do not help plan and run the programs of [a local private welfare agency]."
		COMPOSITE SCALE
59%	56%	Rate local institutions "*low*" in present performance.
		B. *Evaluation of Recent Change in Local Institutions*
70%	73%	6) Feel "the chances of getting a job or of changing jobs are better now than they were 5 years ago."
63%	60%	7) Feel "the places that hire people from here . . . are doing more than they did 5 years ago to help people get jobs or better jobs."
51%	57%	8) Feel "the schools pay more attention to the parents than they did 5 years ago."
34%	36%	9) Think schools have gotten better in the last 3 or 4 years.
50%	18%	10) Can name a "particular employer" who has "gone out of his way to help people get jobs or better jobs."
40%	37%	11) Feel "the police treat people a little (or much) better now than they did 5 years ago."
		COMPOSITE SCALE
61%	57%	Rate local institutions "moderately high" on change over past 5 years.

*Figures calculated on the basis of those answering and not giving "don't know" answers.

schools are measurably better than five years ago; over half feel that school officials show more responsiveness than before. Almost three quarters felt when asked in 1969 that "the chances of getting a job or of changing jobs are better now than they were five years ago." One resident in five can name a specific firm that is doing more to help people get jobs. Half of leaders can. Overall, about 60 percent of residents and leaders rated recent change in local institutions moderately high. In another setting this might seem damning with faint praise. Because of our evidence concerning actual institutional change, however, we can see it rather as a generous sentiment concerning a dismal reality.

IDEOLOGIES OF LOCAL CHANGE

The separation of institutional evaluation into two parts, firstly, that concerning the present situation and, secondly, that concerning recent change, enables us to describe more fundamental ideologies of local change. Four combinations of these two evaluative dimensions are possible as shown in Figure 1.1.

Using this scheme we can locate the viewpoints of various subgroups on an ideological issue important to local leaders, community organizers and outsiders concerned with change at the neighborhood level. If an active discontent with the present state of institutions did not exist (to match the active disarray of the services themselves), creation of discontent would seem to be the first order of business. It is thus hard to imagine leaders of the poor falling into the categories of status quo or optimistic satisfaction. The possibility that the poor at large are fundamentally apathetic cannot be rejected so easily, however. Radicals might argue that cynical discontent would be a positive resource for change. The combination of deep dissatisfaction with the present state of affairs and hostility to the reformism which has characterized change to date would lead naturally to a full-scale critique of society. To those in government, however, widespread cynical discontent might suggest that programs emphasizing cooperation between public agencies and local persons are doomed from the outset. To the community organizer, a critical reformist attitude might seem the most positive, combining as it does angry insight into the local situation with an openness to the possibility of change. The same attitude should appeal to sympathetic professionals who understand how hard-headed realism can keep honesty in programs, but who fear total cynicism concerning the potential of efforts for change.

FIGURE 1.1 IDEOLOGIES OF LOCAL CHANGE

*Evaluation of Recent Change
in Local Institutions*

	low evaluation	high evaluation
low evaluation	CYNICAL DISCONTENT	CRITICAL REFORMISM
high evaluation	STATUS QUO SATISFACTION	OPTIMISTIC SATISFACTION

*Overall Evaluation of Present State of
Local Institutions*

Figure 1.2 places several groups in this matrix of ideological types: the poor in general, youth, political elites, and community workers.[41]

The white poor we interviewed fall just within the status quo satisfaction quadrant. They are led by an elite on the borderline between critical reformism and the more passive optimistic satisfaction viewpoint. White youths, with viewpoints quite close to those of blacks, are less patient than their elders. Community workers appear to have a unique role in white neighborhoods. They alone fall in the critical reformist sector. They alone pull the local consensus in that necessarily ambiguous direction which sees the present situation as deplorable but change as possible.

Blacks as a whole, by contrast, fall into the cynical discontent category. Only about 40 percent of the blacks we interviewed rated either the present state, or recent change in, local institutions moderately high. Black political elites, and even more, black community workers, however, influence community values strongly in the direction of critical reformism. Both these groups are a little less generous in evaluating institutions as they stand but much more willing to acknowledge signs of change (28 percent more black community workers than residents at large rate recent change "moderately high"). Interestingly, black youth, unlike white youth, differ from older persons not in being more cynical, but in being more optimistic, probably because of their greater participation in concrete actions for community development. The "critical reformist" outlook has strong allies in black communities, then, while in white areas it gains support only from local community workers.

With our summary of institutional change and attitudes toward it completed, we move on to the establishment of a typology of community political systems and then to an evaluation of strategies for promoting evolution in neighborhood institutions.

FIGURE 1.2 IDEOLOGIES OF LOCAL CHANGE (DATA)*

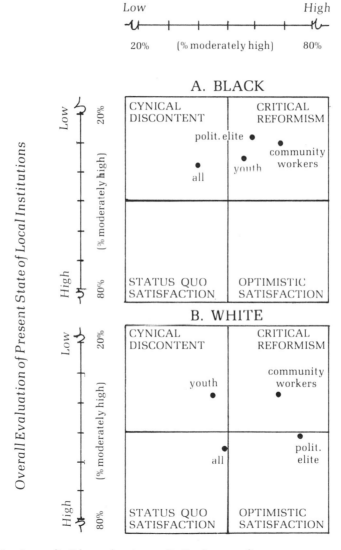

*See Appendix B for scales, Appendix C-5 for exact figures.

2 Does Militance Pay?

The early actions of the Johnson administration's War on Poverty suggest that the Federal government made a decision, however haltingly, to back neighborhood protest as a tactic for breaking the vicious circle of poverty. More recently, this strategy has fallen into disrepute, politically and ideologically. Local participation is now being dealt by a power structure experienced in sidetracking power to "local" professionals, "local" politicos, "local" bureau chiefs, "local" service managers and so on.

The last chapter presented good reason for doubting the success of the War on Poverty. Meaningful institutional change was found in only a minority of communities. The fact that ardent political activism is equally rare, however, suggests the central question of this chapter: is it only militant communities that have accomplished changes? In policy terms, has "maximum feasible participation" been stymied because it did not work, or precisely because it did? Moynihan, himself a partisan of the former view, admits that good evidence is rare: "from the point of view of social science, quite the most pernicious effect of the poverty ideology has been its tendency to discourage rigorous inquiry into the social process that keeps men in poverty and leads them out of it."[1] We present an analysis of the Local Change data in this chapter which supports the latter interpretation, that the government opted out of a strategy which might have accomplished little (because it invested little) but was on the right track in supporting local militance as an effective tool for changing institutions in poor neighborhoods.

We will begin by establishing a typology of political systems in poor neighborhoods. The categorization process will itself be a form of analysis, for we are presenting not ideal types, but types that emerged from facts concerning a hundred real communities. We can thus estimate the prevalence of each type nationwide. A set of hypotheses linking kinds of action with actual change will be suggested by the typology. The information on local institutions, reported in the last chapter, concerning changes in governing structure, service program and clientele will then be used to test these hypotheses. The analysis will point to conclusions concerning the effect of region, radicalism and race on the efficacy of political action. In the final section we will turn from communities to individuals, to describe characteristics of typical leaders in neighborhoods that have been successful in achieving change. The result will be an outline of what might be called the "political culture of activism."

A POLITICAL TYPOLOGY OF POOR COMMUNITIES

Our goal is a typology of neighborhood political systems which will help us understand the dynamics of political change. Hopefully, each variety of community in our typology will be defined by a distinguishable socio-demographic context, a particular kind of political mobilization and a unique pattern of change in local institutions. If we are successful, an examination of the typology will reveal much about the efficacy of political mobilization in accomplishing change at the neighborhood level.

It should be noted at the outset that two levels of phenomena will not be included in the paradigm—the most local and the most national. At the local level are the myriad ways in which particular neighborhood institutions differ from each other. Some agencies are led by persons of unusual dynamism, others by persons who are merely biding their time. Some suffer from overweight bureaucracies and sclerotic channels of communication. Others—often newly funded programs—are open to new ideas, responsive, self-critical. As important as these concerns are to those on the scene, it is not possible to include them in a paradigm which deals, not even in communities, but in groups of communities with shared attributes.

At the other extreme are secular trends in national politics.[2]

The first years of the period covered by the Local Change Study saw the onset of large scale urban rioting, the inauguration of the War on Poverty and a last spurt of New Deal energy under the Johnson administration.[3] The last years witnessed a closing of the cycle, as courage and budgets were emptied by an aggressive war no one would end. This larger national and historical context is central to an understanding of American poverty.[4] We cannot insist too strongly that the focusing of our data and analysis on neighborhood politics should not be taken to imply that poverty can be understood or solved at the local level. It is a national heritage of belief in individual enterprise and hostility to government initiative that keeps so many Americans living in poverty at a time of unparalleled national wealth. It is also national initiatives in employment and service programs that are most likely to bring economic justice. These considerations, however, cannot be incorporated into the framework of this typological analysis. For the moment, we rely on the assumption that this larger national and historical context affects all of our cases more or less equally. Midway between local focus and the national context, however, is a level of political reality which will occupy an important place in the analysis to follow: the city. The American federal system is not a harmonious whole. Kotler argues that the relationship between neighborhoods and cities is in fact a kind of imperialism.[5] Municipal "annexation," to Kotler, is aggrandizement by seizure. Revenues secured from neighborhoods throughout the metropolitan region are used disproportionately, to pay for the services of the downtown area. The Imperial City, in Kotler's phrase, has slowly robbed its neighborhoods of their own political vitality. Students of comparative political development have pointed as well to the tendency of urbanization to erode community involvement at the local level.[6] Two aspects of the relationship between the neighborhood and the city will be included in our typology.[7]

City Size

Our first indicator of city context is city size. All of the hundred neighborhoods under analysis here were selected from cities over 50,000 in population. Cities at the lower end of the scale, 50–100,000, however, differ in a great many ways from larger metropolitan complexes. They have, for example, older, stable populations whose growth has by and large levelled off. Typical of their political problems are redevelopment of an ailing city square, shopping center sprawl and relations with a few absentee industrial lords on whose good graces the town often depends. Pressures for involvement in federal antipoverty efforts are weaker than in larger cities. Failing high-powered city leadership, these smaller cities are likely to be ignored by federal programs (only eight percent of Americans live in the 300 cities between 25 and 100,000 population). Larger cities, by contrast, are often side-shows of ecological and human disruption. Many have burned-out neighborhoods at their core, superhighways abandoned mid-plan, polluted air and water. Most are suffering second generation crises from federal aid programs that smaller cities never got in the first place.[8] Yet with greater problems has often gone stronger commitment to action.[9]

Municipal Expenditures Per Capita

Varieties of city political culture have been studied more thoroughly than those at the neighborhood level.[10] The fate of some recent typologies of state government holds an important lesson for our effort to typologize political systems at the local level. V.O. Key's work on Southern politics began a 20-year tradition which sought in "factionalization" and "competitiveness" the central characteristic of state political systems.[11] Later research, however, points to quite a different interpretation. Recent attempts to explain policy outputs, such as school expenditures and welfare benefits in terms of political structure have found this factor completely overshadowed by differences in wealth. Richer states do more, irrespective of their political complexion.[12] It seems important, then, in our exploration of the city context of neighborhood politics to see the factors in the economic base influencing policy outcomes.[13]

The Local Change Study did not collect indicators of city political culture for the hundred cities surveyed. It would have been a complex and costly extension of research effort in an area with no widely accepted standards. We include in our typology of communities only one indicator of city political culture, but one which takes some account of variations in both the responsiveness and the resource base of communities: municipal expenditures per capita.

Proportion of City Population Black

The final dimension of city variations included in our typology is racial composition. Cities such as Gary, Buffalo and Newark, where blacks will soon be a majority, were felt to provide special contexts for neighborhood political systems. The percentage of blacks in a city's population according to the 1960 Census was included in our typology to capture this variation.

Hierarchy of Neighborhood Leadership Structure

Although city attributes (size, percent black, and municipal expenditures per capita) are prominent in our typology, variation at the neighborhood level is accorded nearly equal weight. The characteristic of local political culture deemed most critical is the degree of leadership centralization, measured by the average number of times the typical leader in a community was attributed leadership by the man-in-the-street. The figure varies a great deal from place to place. In one area we studied, the Market Street of Houston, the 40 residents interviewed named 41 different leaders, but only one leader was named more than once. In the neighborhood we interviewed in Las Vegas, there was a more even distribution. One leader was named by five persons, another by three, six more by two, and the remaining twelve by one, giving an average frequency of attribution of 1.6. East Baton Rouge falls at the other, centralized extreme. Perhaps its influence structure was affected by a crisis the neighborhood was experiencing during the period surveyed (residents were protesting the slaying of a 16-year-old youth by a local policeman). For whatever reason, the influence structure revealed by our survey was extraordinary. One man was named leader by 10 different residents (among the 40 we interviewed) and two were named six times each. The typical leader in East Baton Rouge was named by five persons, or 13 percent of all residents. Leadership hierarchy has several advantages over another measure with some appeal: total size of neighborhood leadership structure. There are serious problems of interviewer bias in the touchy area of leadership attribution, but such bias distorts a "hierarchy" measure less than one based on absolute numbers alone. An interviewer's inability to elicit names from a respondent affects the number of names he will be given, but has less effect on the overlap in names that are given.

First Characteristics of Community Types

We begin our search for community types with four variables—
the city population, percentage of black citizens, municipal expenditures per capita and the hierarchy of local leadership (weighted
twice). A numerical taxonomy program was used to reveal subclusters similar along these dimensions among the hundred communities surveyed.[14] As Table 2.1 indicates, five types emerged
from the analysis: one larger group, the passive center; two middle sized groups, reformists and defiant militants; and two smaller
groups, pragmatic militants and idle radicals.

The 13 Pragmatic militant communities (see row 1, Table 2.1),
are neighborhoods with strongly hierarchical leadership structures located in sizeable cities with large black minorities. The
idle radicals (row 5), are a group in which power is highly centralized
but which tend to be located in smaller cities without significant
black minorities. Strong differences emerge when we turn to
measures describing political action in each community type.[15]
Part B of Table 2.1 describes the political mobilization of each
community type on the basis of information collected by the National Opinion Research Center from three organization heads
per community. (Scales used in the analysis are described in
Appendix B.)

Pragmatic militant communities are active in every respect.
Over half score "moderately high" on militant acts; 62 percent
(32 percent more than any other type) show a "high" level of
intergroup coordination. They have, in comparison with other
community types, the highest frequency of contact with city officials. In over half the communities included, residents participate
in most of the following groups: welfare and tenants rights organizations, civil rights groups, PTA associations and nationality
groups. This forceful combination of broadly based organization,
strident protest and conventional political activity prompts the
description pragmatic militant. South Akron, the Hough District
of Cleveland, Pittsburgh's North Side and Case in Washington,
D.C. are among the 13 communities from our sample that fall into
this category. Appendix B presents the complete list of communities in each category.[16]

Like the pragmatic militants, the defiant militant communities
(in Row 2) are broadly organized and deeply involved in protest
activities. Unlike the pragmatic militants, however, they show
little concerted local activity among groups. Because these com-

munities are also extremely low on visits to city officials, we emphasize the anti-establishment nature of their activities in the name, defiant militants. (Evidence concerning the political world view of leaders of the poor in these neighborhoods will corroborate the decision.) San Francisco's Western Addition, Northeastern Heights in Waterbury Connecticut, Newhallville in New Haven, and the Grove Center Area in Wichita, Kansas all fell into this subcluster.

Reformist communities, 20 percent of the total, show another distinctive pattern. They are quite high on visits to city officials and average in breadth of community organization, but rather low in both militant acts by local groups and cooperative actions among groups. Emphasis is on individual political activity and administrative lobbying rather than organization and protest. Among the communities falling in this category are Riverside, Cambridge; Eastside, Youngstown; the Pruitt Igoe development area in St. Louis and Oakland's Fruitvale neighborhood.

Passive center communities form the largest of the five subclusters and score at a lower middlepoint on all levels of activity. Only one in six is moderately high in visits to city officials, one in three in militant acts by local groups or breadth of local organization. As Chapter 1 indicated, scores at the lower end of these scales of mobilization are low indeed. Racine, America Park in Lynn, Central Erie, Park Lake Seattle and Mt. Vernon in San Bernardino are all indicated as falling in this group.

The fifth and final group is unusual. On three of our four measures of activity it scores lowest of all, falling as much as 54 percent behind other community types. Only one neighborhood in ten of this type has even a moderately high level of militant acts by local groups; in even fewer is there a high level of coordinated, intergroup activity. The first half of our summary title, idle radicals, is firmly warranted by the data. The case for including "radical" as well must await the presentation of further evidence. Some of the communities that fall in this group are Logan, Santa Anna; the Hoosick Street District of Troy; South Amarillo; and Hillside, Duluth.

Figure 2.1 presents the proportions of poor communities falling into each of our five categories. The display places overall levels of mobilization among America's poor in a new perspective. Almost half of poor neighborhoods fall into two types in which political activity is desperately low—passive center and idle radicals. In a

TABLE 2.1 MAJOR ATTRIBUTES OF COMMUNITY TYPES*

(All entries are percentages of communities having a particular characteristic.)

Community Type	N	% of All Communities	A. Defining Characteristics				B. Local Political Action				
			% in Cities over 300,000 pop.	% in Cities Spending $143 up/person	% in Cities over 18% Black	% with Hierarchical Neighborhood Leadership Structure	Militant Acts (moderately high)	Intergroup Alliances (high)	Visits to City Officials (moderately high)	Breadth of Local Organization (moderately high)	Presentations Before Agencies (moderately high)
Pragmatic Militant	13	13	71	50	64	93	54	62	54	54	42
Defiant Militant	20	21	25	50	0	5	47	25	16	58	33
Reformist	20	21	25	15	70	0	21	25	47	40	39
Passive Center	32	33	47	31	31	0	29	28	16	32	46
Idle Radicals	12	12	0	42	0	100	11	8	33	22	13

*First three characteristics derived from census data (1960) in the *City and County Data Book.* For other scales see Appendix B.

TABLE 2.1 (Continued)

Community Type	C. Race**				D. Radicalism**					
	% Black in Neighborhood	Race Identity (high)	Support for Race Policies	Militant Word for Race	Major Changes Needed in Country	Poverty Caused by Political Factors	Anger at Local Situation (very angry)	Disaffection from National Government (high)	% Not Belonging to a Political Party	Alienation from Local Government (some)
Pragmatic Militant	57	35	44	60	74	26	39	26	19	20
Defiant Militant	30	34	54	58	71	33	47	50	36	45
Reformist	45	14	26	29	58	19	26	34	24	30
Passive Center	25	18	50	50	56	19	32	42	28	45
Idle Radicals	42	27	55	86	75	34	39	49	43	54

**Entries are percent of all Leaders in a community type with a given attribute.

FIGURE 2.1 TYPES OF POLITICAL CULTURES IN POOR NEIGHBORHOODS

(Figures are percent of 100 communities studied falling into each type)

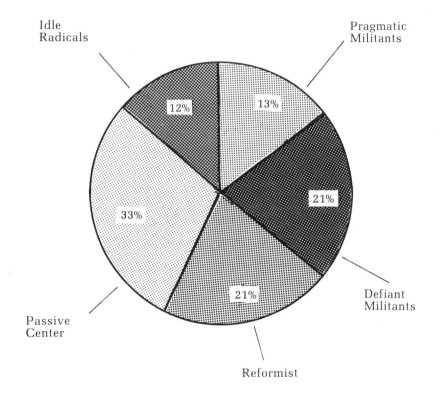

third of these communities there have been, for example, no expressions of demand whatsoever in the areas of tenants rights, welfare rights, or community control of schools. In 40 percent not a single local group conducted a sit-in, boycott, demonstration or mass march in the five years prior to 1969.

In poor communities that are active, it appears that protest oriented activity dominates the political scene. Only reformist communities (38 percent of active neighborhoods) shun protest altogether. In some cases protest is linked with a broad spectrum of political tactics but more often it appears to be emphasized to the exclusion of traditional forms of activity. In order to test empirically the effectiveness of these activity patterns we will next formulate several hypotheses concerning neighborhood militance and institutional change.

DOES MILITANCE PAY?

Any tactical political decision is based on a variety of considerations: the requirements of the issue at hand, lessons from prior action, the local balance of allies and opponents, ramifications in other areas of concern, and so on. There is an important debate, however, between those who feel that success in American politics demands compromise, cooperation and respect for the plural nature of political interests, and those who hold the opposite, that success comes primarily to those who dare to upset the balance, those willing to push others to their limits and beyond. The issue is too complex to be resolved from a single perspective, but some community organizers of a more theoretical bent have tried to outline techniques for making tactical decisions which reconcile all the elements of a specific situation.[17]

We will be examining the argument in favor of compromise or conflict at a *general* level, but with *concrete* data. The results will thus be of less interest to those seeking guidance in specific situations and of greater relevance to those seeking to evaluate or set policy at a more general level.

A Defense of Conflict Strategies for Change

> "Those who profess to favor freedom, and yet deprecate agitation are men who want crops without plowing up the ground."
>
> Frederick Douglass[18]

Overt conflict in human affairs is generally viewed as evidence of failure, the breakdown of trust and communication. There are those who argue, however, that conflict and violence are pathological only among people who form a true community, people who agree on major values. Data collected in a CBS poll in 1968 highlights the degree to which this assumption does not pertain between black and white America.[19] It reveals that three-quarters of blacks favor a minimum family income while only one white in five does. When issue dissensus is marked, a large uncommitted segment can have an equilibriating influence. Here, this silent center is exeedingly small. Half of the whites polled actively opposed such an income plan while only five percent of blacks did so. Opinions on busing and public housing were similarly divided, although concerning housing, a 38 percent minority of noncommittal whites suggests potential for compromise.[20] The survey is of particular relevance as it shows that evading issues with conflict potential would strike crucial items from the agenda of poor and blacks.

In situations of natural dissensus, actualizing latent conflict can be a progressive move. In such situations, conflict can actually promote communication among participants. Conflictual interactions have their own specific media, not discussion and debate, but legal briefs, petitions, statements to the press, and slogans.[21] Conflict can be useful to the community organizer. Events which would quickly be forgotten become newsworthy when accompanied by open conflict. A person can be ignorant of any number of public issues affecting him and still respond to conflict. People with little awareness of common ties can gain an important glimpse of solidarity in a moment of crisis. One reason for the Black Panthers' early emphasis on armed defense was the ability of this issue to move potential supporters in the black community.[22] In the words of a black professional leader in San Francisco, "It's not my style, this violence and filthy talk. . . . But, man, it makes me PROUD they stand up."[23]

Protest can sometimes be an effective means of communicating with those in power. Killian notes that in early phases of black activism in Southern communities, local elites often refused steadfastly to negotiate with the rising cadres of militant leaders. "As long as this situation prevailed," he suggests, "the structure of the situation seemed to permit only one kind of communication between the Negro community and the white power structure: formal, preemptory demands backed by the threat of legal action, political reprisal or economic boycott."[24] Matthews and Prothro found that Southern whites often respected militant blacks more than old line leaders of the black community.[25]

Saul Alinsky, perhaps the foremost strategist of political conflict in community organization, emphasizes its utility as a bargaining tactic. "A People's Organization is a conflict group. . . . The creation of any new power group automatically becomes an intrusion and a threat to the existing power arrangements . . . it is imperative that the organizers and leaders of a People's Organization not only understand the necessity for, and the nature and purpose of conflict tactics, but become familiar with and skillful in the use of such tactics."[26] Again, according to Laue, "In virtually every case of desegregation in the United States, change has come only after the development of a crisis situation which demanded rapid resolution by a community's leadership structure."[27] Frances Piven argues that advocate professionals, schooled in the liberal tradition, often fail to understand the function of conflict for the poor. Efforts of such persons to direct disorganization and frustration into "appropriate social channels," she maintains, too often short-circuit the only power left to the poor, that of disruption. More progress could be made, she suggests, if professionals would "assist the poor to get as much as possible out of turmoil."[28]

The defense of conflict-based politics can be turned into testable hypotheses concerning how much progressive change in local institutions should be expected in each of the five community types discussed earlier. Those, like Piven, who insist on disruption as the major political resource of the poor, would predict most progress in the defiant militant group where this tactic is employed to the exclusion of others. Those emphasizing the need to link protest with activities designed to consolidate gains would predict that the pragmatic militant group, in which all forms of activity are advanced, would have experienced the most change. Both, however, would agree that these communities should score higher on change than the reformist group which emphasizes conventional politics to the exclusion of protest.

The Case for Meliorative Strategies for Change

Belief in conflict is the exception, not the rule, in American politics. Conservatives, law and order partisans, and the vast majority of elected representatives and officials disagree fundamentally with disruptive political strategies.[29] Confrontation is criticized on many levels. First, it is held to be an insensitive instrument of politics, one which pursues the wrong issues, alienates potential allies, and distorts organizational priorities. Its premises are called into question as fundamental misinterpretations of American political reality. Finally, the bad money of disruption is seen as driving out the good currency of hard bargaining, debate, and compromise—the only effective techniques for accomplishing political change.

The first charge concerns the practical problems of protest tactics. Because it relies on numbers, the argument begins, protest can never be finely regulated.[30] It is difficult to get started, and once set in motion, often difficult to stop. The fires of protest burn brightly when lit, but can wane long before slow moving public disputes have been settled. Some see disruptive activity as closely tied to psychological needs, making its adjustment to changing situational realities that much more difficult.[31] Protest strategies might mobilize the more volatile elements of society, but they put off the important task of building strong organizations dedicated to persistent action on concrete issues. Pursuit of militance has become a fashion, argues Kenneth Clark, when concern for what is and isn't militant often only reduces the range of alternative actions.[32]

Protest, its critics point out, is not neutral with respect to the ends of political activity. Immediate problems such as garbage removal gain precedence over long-term ones such as new housing. Tangible abuses that can be dramatized, such as police brutality, can prevail over indirectly administered ills, such as welfare cutbacks. Status issues, such as discrimination, are favored over welfare issues such as health care.

Disruptive tactics are seen as a strategic misreading of American politics, whose genius is to accommodate diversity, make room for new interests, adjust. Protest and disruption consolidate the system. Politicians who would have responded quietly to new realities balk at capitulation to hostile forces. Aggressive demands, threats of violence, and verbal intimidation are inevitably taken personally. Alinsky's mistake, argues Kotler, himself a strong partisan of neighborhood activism, is "to imagine that a neighborhood can succeed militarily where it has failed politically."[33]

A movement's appeal to conscience is seen as irretrievably

blunted when conflict and violence intrude. Americans do not interpret disruption as evidence of concrete grievances. Matthews and Prothro, for instance, point out that half of Southern whites believed sit-ins were caused by outside agitation.[34] Penal reform is thus set back by threats to hostages; housing reform delayed by illegal squatters; governors hardened to reform by the sight of armed protestors in the halls of government.[35]

What would be the predictions of this point of view about which communities would have achieved progressive change in local institutions. Reformist communities, well organized politically and less inclined to disruption in general, would certainly be expected to have experienced the most change, defiant militants who follow the opposite program would be expected to be the least successful. It would be more difficult to hypothesize the success or failure of change in the other community types. Persons favoring any action over apathy might rank pragmatic militant communities second, while those trusting most strongly in secular forces for change might predict that even this form of activism is likely to keep communities from the "normal" progress of more patient neighborhoods.

Evaluation

Using the Local Change data we can test these predictions derived from the conflict and meliorative approaches to social change in poor neighborhoods. Each community type can be associated with the actual amount of change in local institutions achieved over the period 1964–1969. Table 2.2 presents the results.

TABLE 2.2 CHANGE IN LOCAL INSTITUTIONS BY TYPE OF COMMUNITY

Community Types	*Change in Local Institutions** (percent in upper third of all communities)
Pragmatic Militant	55
Defiant Militant	54
Reformist	35
Passive Center	22
Idle Radicals	17

*See Appendix B for scales and Appendix C-7 for exact figures.

There is a clear differentiation between types.[36] Pragmatic militant communities rank high in institutional change.[37] It appears that the combination of protest and conventional activity plus strong intergroup cooperation is powerful in bringing about change at the neighborhood level. Most significantly, the defiant militant group, in which protest is emphasized to the exclusion of conventional activity, ranks far ahead of the reformist group in which priorities are reversed. As expected, all activist communities rank above the remaining two groups in which action of any sort is less frequent.[38] Appendix C-12 presents several graphs which highlight the associations of militance, intergroup cooperation, presentations before agencies, and visits to city officials with institutional change.

Is it possible that our procedure, which looks exclusively at *clusters* of communities, obscures rather than clarifies issues? Fortunately, we have a check. John Mollenkopf examined these data through a straightforward research design focusing on individual communities and arrived at conclusions similar to those outlined here.[39]

The great importance of militant acts and intergroup cooperation in promoting change can be observed in Table 2.3 which plots these variables against each other on a community basis.

TABLE 2.3 RELATIONSHIP OF INTERGROUP ALLIANCES AND MILITANT ACTS TO CHANGE IN LOCAL INSTITUTIONS*
(Entries are percents.)

		Change in Local Institutions			
		Low	Medium	High	
	Low	46	25	29	100%
Militant	Medium	32	38	29	99%
Acts	High	22	31	47	100%
	Low	52	36	12	100%
Intergroup	Medium	40	25	35	100%
Alliances	High	11	32	57	100%

*See Appendix C-8 for citation and details.

Nearly half of communities high in militant acts score high in institutional change, while only 30 percent of those low in militance do. A community high in cooperative group action is four times as likely to have achieved a high level of institutional change as one where there is no such program.

These relationships can be observed as well in Table 2.4 which presents correlations on a community basis between institutional change and a variety of community attributes.

TABLE 2.4 INDEPENDENT CONTRIBUTION OF LOCAL POLITICAL ACTION TO CHANGE IN LOCAL INSTITUTIONS

	*Relationship to Local Institutional Change**		
	A] *Isolated Relationship (r)*	B] *Relationship Controlling for 1-7 (B wt.)*	C] *Significance of B weight*
Variables			
1) Intergroup Alliances	.42	.42	.001
2) Militant Acts in neighborhood	.19	.19	.04
3) City Government expenditures per person	.27	.14	.15
4) Blacks in city	.17	-.03	ns
5) Population of city	.14	.07	ns
6) Size of typical community political organization	.14	.07	ns
7) Number of presentations before local officials	-.06	-.20	.04

*See Appendix C-9 for data citation and details and Appendix B for scales.

The size and militancy of community organizations relate to change, but significantly, presentations before local agencies (Mollenkopf's indicator of conventional political activity) plays a much smaller role.[40] A new theme emerges as well in Table 2.4: the powerful impact of cooperation between community groups on a neighborhood's ability to achieve change. The validity of this theme is emphasized by the evidence of column B which searches for a factor's contribution to change controlling for the influence of all other factors.[41] On this basis, intergroup cooperation is seen to be the most important contributor to change. We see again that it is militant acts and not presentations before local officials which promote change.[42]

All evidence speaks clearly. In big cities and small, generous cities and tight, cities with large ethnic minorities and those without, concerted protest action by local groups helps bring change in institutions that serve the poor. The data does not counter the charge that protest alienates the powerful, but it does counter the charge that it will not bring results. At this point in time it appears to be the most effective tactic open to poor communities to change the institutions that serve them.

Changing Schools, Private Welfare Agencies and Employers

Analysis has dealt to this point in aggregate change. In this section we examine the possibility that different institutions respond in different ways to patterns of community political action.[43] Figure 2.2 indicates the degree of change experienced in each institutional sector by each community type.

While the overall pattern derives from our previous conclusion that institutional change accompanies political mobilization, there are, however, some interesting variations by institutional sector. Schools, for example, seem especially responsive to a mobilization which covers the full range of political tactics. Two-thirds of pragmatic militant neighborhoods, in which mobilization is broadly based, fall into the upper third which have successfully brought about changes in their schools, while only eight percent of idle radicals can show such a record. This suggests that pressures of a conventional kind, such as PTA resolutions, letters to the principal, and presentations downtown, are unlikely in themselves to effect rapid change in massively bureaucratized public school systems. Administrators cultivate the fiction that schools are educational, not political institutions. Indeed, all roles in the hierarchy from teacher-aide to superintendent, tend to be integrated into a system of responsibilities and values defined by the educational hierarchy. It is, however, just such "responsible" institutions that become the most political. It is these institutions which grow inflexible, unable to adapt without a struggle to suggestions for change. Schools are most effectively changed, our data suggest, not by action within accepted channels alone, but by adding to such action protest of a more aggressive sort. Only the two combined are capable of bringing about even nominal change in public education.

Jeff Raffel's analysis of the Local Change school data for OEO arrived at the same conclusion. An increase in political activity

FIGURE 2.2 VARIETIES OF CHANGE IN NEIGHBORHOOD TYPES*

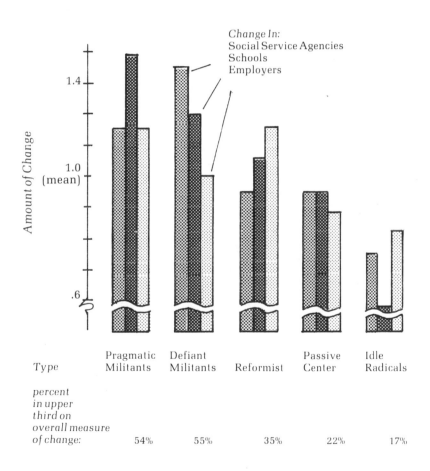

Change In:
Social Service Agencies
Schools
Employers

*Each index includes some 20 sub-areas of change. See Appendix C-10 for exact figures and n's, and Appendix B for scales.

by parents, Raffel discovered, is a better predictor of change in local schools than municipal expenditures, city size, or, importantly, increase in PTA activity.[44]

Social service agencies, in contrast to schools, seem particularly sensitive to protest tactics whether or not accompanied by more conventional political activity. Defiant militant communities have accomplished more change in private welfare agencies than any other group, including pragmatic militants, while reformist communities rank little ahead of the passive center.[45] Compared to schools, private welfare agencies are less bureaucratic, less dependent on public values, more decentralized and client oriented, all of which foster responsiveness to the local political situation. The climate of tension created by community militance appears ideally suited to inducing welfare agencies to move in creative ways to meet the needs of consumers.

Employers, as might be expected, show the least responsiveness to community militance. Businesses are service organizations only to their customers, not to their employees or neighborhoods. Most of the companies we investigated are large enterprises and thus inevitably more responsive to national economic and political currents than to local events where they happen to reside. Because business enterprise is rigorously hierarchical, it seems likely that pressures from below would have less impact on their operations than appeals from above.

THE DYNAMICS OF COMMUNITY MOBILIZATION

We have avoided characterising community types by leadership attributes. It was important, in establishing the typology, to emphasize stronger evidence concerning structural change in institutions and the levels of political mobilization.[46] It is now possible to examine political action in its cultural context. In each of the five community types we held interviews with between 52 and 216 leaders of the poor. Our strategy in this section will be to identify those attributes of political culture which accompany mobilization on a community wide basis. For this analysis we will consider community types listed on Table 2.5, to be ranged along an ordinal scale of increasing mobilization.[47] Table 2.5 presents profiles of leaders of the poor in each type of community. All entries are percentages [for example, 47 percent of leaders in pragmatic militant communities have some college education].

TABLE 2.5 POLITICAL CULTURE AND COMMUNITY TYPE*

Community Types	A. Factors Bearing Little Relation to Community Mobilization						B. Factors Contributing to Community Mobilization						
	Education (% any college)	Income (% over $6,000)	Belief in Self (% feeling they can change their life)	Belief in Planning	Sociability (% knowing a lot of neighbors)	Race (% over 81% black)	Perception of Local Problems (% naming 3)	Political Information (% moderately high)	Talk often about Community Issues	Daily Accessibility of Leaders (% high)	Articulateness (% very)	Group Membership (% belonging to 2 or 3 groups)	Action Group Members
Pragmatic Militant	47	43	72	38	85	57	75	81	83	68	84	49	79
Defiant Militant	48	53	74	42	81	30	57	70	74	44	56	36	74
Reformist	48	51	72	32	79	45	51	54	72	43	72	30	51
Passive Center	38	55	70	34	75	25	36	41	52	48	51	23	42
Idle Radicals	42	55	65	42	89	42	46	67	86	33	42	32	

*Data drawn from Leaders of the Poor in fifty cities. See Appendix C-11 for N's, & Appendix B for scales.

Most of the attributes to be discussed here will be the subject of extended analysis in the chapters to follow.

Several factors appear unrelated to community mobilization. There is little variation in income or education of leadership by type of community. The socio-economic status of community leadership as a group seems to play little role in determining how active a community will be. The Local Change study did not seek elaborate measures of personality attributes. Included in the questionnaire, however, were questions dealing with the respondent's belief that he could "change his life," and whether or not he felt it best "to live for today and let tomorrow take care of itself." No differences were found between community leaders on either question. The data thus offer no support for theories of community development emphasizing "present" versus "future orientation," or differences in attitudes toward self-improvement.[48]

Region

Before examining some aspects of political culture that did emerge as sigificant, we pause briefly to consider a demographic factor that bears an intriguing relationship to political mobilization: the region of the country in which a community is located. Communities of the passive center are found equally in the West, the Midwest, the Lakes Region, the South, and the Northeast.[49] As might be expected, the Northeast claims slight disproportions of defiant militants and idle radicals (forty and fifty percent) while something over half of pragmatic militant neighborhoods are found in the South. The proportion of communities falling into the three activist types varies little by region.[50] We found no pragmatic militant neighborhoods in the West or Midwest, however, and only one defiant militant community in the Midwest. Differences between regions thus seem to lie not in the extent of activism but in the extent to which activism has moved into militant phases. It is likely therefore that some diffusion of militance is underway, moving from home bases of local activism in the South and Northeast to other parts of the country.

Race

White ethnic activism is gaining recognition in working class communities. Among the poor, however, political militance is often felt to be the exclusive domain of blacks. Our data indicate this is only partially true. While only one in five of the fully mobilized, pragmatic militant neighborhoods is white, there are as many white neighborhoods among reformist and defiant militants as in the sample at large.[51] Again, a diffusion of militance would account for the differences, with white communities gradually adopting patterns of mobilization most fully actualized in black neighborhoods.

The dialogue, within black communities, between race values and political mobilization is a fascinating one. The fact that race identity is high among leaders in pragmatic and defiant militant communities supports our earlier conclusion that race identity is a central concomitant of political activism for blacks. Note, however, that reformist communities are *lowest* of all types in race identity. It appears that there is a path to activism, although followed by a one in five minority of active black communities, which bypasses appeals to race consciousness. Reformist communities, it should be pointed out, are not conspicuously successful in achieving change in local institutions (See Table 2.2). Idle radical communities present another interesting sub-pattern, for they are at the bottom of the heap in activism and change, yet moderately high in race identity, and extremely high in support for race political goals. For the one black community in eight in this category, heightened race consciousness is not part of a larger syndrome of effective political mobilization.

From a slightly different perspective, these findings support a conclusion to be elaborated in Chapter 3, that while race identity plays a central role in the political mobilization of blacks, support for race policies does not. Only defiant militants, of the three active types, show unusually strong support for race policies (black teachers in black schools, race voting). Black communities are not generally trapped, as some have maintained, by a narrow definition of policy objectives along race lines.[52]

Radicalism

There is an interesting interplay between political mobilization and radicalism, although the latter is a most difficult term to define adequately. All common ground in political discourse trembled when Nixon stated, as he did in 1968, "Hubert is a pleasant man, he's a plausible man, but Hubert is a sincere, dedicated, radical." For purposes of communication, a precise defini tion of terms is in order. We will use a commonly accepted definition which sees in radicalism three kinds of attitudes: belief in the necessity of large scale changes in society, class awareness, and non-support of the political system. Only two types of communities evidence a consistent strain of radical thought among local leadership: defiant militants and idle radicals. (We arrive finally at the characteristic of the latter group emphasized in its name.) Leaders in these communities, more than those in others, believe that poverty is caused by political factors and that the lot of the poor is unlikely to improve without major changes in the way the country is run. The leaders in these communities are more alienated than other leaders from national and local government.[53] The fact that the two community types in which these attitudes are found differ so profoundly suggests that radicalism among the poor appears in two distinct forms. The dominant pattern, accounting for 20 percent of all communities, adds to ideological radicalism a strong involvement in direct political action. The result is a highly successful strategy for achieving change in the local environment. A second pattern, however, which characterizes 12 percent of all communities, is quite different. In it, alienation from government and support for radical change is accompanied by an almost total absence of political activity, conventional or protest. The result is disastrous; 58 percent of these communities fall into the lowest third on institutional change. Communities in which ideological radicalism is one component of successful political mobilization outnumber those for whom the term "idle radicalism" seems more appropriate. Radicalism as such, however, is not as central to mobilization as race or the several factors to be discussed in the following section.

SUMMARY

It is not difficult to find ways in which mobilized *individuals* differ from those less active. Our search for differences between individuals living in mobilized *communities* and those who do not has been less rewarding. Class and personality do not make much difference. Race consciousness and radicalism are concomitants of action, but cut both ways. We turn in summary, however, to some clear themes in distinctions between leadership in mobilized and unmobilized communities: the importance of perceiving the concrete ills besetting one's own community; the necessity for widespread information about local political activities, and the central role occupied by local action organizations. Taken together, these distinctions form a distinct political culture of activism.

Among leaders in communities of the passive center, only 36 percent chose to describe three community problems when asked to name "the most serious problems affecting the people in this neighborhood." Twice as many in pragmatic militant communities did so. Less than half of local leaders chosen by the man-on-the-street in passive center communities have a "moderately high" level of information about local political events, whereas 81 percent of pragmatic militant leaders do.[54] Perhaps the most striking concomitant of mobilization, however, is participation in the congeries of block, militant ethnic, welfare, tenant and civil rights organizations we call "action groups." Out of ten typical leaders of passive center communities, only four belong to action groups; the figure rises to five in reformist communities; to seven in defiant militant communities and to eight among pragmatic militants.

A further difference between mobilized and unmobilized communities is found in the "localism" of community leadership. We asked each leader whether he would have been in the neighborhood "yesterday about this time" and "yesterday in the day/night." Sixty-eight percent of leaders in pragmatic militant neighborhoods said they would have been in the neighborhood both times. Only a third of leaders in idle radical communities and about 45 percent of those in the remaining types were equally as available. The results are only indicative (more precise measurement of this characteristic is possible), but they do suggest the danger of relying on leadership not committed to living and working in the local area.

The successful assault on local institutions is a political act. The political culture from which it emerges has distinctive characteristics: committed leadership with keen perception of local problems, politicized group life and militant action.[55]

Part II
DYNAMICS OF
POLITICAL REVITALIZATION

3 Political Culture in Poor Neighborhoods

In this chapter, we begin our inquiry into aspects of political mobilization with a look at the values and activities of residents of poor neighborhoods. Although some signs of potential for mobilization will be found, the overall picture will not be an optimistic one. The world view of the poor will not emerge as highly politicized—typical listings of neighborhood problems and their causes show an almost benign acceptance. Adequate information concerning local events will be found the exception, not the rule. Undercurrents of potential for revitalization will be revealed as well, however: a proto-radicalism, a strong sympathy for direct action tactics, and, among blacks, a pragmatic race consciousness, discriminating in content and strongly supportive of collective action. Succeeding chapters will focus on ways certain neighborhoods have achieved political revitalization in this environment of ambiguous commitment to political self interest.

SOCIO-ECONOMIC RESOURCES FOR POLITICAL DEVELOPMENT

Political involvement is social behavior. The personal resources that underwrite social success promote political success as well. People with education, wealth and status are, for those reasons, more likely to see their values and interests prevail over those with low status, little education and reduced income. In this section we review briefly the socio-economic status of persons interviewed in the Local Change Study to help place remaining analysis in the perspective of the objective poverty in the areas under study. Table 3.1 lists major demographic characteristics of persons interviewed.

Only seven percent of the general residents interviewed have attended any college: for other Americans the figure is close to one quarter.[1] At lower levels, free public education has reduced disparities in formal schooling greatly, although, as chapter 1 indicated, there is little cause for optimism concerning the responsiveness of ghetto schools to the needs of the poor. The difference between family incomes surveyed and those of Americans at large is $4,000. Job insecurity is widespread. Seventeen percent of those we interviewed told us they were unemployed. One in three have applied for public assistance or welfare. The same proportion have sought unemployment insurance. Over half use the state employment service for help in finding work. Scores on a composite scale indicate that one person in two faces a productive life marked by insecure employment.

The nature of community life and group involvement in the neighborhoods of the Local Change Study is the subject of Chapter 5. Here we note only the impediments to active group life implied in the demographic complexion of poor communities. Higher socio-economic strata can rely on work situations for social support: company leagues, paid vacations, union halls and so on. For poor people, however, work is frequently an isolating experience—"I only work here."[2] Underemployment, anxieties over seasonal layoffs, the affront of menial work positions, inadequate compensation—these consume rather than create resources for social involvement. Later we will ask whether other factors, such as the centrality of friendship to lower class value systems, or the politicization of group life, can overcome these obstacles to organizational vitality.

POLITICAL VALUES AND ACTIVITIES

Agenda of Community Concerns

Because policy priorities affecting the poor so often trickle down from above, it is important to ask what the poor themselves consider to be the major problems affecting their neighborhoods.[3] The first question put to respondents in the Local Change Study was an open-ended one: "What do you think are the most serious problems affecting people in this neighborhood?"

TABLE 3.1 DEMOGRAPHIC CHARACTERISTICS OF PERSONS INTERVIEWED*

Sex ratio
    55% are women.

Education
20%	None or Elementary School only
23%	Junior High School Graduate only
50%	High School or Trade School diploma
7%	Attended any College
0%	Attended Graduate School

  100.0%

Age, Median = 36
36%	16-29 years
35%	30-44 years
19%	45-59 years
11%	60 years up

  101%

Residence, Median = 11
24%	0-3 years
25%	4-10 years
23%	11-20 years
28%	over 20 years

  100%

Work Situation
  Income, Median = $5,200
11%	0-$2,000
20%	2-$4,000
32%	4-$6,000
30%	6-$10,000
7%	$10,000 up

  100%

Occupation
17%	Unemployed
22%	Housewives
14%	Retired, disabled
12%	Unskilled
19%	Skilled
2%	Community workers
11%	White collar
4%	Professional

  101%

Job Insecurity
33%	Have applied for public assistance or welfare
52%	Have applied for unemployment insurance
54%	Have gone to state employment service
49%	Experience "some" job insecurity

*Based on 1,114 general residents in five poor neighborhoods.

TABLE 3.2 POLITICAL CONCERNS OF RESIDENTS IN POOR COMMUNITIES*

Political Concerns
Number of "problems affecting the people in this neighborhood" described by residents.

17%	0
38%	1 problem
28%	2 problems
17%	3 problems
100%	

Kind of Problems cited.

17%	None
28%	Qualities of People in Neighborhood
26%	The Neighborhood Environment
10%	Bad Public Services
10%	Employment
5%	Discrimination, Oppression
4%	Educational Facilities
100%	

"Major problems about job around here."

16%	None
31%	Low Education and Training Level of People
21%	Employer Practices
15%	Operation of the Economy
11%	Personal Inadequacies of People
6%	Discrimination, Oppression
100%	

*Based on 1,114 General Residents in Five Poor Neighborhoods. See Appendix B for scales.

The answers given are listed in Table 3.2. Interestingly, the category of problems mentioned most frequently by people at large concerns attributes of their neighbors: young people, "kids are rough and there's no discipline," "kids on dope, foul language;" people at large, "the people need to clean up," "people never put down roots, don't care," and local crime. Next in importance (mentioned first by 26 percent) are aspects of the neighborhood as a living environment, poor housing most of all, but other problems as well: "the smell from the dumps is terrible," "lack of street lights," "improved roads." Poor public services are cited as problems by 14 percent of persons: "no day care centers," "very poor bus service," "police don't protect you." Another 10 percent note aspects of the economic situation: "no jobs," "old age pensions and welfare aren't enough for the sick people." Only five percent point to people or institutions outside the area as problems: "plant jobs discriminate," "racism," "poverty programs are just pacifications."

The apolitical nature is most striking. Almost one person in two either mentions no problem at all or one directed inward, at the community itself. The vast majority of those remaining are concerned with objective situations, conditions that can be remedied. The poor conceive their problems not as irreconcilable political conflicts but as problems needing remedy.

Respondents were also asked what they felt were the "major problems about jobs around here." The largest category of responses were concerned with the lack of education necessary to qualify for employment: "kids quit school," "the educational level makes it hard to qualify for jobs," "lack of education."

The fact that certain social groups are more likely to be poorly schooled than others makes education a deeply political issue. The American dream that every man can pull himself up by his bootstraps, backed by an image of education as the great social leveler, has taken the political bite from unequal opportunity. The belief of lower and working class Americans that if they had only "stuck it out in school" things would have been different diverts attention from the *institutions* of miseducation, schools and employers. "Education requirements are high, but this is so everywhere, not just here," said one respondent. Competition is tough, the attitude goes, who can blame employers for choosing the most qualified person? When responses mentioning education are added to others which state that there are no job problems at all and to those which cite other attributes (laziness, language problems, little job experience), there are 58 percent citing problems which have no political content. Even the comments (15 percent) that cite "operation of the economy" are by and large free of political content: "businesses moving out," "plants laying off people" or simply "not enough jobs," or "no work." About one person in four describes an employer practice as the major problem: "women can't get hired," "company won't train you," but only six percent of the total population mentions the deeply political issue, race discrimination.[4]

There is, of course, great variation between individuals in how problems are perceived. A black woman we spoke with in Passaic's First Ward told us, "In this neighborhood you just don't have that, not here, it's outside," and a man living nearby told us in the same vein, "I don't have the slightest idea, I don't know too many people here." Yet in the same community, a Puerto Rican man began tentatively with "It's nice around here," but continued, "the housing ain't too good, you know, everything could be better. The rent's kinda steep." Another person stated forthrightly, "drugs, crime, housing, and a fucked-up police force." Finally, in the same community, a black woman had an even longer list of grievances: "drug addiction, discrimination, unfair housing, lack of employment opportunities, discrimination in medical facilities and public services."

It is quite natural that there should be variation between individuals in problem perception. People living side-by-side can have different landlords, different jobs, different family needs. Furthermore, the ability to face and articulate life's dilemmas has a great deal to do with the ego defenses and rationales which stand watch over an individual's sense of basic security. The question thus arises, is it possible for a *community* problem consensus to emerge from the chaos of individual perceptions. We already have evidence, from the community typology of chapter 2, that the answer is yes. Communities of the "passive center" (1/3 of the total) show relatively little concern for neighborhood problems. Only 36 percent of leaders in such communities describe three different community problems. In another group, the "pragmatic militants," fully 75 percent of leaders fall into this same category.[5] It is important to note, however, that it is among *leaders* that differences between communities are strong. Bringing depth and order to the articulation of local concerns is a critical function of leadership in poor areas.[6] We return to this theme in Chapter 4.

Political information

Earlier analysis pointed to the importance of political information for community mobilization. Others have come to similar conclusions.[7] Matthews and Prothro hold, for example, that information is more important than schooling in contributing to political participation among Southern blacks.[8] Bobby Seale's highest praise for Huey Newton, his ideological mentor, concerned his facility in "rapping off information and throwing facts." "I followed Huey because he clarified . . . things to me," says Seale.[9] In an important sense, the communications media are the contemporary community organizer's best ally. Eight out

TABLE 3.3 KNOWLEDGE OF LOCAL EVENTS IN POOR COMMUNITIES*

Local Political Information
78%	Very low
15%	Moderately Low
7%	Moderately High
1%	High

101%

Knowledge of "important groups" that people in this neighborhood belong to"

63%	could name none
22%	named 1
10%	named 2
6%	named 3

101%

Knowledge of Community Action Programs

33%	have heard of local CAP Neighborhood Center.
4%	can name head of local CAP project.

Knowledge concerning Local Service Institutions

57%	know some "children who have been helped by local school programs.
34%	know a "way that people in this neighborhood can get free advice from a lawyer."
24%	can name 1 group "working to solve job problems."
24%	can name a local community newspaper.

*Based on 1,114 General Residents in Five Poor Neighborhoods. See Appendix B for scales.

of ten of his constituency are likely to have televisions, everyone radios.[10] Many will be familiar with the heroes, villains and historic events of the subculture through the national media. Eldridge Cleaver, as Cruse notes, "like many others, was first legitimized by the very mass media whose social role most of us attack as the corrupting propaganda agency of the power structure". What Third World leader, he continues, would not ". . . find Cleaver's access to publishing houses and television studios incomprehensible."[11]

There is, however, great irony in the contrast between widespread knowledge of national personalities and the desperate lack of information concerning local political events evident in the data of Table 3.3.

While three-quarters of blacks have heard of Rap Brown, Stokely Carmichael and Ralph Abernathy, 63 percent of persons we interviewed could name no important group that people in their neighborhood belong to.[12] Only a third of poor persons we talked with knew of the neighborhood center in their area or how to get free advice from a lawyer. The proportion of blacks who have heard about Ron Karenga is the same as the proportion who can name the head of the community action program in their neighborhood.

The figures do not augur well for politics in poor neighborhoods. The heightened political consciousness fostered by the national media is no substitute for familiarity with activities and issues on the local scene. Political mobilization can be imagined independent of the former, but the latter seems irreplaceable. We will consider a high level of political information in a particular social role or organization an important first sign of potential contribution to political mobilization.

Perception of problems and familiarity with local events are, in a sense, pre-political dispositions. We turn now to some more purely political aspects of local culture: views on what is and isn't political, attitudes toward the causes of poverty, and political radicalism. Some data on direct action and the kinds and amounts of political activity actually undertaken will conclude this section.[13]

Political World View

When asked directly, "What do you think of when you hear the word 'political'?" the poor answer in benign terms (see Table 3.4). A third of responses have no content at all: "just a word," "a job," "never gave it no thought." Another third refer to American political institutions: "The Congress," "the White House," "voting and elections." Only one response in five, like Bobby Seale's definition, "Politics is war without bloodshed," has a sense of the process behind politics: "debate and argument," "the means of continuing government," "the best man wins." An even smaller minority give variations on the theme of politics as unkept promises: "crooks," "living off the people," "jumping on each other's throats." Respondents were asked if they felt any of a series of specific institutions were political (see Figure 3.1). Institutions of national government receive unanimous nomination as political (although one person in ten felt the Presidency was above politics). At the other extreme, less than a quarter see either movies or libraries as political. In the middle range we find more of the tendency, already noted, to define problems facing the com-

TABLE 3.4 ATTITUDES TOWARD THE POLITICAL WORLD*

A) Definition of "Political"
   - 34% No content
   - 34% Reference to American political institution
   - 20% Process oriented answer
   - 13% Negative reference

   101%

   Views on what institutions are 'political'
   - 97% See the U.S. Congress as political
   - 65% See the Courts as political
   - 56% See schools as political
   - 48% See welfare as political
   - 36% See hospitals as political
   - 23% See movies as political

B) Views on "the most important reason that people in this city are poor"
   - 26% The job situation
   - 21% Poor education of people
   - 19% Personal character of people
   - 10% The political system
   - 10% Fate
   - 10% Discrimination, Oppression
   - 5% Don't know

   101%

*Data drawn from 1,114 General Residents in Five City Neighborhoods. See Appendix B for scales.

munity in pragmatic, nonconflictual terms. The quality of hospital care for the poor, the workings of the welfare system, job and educational opportunities are patently political issues, yet only half the persons we interviewed labelled them so. Note, however, the interesting differences between residents and their leaders. There is little difference between leaders and rank and file at the extremes. In the middle realm, however, on the cutting edge of issues affecting poor neighborhoods, community leadership is significantly more sensitive to the political component of local problems. Again we see the importance of community leadership in achieving political mobilization in the socio-cultural environment of poor neighborhoods.

We also asked respondents to reflect on the fundamental causes of the poverty that surrounds them. While it might often be astute politically to describe *problems* in nonconflictual terms, the wisdom of extending this thinking to the *causes* of problems is

FIGURE 3.1 VIEWS ON "WHAT IS POLITICAL" AMONG RESIDENTS AND LEADERS*

(Arrow at top of backet points to percent of leaders feeling an institution is political; arrow at bottom of bracket points to percent of residents who feel the same institution is political.)

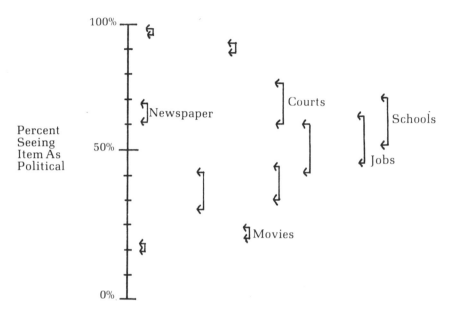

*Sample is Five City General Residents and Leaders. See Appendix B for question.

much less clear. Yet the views of the poor on the causes of poverty are as benign as their views on the problems that beset their communities (See B in Table 3.4). A quarter respond merely by citing a definitional concomitant of poverty, "not enough money," "no jobs." Four out of ten turn their attention inward, toward the community and its people, with lack of education and poor motivation receiving roughly equal emphasis. Another ten percent evidence a hopeless resignation: "you got to have some poor people," "born poor, die poor," "we were meant to be poor." A full 80 percent of people are accounted for before we find analyses which implicate government, class interest, or racial discrimination as causes of poverty.

Radicalism

We will attempt no comprehensive judgment on the radicalism of the poor here. The Local Change Survey, however, did collect strong evidence concerning aspects of a radical outlook described earlier—belief in the need for large scale change in society, class awareness and nonsupport of the political system.[14] By all these criteria there are strong undercurrents of radicalism in the political outlook of the American poor (see Table 3.5). Three-quarters of persons we interviewed find aspects of their situation which "make a person angry." Almost half feel that things will not get better without "major changes" in the way the country is run. Few are under any illusions concerning class conflict in American politics. Eight in ten agree that no matter how hard some Americans work they will never get rich. Just as many think that poor people and rich people do not agree about what the government should do.

Disaffection from national government is monumental. Seven out of ten say they don't have much voice in how the government is run, half that government is doing very little to help poor people. A quarter say they are not sure their country is worth fighting for. Seventeen percent find some truth in the "rumor about concentration camps being set up in this country."[15] Nor is support for local government strong. Four in ten feel that there are not any government officials in the city "who really care about what people in this neighborhood want." Over half say that people in the neighborhood have "very little" or "no" say about decisions made by the city government."

Remembering the benign quality of problem concerns of the poor and their hesitancy to politicize reality, we must be careful not to over-emphasize the radicalism of poor neighborhoods. The fact that on composite scales only 13 percent score "very high" in national alienation and 19 percent show a "great deal" of local alienation is instructive. If hostility to government formed a more coherent syndrome of attitudes, there would be less "deflation" of scores on composite scales. Almost three quarters acknowledge allegiance to a political party (8:1 Democratic). When we asked those who felt major changes were needed in government what those changes should be, less than half stuck to the theme of systemic transformation. Modest changes in government ("better men in office," "more honesty"), or improvement in the employment

TABLE 3.5 RADICALISM OF POOR COMMUNITIES*

A) Views on Political Change
   - 78% agree, "there are things around here which make a person angry."
   - 46% agree, "things will never really get better for poor people without major changes in the way the country is run."
     Description of this Major Change
     - 19% a revolutionary change in government
     - 11% an incremental change in government
     - 10% a change in the employment situation
     - 6% a change in the personal characteristics of people

     46%

   Some Political Demands
   - 79% believe "everyone in this country has a right to have a nice home even if he doesn't earn much money."
   - 54% believe "all people have the right to have enough money to live on, whether they are working or not."
   - 15% think it would be good if everyone got paid the same amount of money, no matter what his job was."

B) Class Consciousness
   - 77% do not think that "for the most part poor people and rich people agree about what things the government ought to do."
   - 80% agree, "in the United States, no matter how hard some people work they will never be rich."

C) Alienation from National Government
   - 72% agree, "people like me don't have any say in what the government does."
   - 68% disagree, "all in all I'm pretty satisfied with the way the country is run."
   - 57% feel the U.S. government is "doing very little to help poor people."
   - 26% do not "personally feel that this country is worth fighting for."
   - 12% feel the U.S. government is "trying to keep poor people down."

D) Alienation from Local Government
   - 52% feel "people in this neighborhood have very little or no say about the decisions made by the city government."
   - 40% feel there are not "any government officials in this city who really care a lot about what people in this neighborhood want."
   - 24% feel that complaining to a public official about an instance of local job discrimination would not help.

*Data drawn from 1,114 General Residents in Five City Neighborhoods. See Appendix B for scales.

situation, or change in people ("more education," "coming of the Kingdom of God") were more often cited. Nor are these attitudes translated aggressively into policy demands. As shown in Table 3.5, almost eight out of ten poor persons believe "that everyone has a right to a nice home even if he doesn't earn much money." A national minimum income, on the other hand, is supported by only a slim majority; and only one in six will agree that "it would be good if everyone got paid the same amount of money no matter what his job was."

The radicalism of the poor is a hesitant proto-radicalism, unconverted into strident policy demands. One of its constituents, alienation from *local* government will later emerge as actually inimical to political involvement. This nascent radicalism is nevertheless an important sign of class and political awakening, an important resource for community organizers to contemplate.

Direct Action

An important contribution to American politics by poor and ethnic minorities has been the rejuvenation of direct action political tactics. The civil rights, black liberation and community organization movements have now rewritten the script of political conflict to include marches, picketing, haunting, boycotts, community filibusters, rent strikes, and all the other techniques for turning committed bodies to political account. As social groups, from convicts to secretarial pools, feel the weight of powerlessness, they are turning more and more to the experience poor neighborhoods have accumulated in these new forms of political action.[16]

We have already shown the efficacy of direct action tactics in bringing about change in local institutions. Here we will examine the attitude toward and participation in such activities by residents of poor neighborhoods (see Table 3.6).

The Local Change Survey found belief in the efficacy of direct political action widespread among the poor. Each respondent was given, as a hypothetical situation, that a big supermarket in his area would not hire blacks/chicanos/Puerto Ricans.[17] He was asked if he felt any of a series of direct actions might help. Three-quarters said that under such circumstances a boycott would help, over 60 percent that picketing or complaining to the manager or a local official would help. Respondents were also asked, with

TABLE 3.6 POLITICAL ACTION AND POLITICAL VIOLENCE IN POOR COMMUNITIES*

A) Efficacy of Political Tactics
   In a hypothetical situation concerning a big supermarket that would not hire (respondent's subgroup).
   76% feel a boycott would help.
   66% feel complaining to a public official would help.
   64% feel picketing the market would help.
   63% feel complaining to the manager would help.

B) Overall Level of Political Activity
   5%   Very Much
   10% Great Deal
   31% Some
   54% Little
   ———
   100%

C) Frequency of Discussion of Community Issues
   16% Often
   36% Sometimes
   48% Seldom, never
   ———
   100%

D) Participation in Various Forms of Political Action
   12% have complained to a manager.
   11% have complained to an official.
   16% have picketed.
   32% have boycotted.
   8%   "would" threaten damage.

E) Political Violence
   28% do not feel "black people today can win their rights without using violence."
   14% would join a disturbance like the ones that occurred after the assassination of Martin Luther King.
   8%   would agree to threaten damage to a store to get the proprietor to change discriminatory employment practices.

*Data drawn from 1,114 General Residents in Five Poor Neighborhoods. See Appendix B for scales.

reference to each type of activity, "Would you agree to do it?" and "Have you ever done it before?" The "gap" between responses to these two questions is a good indicator of unfulfilled potential for political involvement in poor neighborhoods. Figure 3.2 indicates this "political action potential" for each form of involvement. In every instance it is large. Of 100 poor persons, 40 would agree to participate in a boycott or picket but have not yet done so. Almost six in ten say they would agree to take a complaint to a manager or official but have not yet done so. At first glance Figure 3.2 seems to be all gap and no action, but a comparison with levels of political involvement for Americans in general indicates this is not so. The proportion of poor persons who have participated in pickets and boycotts is twice as large as the proportion of Americans who have worked or contributed money to a party or candidate.[18] About the same proportion of poor persons have complained to a manager or official as Americans at large have written or talked to a public official over the last year. A small minority of the poor (16 percent) say they talk "often" with neighbors about community issues, but only 21 percent of Americans at large report "frequent" discussion of public issues in which they take an equal part.

FIGURE 3.2 POLITICAL ACTION POTENTIAL IN POOR COMMUNITIES*

(Top of bracket points to the percent of poor persons who "would agree to" a political action against a local supermarket, bottom points to percent who have ever done it before.")

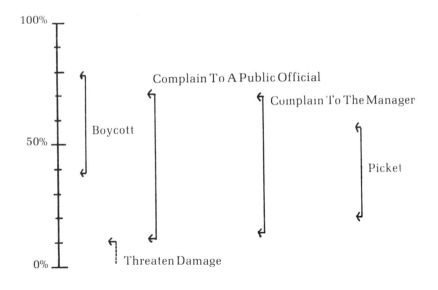

*Based on 1,114 General Residents in Five City Neighborhoods.

Widespread dedication to violence as a political tactic would be inconsistent with the aspects of political culture already described. The final political tactic we questioned respondents about was "threatening the manager with damage to his store." One person in seven said yes, he felt threatening damage would help, half this number indicated they would agree to do it. Violence finds greater support among blacks than whites. More than one black in four accepts the likelihood that the prosecution of his cause will involve violence.[19] Only 14 percent of blacks say they would join a "disturbance like the ones that broke out after the assassination of Martin Luther King," but almost half feel that such disturbances have "helped the cause of rights for black people" (see Table 3.7). Few neighborhoods investigated in the Local Change Study seemed on the brink of large scale violence. For every person who told us he would join a disturbance, another said he would "try to stop it." On a composite scale of propensity to violent political activity only five percent of blacks (whites were not scaled) scored "very high," and only 25 percent showed even "some."

It is not difficult to understand these levels of political violence. Poor neighborhoods are not peaceful places. Residents are often the objects of violence to person and spirit: from police, case workers, employers, merchants, landlords. "Fear" rather than "love-oriented" child rearing techniques prevail with the resulting stress on physical rather than internalized behavior controls. Masculine competitiveness, often diverted into striving for economic success in middle class society, remains more closely linked to physical prowess in street corner society.

RACE IN THE POLITICAL CULTURE
OF POOR NEIGHBORHOODS

How important is ethnic loyalty to political behavior? For whites, a popular theory goes, it is not very important. The "assimilation theory" argues that with the attrition of ethnic identification in second and third generation immigrants, the narrow perspective of ethnic loyalty has been virtually eliminated from American politics. Recently, however, the assimilation theory has come under heavy criticism. It is belied, some point out, by the persistent habit of political pros to balance tickets along ethnic lines. Others note the quite recent revival of ethnic voting in cities where domination by white Anglo-Saxon elites has only delayed its emergence.[20] More contrary evidence comes from Converse's intriguing study of belief systems which points to the central place of group solidarity in structuring political opinion. When persons are asked identical questions about basic policy preferences at a four year interval, Converse discovered, only ". . . thirteen people out of twenty manage to locate themselves even on the same *side* of the controversy in successive interrogations, when ten out of twenty could have done so by chance alone."[21] Only when its object is a *social group*, especially blacks, does opinion grow stable over time.[22] For many Americans, it appears, group loyalty is indeed a fundamental generator of political values. It is not surprising, then, that race consciousness has been so salient in the political mobilization of poor black neighborhoods. We will return often to the fundamental question: Has black consciousness invigorated politics in poor neighborhoods or, as Banfield has suggested, tended to seduce blacks with false issues and counterproductive strategies for change.[23] In this section we investigate the following aspects of this issue: How fundamental is race to the political world view of poor blacks? How salient are race political goals? Does race consciousness contribute to political involvement? Finally, how important is race to the support of an active community leadership? Table 3.7 presents opinions on race issues of 769 poor blacks interviewed in the three cities of the Local Change Study chosen for intensive analysis.

Sympathy with aggressive race consciousness is not a majority sentiment among poor blacks. Only 55 percent of persons we interviewed said they favored "black power," for example. When Aberbach and Walker asked blacks in Detroit to define "black power" they also found about half the responses to be positive (equally divided between emphasis on "racial unity" and "getting a fair share of resources.")[24] We asked respondents what word they would use to describe their race. Less than half responded "black," "Afro-American," or "black American."[25] A composite scale of "Race Identity" was formed from several items. A "high" score required use of these terms for one's race, belief in black power, and disagreement with the proposition that blacks blame too many of their problems on whites.[26] According to these criteria only one poor black in seven actively embraces the new race identity and two out of three show little or no impulse toward it.

Both deep suspicion and great patience mark the racial world view of poor blacks. Marx found over seven out of ten blacks agreeing that "most whites want to keep Negroes down as much

TABLE 3.7 RACE VALUES IN POOR BLACK COMMUNITIES*

A) Racial Identity

        Summary Measure of Racial Identity

          14% High

          19% Moderately High

          39% Little

          28% None

        100%

    55% feel "Black Power is a good idea."

    48% disagree, blacks blame too many of their problems on whites.

    40% use black or Afro-American to describe their race.

B) Racialist World View**

    45% feel there are not any white people who really want to see the black man get what he wants in this country.

     5% describe problems concerning discrimination or oppression when asked "what . . . are the most important problems affecting people in this neighborhood."

    10% describe race oppression as "the most important reason people in this city are poor."

     6% cite discrimination as a "major problem about jobs around here."

C) Support for Race Policies

        Overall Support for Race Policies

          18% Low

          35% Moderately low

          28% High

          19% Very High

        100%

    60% feel "stores in a black neighborhood should be owned and run by black people."

    38% feel schools with mostly black children should have mostly black teachers.

D) Race Voting

    79% feel "black elected officials generally can be trusted."

    62% agree "black people will have very little say in the government unless they all decide to vote for the same candidates."

    31% agree "black people would do better if they voted only for blacks."

E) Race Political Actions

    69% feel "black people are more angry about life in this city than 5 years ago."

    66% feel "blacks are treated with more respect by whites than 5 years ago."

    46% feel riots have been of positive value in aiding black advancement.

If a disturbance broke out "like the ones that occurred after the assassination of Martin Luther King,"

TABLE 3.7 (continued)

57% would stay away from it
19% would try and stop it
14% would join it
F) Black Separatism
    Scores on composite "Sympathy for Black Separatism" scale
52% none
33% very little
12% some
  3% very high
100%

*Data drawn from 769 black respondents in 3 poor neighborhoods.
**These are averages over 3 open-ended responses to each question.

as they can."[27] Forty-five percent of poor blacks we interviewed say they do not feel there are "any white people who really want to see the black man get what he wants in this country." The most frequent human reactions to perceived hostility are stereotyping, defensive posturing and heightened sensitivity to "losing face." These do not, however, seem to be the dominant responses of blacks to their perception of white malevolence. Seven out of ten are willing to grant, for example, that white attitudes have changed for the better in the recent past and will continue to do so.[28] Earlier evidence, suggesting that only one black in ten spontaneously mentions racial matters when speaking of neighborhood problems and the causes of poverty, should be remembered as well.[29]

Poor blacks are thus characterized by a "pragmatic racism"— clear perception of racial antagonism combined with a willingness to approach each problem on its own terms and an ability to recognize and accept racial good will when it occurs. Race, for blacks, is a political weapon. A majority of blacks feel that members of their race are "more angry about life in the city than five years ago," but also that "blacks are treated with more respect by whites than five years ago." Sixty-two percent feel blacks should vote for the *same* candidate, but consistent with a pragmatic race

consciousness, only half as many insist that the candidate supported should always be black. Eight out of ten say black elected
officials can generally be trusted.

There is almost no enthusiasm for full political separatism as
a solution to race problems. Only three percent meet our criteria
for "very high" support of black separatism: use of an identity-
conscious race name, having qualms about fighting for the United
States, and belief that a "separate nation inside America run by
black people is a good idea."[30] Only 12 percent more meet even
two of these criteria. Support for race-oriented public policies is
high but discriminating. Almost 70 percent feel that stores in
black neighborhoods should be owned and run by black people,
but less than 40 percent that "schools with mostly black children
should have mostly black teachers." On a composite scale, about
half score "high" on support for race policies.[31]

More important than absolute levels of race sentiment for our
purposes are interactions between race consciousness and other
aspects of political culture. Table 3.8 begins to place race identity
and support for race policies in the context of neighborhood
political mobilization generally. It indicates that blacks who identify strongly with their race do have attributes which contribute
to the vitality of local political culture. Compared to those without
heightened race pride, they are more politicized, more sensitive
to local problems, more likely to know about efforts to resolve
local problems of all sorts, and more likely to belong to local membership groups and engage in political action.[32] Alienation from
government accompanies race pride, but it is most important to
note that hostility focuses on national, not local, institutions. As
later analysis will indicate, this is a configuration especially conducive of political involvement. Also accompanying race pride is
an increased propensity to violent political behavior. Among
respondents with the strongest race identity, 18 percent show
"very high," and 32 percent, "some," propensity to violence.[33]

Although the relationships we have been discussing are all
statistically significant, none are unusually strong. Among community leaders as opposed to general residents, on the other hand,
the same patterns hold, but in almost every instance the strength
of association is doubled. If race plays a role in fostering involvement among people at large, its influence is that much greater in
promoting committed community leadership. While leaders do
not operate at higher absolute levels of race consciousness, their
race values do play a strong role in a larger syndrome of political
awakening and involvement.[34]

TABLE 3.8 RACE CONSCIOUSNESS IN THE POLITICAL CULTURE OF POOR COMMUNITIES**

(Entries are associations (r's) between Race Identity or Support for Race Policies and aspects of political culture listed.)

| | Race Identity | | Support for Race Policies | |
	General Residents	Leaders	General Residents	Leaders
Sources of Race Values				
Education	.28	.22	-.11	—
Age	-.27**	-.36	—	-.28
Income	—	—	-.22	—
Ramifications of Race Values				
Talk about Local Issues	.10	.20	—	—
Perception of Local Problems	.10	.16	—	—
Politicization	.08	.27	.10	.31
Anger at Local Situation	—	.35	—	.23
Disaffection from National Government	.22	.46	.18	.46
Alienation from Local Government	—	.23	.16	.47
Propensity to Violent Political Activity	.38	.58	.30	.44
Political Action	.14	.32	—	.12
Group Membership	.08	—	—	—
Modern Political Demands	—	.23	.18	.13

*Data is drawn from 769 black General Residents in 3 poor neighborhoods and 298 black Leaders in 100 poor neighborhoods.
**Blank entries are associations not significant at the .05 level.

Support for race policies stands in a much more ambiguous relationship to political mobilization than does race identity. It is associated, for example, with alienation from local as well as national government. Compared to race pride it relates less strongly to perception of community problems, discussion of community issues, and involvement in direct political action. Evidently a strong focus on local problems as race issues (not the majority perspective) does not contribute to community mobilization generally.

SUMMARY

The political culture of poor neighborhoods revealed by this brief survey is by no means universally vital. Political involvement of the poor, although different in kind from that of other Americans, is not higher in absolute terms. Compared to a middle class "control group" of 125 persons interviewed by the Local Change Survey in Detroit, the poor are actually more traditional in their definition of politics—*less* inclined to see politics in a negative light.[35] The same comparison shows the poor are no more inclined than others to see discrimination or oppression as a cause of poverty.[36]

Our survey, however, has revealed unique potentials for mobilization as well. The proto-radicalism of the poor is not shared by Americans at large. The middle class sample shows half the disaffection from national government and one fourth the anger at local events we found characteristic of the poor.[37] Explanations of events gravitate toward the personal, hesitating before political interpretations which would place blame more squarely on social forces and collectivities.

Perception of problems by the poor as revealed in the Local Change Data might not seem high, but it is three times as great as that of middle class persons.[38] In black areas, race consciousness is an important resource for political mobilization as is the firm belief in the efficacy of direct political action discovered among the poor generally.

In the next two chapters we turn from the investigation of political culture as embodied in the values and activities of the man-on-the-street to several sources of special energy for political revitalization: neighborhood leadership and local membership groups.

4   Neighborhood Leadership

At a time when the movement for racial and economic justice is digging in at the neighborhood level, studies of the leadership of the movement remain pitched at a national scale.[1] Polls concerning leadership of the race liberation movement, for example, typically ask nation-wide samples of blacks how they feel about nationally known black leaders.[2] In earlier years, these polls were conservative—*important* people in the movement, they reassured the country, are reasonable men, dedicated to incremental change and the principles of non-violence.[3] Now the opposite is probably the case. National prominence has been captured by image-wise radical leaders whose activities and ideas seem irresistible to the media. Public policy is increasingly based on the assumption that poor neighborhoods do not have leadership resources capable of sustained organizational activity. In this chapter we will match that assumption against Local Change data concerning the values and activities of leaders nominated by the poor in one hundred neighborhoods nationwide.[4]

In assessing the vitality of neighborhood leadership we will ask three questions: How much leadership is there in poor neighborhoods? How do community leaders differ from residents at large? And, how representative is leadership? Two analytic approaches will be taken. We will first look at the following strata of the community influence structure:

Unaffiliated persons
Persons knowing local leaders
Community leadership as a whole
Community political elites

We will investigate the number and distinctive characteristics of leaders found at each level. The goal will be to describe the influence structure of poor neighborhoods and the impact of that structure on local political culture. A second approach will view leadership from a more individual perspective. The following five-fold typology of leadership will be presented, based not on "ideal types" of leaders, but on actual groups of leaders found similar to each other in the Local Change data:

Neighborhood radicals
Respectable militants
The uninvolved
Elder elites
Neighborhood establishment

A comparison of these types and their relative occurrence in black and white neighborhoods will reveal some of the interplay between race, disaffection from government, and violence in the political revitalization of poor communities.

INFLUENCE STRATIFICATION IN LOCAL NEIGHBORHOODS

The Unaffiliated

Two questions were asked of residents to elicit names of local leaders. After recording up to three problems that the respondent mentioned as ones people in the neighborhood were concerned about, the interviewer asked "Who do you know around here who is doing anything about these problems?" A second question asked, "Can you think of anyone around here who seems to know a lot of people in the area, someone who talks to a lot of people and gets in on things that are going on?"[5]

A striking 59 percent give no names of leaders on either question. Interpretation of this figure is clouded by two issues, the political sensitivity of the question and the natural tendency of respondents to feel that it is not their meagre knowledge that the interviewer is interested in. Although we were indeed occasionally told that it was precisely from government "investigators" that leaders' names must be kept, political sensitivity was not a major problem. One respondent in four was rated slightly unsympathetic to the project by interviewers, but only six percent seemed highly unsympathetic, and five percent highly "devious" in answering. Interviewers were carefully trained in probing on this question and were probably effective, considering their judgment that 95 percent of respondents were "fairly" or "very" cooperative.[6]

Even considering the likelihood of some inflation through political and social reticence, the 59 percent figure is depressingly high. About half of poor persons say they do not know anyone who has helped out on neighborhood problems or has more knowledge of local affairs than themselves. The influence structure that we found in poor neighborhoods is familiar to only half of local residents.

What distinguishes those who can name a local leader, and thus form the lowest strata of an influence hierarchy, from those completely unaffiliated? Sex and age play little role although those over 50 are slightly under-represented.[7] Affiliation is roughly equal among housewives, blue and white collar workers and the unemployed.[8] Knowledge of leaders tends to peak among people who have lived in the area about 15 years, indicating that in most communities neither newcomers nor the longest term residents monopolize local influence. What does characterize the affiliated are three political traits: keen perception of problems confronting the neighborhood, involvement in community groups, and holding a position as a community worker.[9] Here are several themes that will recur throughout this study: that organization into membership groups and outside support of community service occupations are important contributors to community mobilization.

Community Leaders

We turn now to that group of persons identified as leaders by the man-on-the-street.[10] When a respondent gave us the name of a leader, we asked several questions to help specify the nature of his "affiliation" with the person named. Answers given indicate that leadership in poor areas is local, grounded in personal acquaintance, problem oriented, and organization based.

An easy familiarity characterizes relations between community leadership and the affiliated half of the population. Two-thirds of this affiliated group say they have spoken with a community leader over the last few months. When asked how they knew the leader they named, a third mentioned contacts through meetings, activities and the media, but over half spoke of more informal knowledge, "occasional contacts, friendships or family relations."[11] Community leadership is deeply involved in the concrete problems affecting local people. We asked those who gave us the name of a local leader what specifically that person had been doing about local problems. Answers covered the full spectrum of community concerns: housing, neighborhood conditions, community organization, jobs. But even among leaders who were nominated as "knowledgeables" as opposed to "problem activists" (see leadership questions above), the proportion not active on local problems never rises above 15 percent.[12]

The largest single category of problem activities mentioned by leaders is "community organization" (30 percent), but even this figure understates the importance of organizational affiliation to the maintenance of local leadership among the poor. When asked to specify whether a leader mentioned was a government official, organization member, relative or friend, residents answered thus:

> 49 percent organization member
> 26 percent friend
> 13 percent government or party official
> 3 percent relative[13]

According to the poor themselves, one half of contacts between leaders and rank and file are mediated by community organizations. Note the small number of people known as government or political party officials. In the next chapter we will return in some detail to the dismal picture of local party organization painted by the Local Change data.

The pattern of values and activities that distinguishes leaders from residents at large is an interesting one (full profiles of general residents, and leaders by race, influence level and leader type can be found in Table 4.1 at the end of this chapter). Although leadership tends to be drawn from a slightly higher socio-economic strata of the community, it is not distinguished from residents at large by political consciousness, radicalism, or race identity. Leaders are, however, more involved in community activities of all sorts, and much more engaged in the daily round of community problem-solving.[14]

The Representativeness of Local Leadership

For several reasons, social groups of all kinds tend to be led by socio-economic elites. High status individuals are more likely to have time and money to invest in gaining power. They are often given preference by other status elites with whom they must bargain. Education and professional training give skills and access to information which are important in certain phases of problem solving. The dilemma is less acute for groups whose members have a relatively elevated social status, more acute for the poor, whose low status is their defining attribute. Can the poor be led by persons sensitive to their true needs? The question is important to those seeking an understanding of the social dynamics of poverty and to those attempting to frame effective anti-poverty policy. If programs at the local level are to be responsive to real needs, they must emerge from, and be channeled through the community. If no local leadership exists, or what does exist is distant from true community needs, community development programs suffer disastrously.

Many have pointed with concern to the unrepresentativeness of leadership elites in poor neighborhoods. Kramer's extensive study of four California Community Action Programs found that ". . . those persons most accustomed to participation in voluntary associations became the nucleus of the organizing committee, thus excluding most of the hard core poor.[15] Results of a Kraft survey of black opinion in Harlem and Watts were interpreted to the Senate hearings on urban affairs in a similar vein. "[Martin Luther King] is a kind of folk hero. He is someone negroes trust. But when it comes to solutions to their problems, the people in the ghetto don't know whom to turn to. . . . The so-called community leaders are very little in touch at all with the people in the ghettos."[16] Studies of race leadership in Southern communities have consistently found some 80 percent of black leadership to have attended college.[17]

Arguments favoring "representative" leadership are complicated by two factors: the importance to the community of persons able to mediate between local activities and relevant professionals, and the depletion of leadership resources in poor areas. Many of the strategies open to poor neighborhoods—injunctions, rent actions, nonprofit corporations, presentations before planning boards, grant proposals—demand high level input by experts. As poverty programs move into bargaining and operational phases, there is a growing premium on having and using professional expertise without compromising local priorities.[18]

It is one of the hardest realities of social life in poor neighborhoods that leadership there is subject to constant attrition. Many of the qualities that enable a person to become an effective leader— sociability, skill in bargaining, useful contacts—can be readily turned to personal advantage. Hustling for the people is good practice for hustling for yourself. Black professionals, notes Bishop Wm. Bonner, ". . . live in Harlem long enough to get their heads above water and then run to suburbia."[19] In the South, migration upward through the class structure is compounded by "lateral" migration of dynamic elements to the North. "The potential leaders among the young people tend to migrate, and the most visible negro leaders are those whose status has made them the accustomed gatekeepers to the white community in a totally segregated system."[20] The concern of government programs that not a penny of poverty money stumble into the hands of those who are not poor exacerbates the problem. Maximum income restrictions for occupancy of government-funded housing units, for example, weed out those few persons who emerge as leaders because of their familiarity with local problems and grievance mechanisms.[21]

Recognizing "depletion of leadership" as a problem places the question of leadership by status elites in a somewhat different perspective. The problem is not just to exorcise "false leadership" but to challenge accomplished persons to reinvest energies in neighborhoods they or their parents worked so hard to escape.[22] "Once I thought it was a disgrace to get involved," a black clergyman told *Newsweek* interviewers, "Now I feel it is a disgrace not to get involved."[23]

Representativeness, then, is a two way street. Our description of political culture among the poor in the last chapter was by no means universally bright.[24] It is important that leadership be of the people, but also important that it be a force for change in critical areas—sensitivity to the full dimensions of poverty problems, for example. Elites will thus be viewed from two perspectives: how they represent, and how they transform, their communities.

An activist judges the "representativeness" of a leader by simply comparing the interests of the people, as he perceives them, against those of the leader, as he perceives them. Our empirical approach is at once more, and less, precise. More precise because data will allow comparison of characteristics as held, not perceived. Less precise because we must deal in collectivities (community leaders, the neighborhood establishment, militant ethnic group members, etc.) that may or may not be relevant in a particular situation.

We will consider three aspects of representativeness: socio-economic similarity, localism, and congruence of belief. *Socio-economic similarity* is defined demographically. Leaders will be considered dissimilar to the extent they differ from the poor generally in occupation, income, education, and age. Age, because it is a less powerful concept than class, will always be viewed in the context of the concrete attitudes and values that accompany it. Education will be examined carefully as well, with the possibility kept open that more education can lead to greater involvement with the problems of the less educated. Of special importance will be the relationship between education and income. A base line will be established which posits a "typical" amount of income earned by persons at each educational level. This procedure establishes two intriguing "deviant cases." Firstly, the individual who has "postponed" the conversion of education to income. We will make a first presumption that such individuals are investing their skills in less remunerative community service work. Secondly, the "hustler" who turns his education to more than average profit. We will investigate this pattern to see if it implies the avoidance of unremunerative community service activities.

Localism will be considered a second aspect of leadership representativeness. We will presume that the poor are best represented by people who live among them and are accessible on a day-by-day basis.

In the last chapter, a picture was drawn of attitudes toward the political world on the part of poor persons generally. The same data are available concerning all leadership groups, enabling precise comparisons along a full range of political attitudes and belief. *Congruence of belief,* our third criterion of representativeness, will be defined as similarity along these dimensions.

In these terms, community leadership in poor areas, although drawn from the upper socio-economic strata of neighborhood society, constitutes a highly local group, and one whose political beliefs are highly congruent with those of the community at large. According to our data, the average leader, at 41, is five years older than the typical resident. His income at $6,200 is $1,000 in excess of the community median (see Table 4.1 containing profiles of general residents, community leaders, political elites, and leader types, located at the end of this chapter.) Differences in educational levels are more marked. Forty-five percent of community leaders have attended some college, compared with only seven percent of residents at large. There are 25 percent more white collar and professional workers among leaders but of equal importance is the fact that almost one in four is employed as a community worker in a local service program. Dissimilarity of socio-economic status does not connote absentee leadership, however. Compared to residents, leaders are *more* permanent members of the community. The average leader has resided in the local area for a full 16 years.

Along most dimensions, the political beliefs of leaders are quite congruent with those of local residents. Leaders are neither more radical, as we have defined the term, nor more politicized. They do not express more personal anger about the local situation or show more disaffection from national government. They show no more race consciousness than residents at large. Leaders as a group are not distinguished by their ideas about what constitutes politics or their reasoning concerning the causes of poverty.

It is not ideology or political belief but community involvement and political engagement that differentiates leaders from residents-at-large. Twice as many leaders know a lot of people locally, and five times as many talk often about local issues with their neighbors. Eight percent of poor persons rank "moderately high" in political information; 58 percent of community leaders so. A third say they talk often with local officials, the same number that they have marched on a picket line. Half engage in a "great deal" of political activity; among residents the same figure is 10 percent.

There exists in poor neighborhoods, then, a leadership strata which is problem oriented but not ideological, politically engaged but not radical. This strata reinforces local political culture at several of its weakest points, community social interaction, formal group membership, and participation in direct political action.

Political Elites

At the top of the neighborhood influence structure is a sub-group of community leaders we label the local "political elite." The group, 20 percent of leaders at large, consists of those persons attributed influence by four or more of the 40 residents interviewed in a given city. How "elite" does this make them? The chance that 10 percent of a sample of residents would pick the same name from a population of 7,000 is, of course, infinitesimal. Persons given multiple attributes, as problem activists and local knowledgeables (the two domains of our leadership questions) are quite likely to be at the center of neighborhood events. Because of their familiarity to the man on the street, they would be important contact points both for outsiders interested in neighborhood affairs and for residents in need of information and help.

How is the image of neighborhood political culture altered by consideration of its topmost political elite?[25] Many of the principles of stratification described so far find extension in distinctions between political elites and community leaders. Black elites are not, for example, more race conscious than leadership generally. The tendency for leadership to be more committed to conventional political activities is heightened at the elite level. Both black and white elites are less alienated from local government than other leaders and more likely to talk with local officials, vote in elections and engage in political action generally. Involvement in community building activities is greater among elites as well. Eighty-five percent of elites are "moderately high" in information about local activities compared with 55 percent of leaders generally, and eight percent of the rank and file. Nine in ten say they know "a lot" of people locally and talk often with their neighbors about local issues. The same proportion belongs to an important local group.

These observations hide intriguing differences that can be observed between leadership in black and white communities, however. Black political elites are actually *lower* in socio-economic status than black leaders generally. They are also angrier, more oriented toward direct political action (like picketing) and have fewer qualms about violence in politics. This is the first evidence we have found in poor neighborhoods of a stratification favoring low status, anti-establishment persons in positions of power. It is an important finding, one highly uncharacteristic of American politics generally and a major distinguishing characteristic of political culture in poor black neighborhoods.

The situation of white political elites is somewhat different. They are drawn, more traditionally, from a higher socio-economic strata of leadership. Three in four have attended college, 28 percent more than white leaders generally; 36 percent hold white collar or professional jobs. The proportion of persons experiencing some job insecurity goes down among elites from 24 to 20 percent (among blacks it *increases* from 38 to 44 percent).

It is important to note, however, that white political elites differ from other leaders in several ways which bring them closer to the views of black elites. White political elites have moved away from other white leaders and toward blacks in making strident political demands and supporting direct action tactics. Compared to other leaders, white political elites are angrier and more likely to feel that major changes are needed in the way the country is run (although in these matters they still fall far behind black political elites). They do speak out as strongly as black elites on demands for a minimum income and public housing. The gap between their views on the efficacy of direct actions and those of other white leaders is enough to bring them in line with black political elites on this important issue. It seems likely that some cultural diffusion is in evidence, with white community elites adopting elements of the activist political culture of poor black neighborhoods. If so, it is a selective process. White elites have not accepted the disaffection from mainstream social institutions at national, city and neighborhood levels that characterizes black political culture. Also resistant to diffusion is the new pattern of organizational membership. Three times as many white as black political elites belong to friendship groups, but only half as many belong to the newer action groups, now carrying the burden of community organization in black neighborhoods.[26] What whites *have* adopted from blacks is a sense of outrage, a shift in tactical thinking, and the willingness to recognize poverty problems as neighborhood realities. The last might sound insignificant, but in older white communities, positive minded "community spiritedness" can be a major obstacle to an aggressive challenge of the economic status quo.

A TYPOLOGY OF NEIGHBORHOOD LEADERSHIP

We turn now from our inquiry into influence strata to a fuller typology which considers many aspects of political attitude and behavior simultaneously.[27] The groups we will be discussing are not "ideal types" but clusters of actual leaders found similar to each other along lines which our analysis indicates are crucial to political culture.[28] Included are the following dimensions of group activity, political belief and political action.

Group Activity

> Membership in traditional community groups
> Membership in action groups

Political Belief

> Anger at the local situation
> Alienation from local government
> Propensity to violent political activity

Political Action

> Participation in protest political action
> Participation in traditional political action[29]

Five types of leaders sharing characteristics along these lines emerged in the data: neighborhood radicals, respectable militants, the uninvolved, an elder elite, and a neighborhood establishment (See Figure 4.1). We will describe each type briefly and then investigate the implications of the typology for several more general issues. Table 4.2 at the end of this chapter gives defining characteristics for each type. Other descriptive characteristics can be found in Table 4.1, Rows 7–11.[30]

Perhaps the most important attribute of our first type is its sheer size. *Neighborhood radicals* (one third of all leaders) comprise the largest single category of leadership in poor neighborhoods. Almost all persons of this type belong to action groups (block, tenant, welfare, civil rights organizations) and avoid traditional groups entirely (PTA's, political parties, professional and civic groups). Two thirds agree "strongly" that there are things around the neighborhood that make a person angry; a majority feel alienated from local government. They are, as a group, very active in politics, conventional and protest, and have

FIGURE 4.1 TYPES OF COMMUNITY LEADERS*

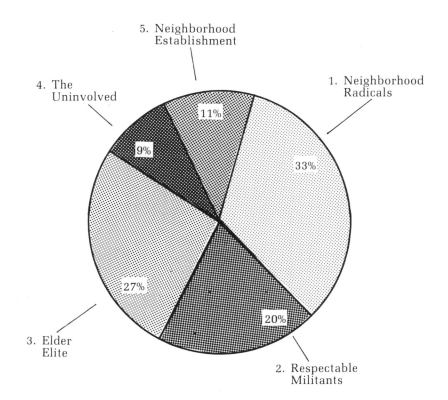

*Data drawn from Leaders of the Poor in Fifty Communities. N's clockwise: 93, 58, 76, 25, 32.

among the leadership types the highest propensity to violent political activity. The term "radical" is applied with some caution. Eight in ten believe major changes are needed in government, and almost half (versus 29 percent of leaders generally) go on to describe that change as a fundamental one affecting the political system. Six out of ten are highly alienated from national government; four in ten have qualms about fighting for their country. For 42 percent, racial discrimination or political oppression comes first to mind as a cause of American poverty. It is interesting that the group defines its leadership role in terms of "community organization," however, and not "getting people angry," and that its analysis of local problems is pragmatic not ideological in nature. Black pride—an important tool of community organization—is highly developed among neighborhood radicals, but support for race policies is not.

Although two thirds believe riots have helped the cause of the black man, there is a fascinating tension between militance and community concern in their attitude toward joining a riot. Thirty-one percent, more than any other type, say they would join a local disturbance, but an even higher proportion, 37 percent, say they would try to *stop* such a development if they saw it coming. As a group they are younger, by six years, than other leaders, and come from a slightly higher socio-economic strata. They are distinctly local, having lived in the neighborhood an average of fourteen years.

One leader in five falls into a second category, the *respectable militants*. Like the neighborhood radicals, these persons are active in protest and conventional politics and belong to local action groups. But they also belong to traditional community organizations and have very little antipathy towards government, local or national. Only eight percent feel that the government is trying to keep the poor down, as against 28 percent of neighborhood radicals who hold this belief. Perception of local problems is at its highest in this group, but this is not translated into vocal political demands. Members are five years older and four years more senior in residence than the neighborhood radicals.

A third, smaller category is more difficult to characterize. Members belong to action groups but are not politically active. They show little alienation from government or anger at existing neighborhood problems. The group, which we call neutrally, the *uninvolved*, is newer to the community than the typical leader but its average age is forty-three. Are members on the verge of greater involvement? It seems likely. The gap between the political activities they say they would engage in and those that they are involved with is much greater than that for other types. Eighty-three percent say there are political activities they would agree to participate in but haven't. Evidently, their involvement with a local action group was the first tentative step on a path that remains to be followed.

The second largest category of leaders we call the *elder elite.* This group averages 50 years in age and is living testimony to the significance of leadership depletion mentioned earlier. With little education and the lowest incomes of any leader type, the elder elite is the end result of a selection process which sees the most dynamic leadership elements leaving the local area. Members of this group belong to neither traditional nor action groups, and participate only slightly in politics. The elder elite is apolitical but all members were nominated by at least some resident as local leaders. Do they contribute to community building in the social sphere? Unfortunately, no. Fewer in this group than in any other say they know a lot of people locally, and their level of information concerning local activities and people is extraordinarily low. The one nominally "radical" attitude of the elder elite is an unusual cynicism concerning local government (perhaps an astute organizer could found a mobilization strategy on this singular disaffection). A community in which the elder elite dominated local leadership would be hidebound indeed.

Our last category, the *neighborhood establishment,* is small but important. Members have the unusual combination of relatively low education but very high income. Few are engaged in community work as a profession. About half are housewives, half employed in white collar or professional positions. Organizational membership is exclusively in traditional community groups. There is little anger or disaffection in evidence. Forty percent define politics simply by citing some branch of government. Half see poverty caused by personal inadequacies. Among all leadership types, the political demands of the neighborhood establishment are the most feeble, their perception of local problems most attenuated. Their danger lies in the fact that they report regular contact with local officials to a much greater extent than any other group. It is hard to imagine worse local persons to have the ear of those in power.

This leader typology provides an excellent tool for investigating the "balance of forces" prevailing in poor neighborhoods. Figure 4.2 indicates the relative proportions of leader types found in neighborhoods by race (chicano, black and white). Pro-change activists (neighborhood radicals plus respectable militants) form the largest subgroup in chicano communities where they outnumber established elites 4:1. In black neighborhoods, the neighborhood establishment is not large but one leader in four is an elder elite. Pro-change forces nevertheless prevail 2:1. Figure 4.2 presents graphic evidence of the difficulties facing community organizers in white neighborhoods, and the distance these communities have to go in order to mobilize for change. Almost one white leader in four is part of the neighborhood establishment, one in three an elder elite. If active, pro-change leadership is a relatively recent development in white communities, then the 35 percent of leaders in this category there represents real change. The present balance of forces in white neighborhoods is nevertheless discouraging. Elder elites can probably be bypassed by activists—their hold on local influence is tenuous. The neighborhood establishment poses a more difficult problem. These persons are more likely to be an aggressive opposition—heading up status quo election campaigns, pushing petitions against rent control, and forming organizations to stop radical educational change. Perhaps one of the few blessings of the greater disorganization of black ghetto neighborhoods is the near total absence of a neighborhood establishment there.

Because we have data on so many levels of disposition and behavior, the same technique which describes types of persons can, from a slightly different perspective, reveal motivational syndromes. We can note, for example, that conventional political activity, protest political activity, and propensity to violence form part of a single syndrome. Not one of our types is high on any of these without being high on them all.[31] We find no cadres in poor neighborhoods dedicated *exclusively* to violent mass action. There are, on the other hand, few individuals who get involved in conventional activity but draw the line short of direct, conflict producing action.

It has become a truism of behavioral political science that political involvement is fostered by system supportive political attitudes.[32] Figure 4.3 indicates how misleading that assumption is for those interested in mobilizing the poor. Neighborhood

FIGURE 4.2 DISTRIBUTION OF LEADER TYPES IN CHICANO, BLACK & WHITE NEIGHBORHOODS

(Figures are percentages of leaders of given race in a leadership type)

Types of Leaders

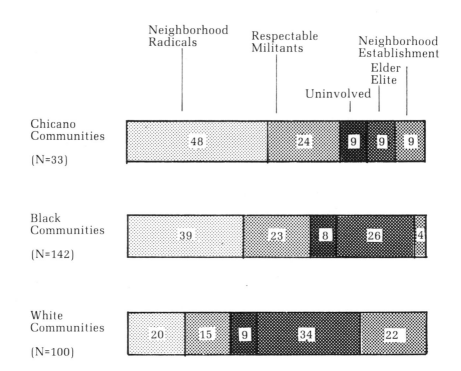

FIGURE 4.3 DISAFFECTION FROM NATIONAL AND LOCAL GOVERNMENT BY LEADERSHIP TYPE*

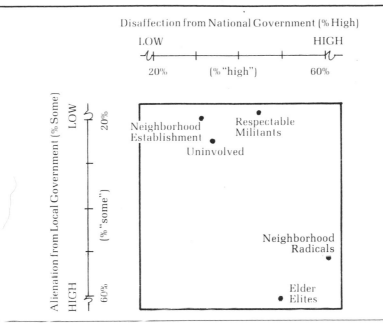

*See Appendix B for scales, Appendix C-13 for exact percentages and N's.

radicals, the most militant leader group, are highly alienated from national and local government. The neighborhood establishment, and the uninvolved, two completely *inactive* types, are low in alienation of both sorts. The moderate disaffection from national government combined with a strong support of local government characteristic of respectable militants is an important syndrome as well—one we found strongly supportive of mobilization among residents at large.

Figure 4.4 indicates, in a similar vein, that there are two positive "ideologies of local change" that underwrite political militance among leaders. The format of figure 4.4, identical to that of Figure 1.1, locates respondents according to their evaluation of local institutions and their willingness to grant improvement in them over recent years. The first positive ideology (that held by neighborhood radicals) is a "cynical discontent" which rates institutions low and refuses to agree that they have improved much over recent years. The second, "critical reformism," (held by respectable militants) agrees that things are pretty bad at present, but that efforts to change things have been paying off. The least effective point of view, as the analysis of chapter 1 suggested, is the "optimistic satisfaction" of the neighborhood establishment. Clearly, some point of view which recognizes how little government and service institutions care for the plight of the poor is a pre-requisite for political involvement among leaders of the poor.

FIGURE 4.4 IDEOLOGIES OF LOCAL INSTITUTIONAL CHANGE BY LEADER TYPE*

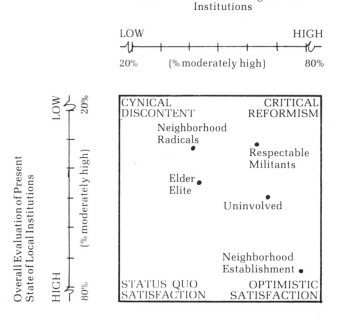

*See Appendix B for scales, Appendix C-14 for exact percentages and N's.

SUMMARY

Our brief survey has revealed important signs of political re-vitalization in poor neighborhoods. Many such areas now boast capable leadership, deeply committed to pragmatic action for community development. Although leaders are drawn from a slightly higher socio-economic strata, they are local, not absentee, and have political beliefs highly congruent with those of the poor at large. Leaders are distinguished more by their activist orientation toward community development than their political beliefs. They thus support a frail political culture (as described in the last chapter) at some of its weakest points.

There are new leadership cadres in poor areas, but equally exciting are novel leadership dynamics. In black neighborhoods nationwide, political elites are distinguished, not by high socio-economic status and conservatism, but their opposites. "Neighbor-hood radicals" comprise the largest, most concerned and active group of leaders; none of them belong to any of the political and civic organizations traditional to the American scene. "System supportiveness," long felt to be a prerequisite for political involve-ment, does not seem to be so in poor neighborhoods. America now has a major interest subculture led by persons more alienated from government than rank and file.

Evidence is not uniformly optimistic, however. Some half of general residents know no one in the leadership group we have been discussing here, for example. The balance of forces in white communities is distinctly more regressive than in black. Five times as many white as black leaders belong to the neighborhood establishment, an upper status group that is highly political yet unsympathetic to poverty problems. Women form a large minority of local leadership but are not as militant or active as men. White women especially are trapped by stereotypes of role and issue activities "appropriate" for their sex (see chapter 6).

Overall, however, the picture is one of strong potential for effective local action toward community development. It is thus ironic that national policy seems increasingly based on the oppo-site conclusion: that programs which decentralize to the neighbor-hood level raise expectations but are inherently defective. The present analysis indicates that defects should be sought, not at the local level, where leadership is ready to move, but at the national level, where policy makers are not.

TABLE 4.1 PROFILES OF LEADERS, POLITICAL ELITES, COMMUNITY WORKERS, IDEOLOGUES, AND LEADER TYPES IN POOR COMMUNITIES*

(All entries are percents except where noted.)

Attributes	General Residents	All Leaders	Black Leaders	White Leaders	Black Polit. Elite	White Polit. Elite	Neighborhood Radicals	Respectable Militants	Neighborhood Establishment	Uninvolved	Elder Elites	Missing Data
A. Sample												
No. of Cities	5	100	100	100	100	100	50	50	50	50	50	—
No. of Respondents	1,114	630	323	225	81	25	93	58	32	25	76	—
B. Demographic												
Age (median years)	36	41	41	42	40	37	35	40	41	43	50	4
Race (Black)	70	54	100	0	100	0	60	59	17	50	50	3
Sex (female)	55	43	41	49	36	32	36	35	57	42	50	2
Education (any college)	7	45	45	45	58	73	63	60	23	46	13	7
Income (median $/1000)	$5.2	$6.2	$6.1	$6.6	$5.9	$6.7	$7.0	$7.0	$8.4	$6.2	$5.9	28
Residence (median yrs.)	11	16	17	15	17	9	14	18	19	11	15	8
Occupation												
Housewife	13	11	5	20	3	4	0	4	44	4	22	6
Unemployed	17	5	6	3	8	0	11	2	0	13	8	6
White Collar	11	23	23	25	27	39	16	20	22	21	23	6
Professional	4	17	17	18	10	17	24	27	19	29	8	6

*See Appendix B for scales. N's can be derived ±1% by applying "Missing Data" statistic to the N of column 2. Empty cells indicate no data, inapplicable to subgroup, or N's too low for reliable data.

**Missing data is artificially reduced by scale construction technique which gives mean values for certain proportion of missing data. Missing Data figures approaching 50% indicate proportion of missing data. Missing Data figures approaching 50% indicate question not asked in first fifty cities.

TABLE 4.1 (continued)

(All entries are percents except where noted.)

Sample	General Residents	All Leaders	Black Leaders	White Leaders	Black Polit. Elite	White Polit. Elite	Neighborhood Radicals	Respectable Militants	Neighborhood Establishment	Uninvolved	Edler Elites	Missing Data
Attributes												
C. Personal												
Applied for Welfare	33	22	25	17	22	21	12	30	7	29	25	2
Feel Able To Change Life	69	70	67	74	68	88	69	69	59	78	59	4
Belief in Planning	65	84***	85	85	88	84	86	89	75	92	73	3
Articulate (Very)	32	61	63	58	78	92	77	80	52	58	33	3
Plan More Education	—	19	20	14	21	12	32	32	6	25	4	0
Job Insecurity Some	49	33	38	24	44	20	33	37	17	29	25	5
D. Community Involvement												
Know Lot of Local People	41	81	82	78	95	84	89	93	71	71	57	1
Talk Often of Community Issues	16	68	71	62	89	88	89	90	59	33	23	1
Belong to a Local Group	16	70	74	62	91	83	76	98	100	87	80	2

***This is one of the few comparisons that differs if we compare Five City Leaders (66% of whom show a "Belief in Planning for Tomorrow") instead of One Hundred City Leaders with Five City Residents.

TABLE 4.1 (continued)

(All entries are percents except where noted.)

Attributes	General Residents	All Leaders	Black Leaders	White Leaders	Black Polit. Elite	White Polit. Elite	Neighborhood Radicals	Respectable Militants	Neighborhood Establishment	Uninvolved	Edler Elites	Missing Data
Leader in a Local Group	—	46	50	39	59	67	45	77	69	50	9	46
Belong to Friendship Group	—	30	29	30	15	50	23	30	47	39	24	48
Belong to Traditional Group	—	34	29	41	38	33	1	100	100	26	0	48
Belong to Action Group	—	58	65	40	89	50	88	98	0	96	1	48
Political Information (mod. high)	8	58	61	48	79	88	75	77	34	50	17	0
Can Name 3 Local Leaders	—	50	55	41	59	67	66	61	43	63	24	54
E. Race Values												
Race Identification (high)	14	—	23	—	27	—	44	28	—	—	20	0
Support for Race Values (very high)	19	—	18	—	15	—	27	3	—	—	37	0
Believe Riots Have Helped	46	—	51	—	72	—	65	64	—	—	32	5
Would Join Riot	18	—	14	—	18	—	31	21	—	—	9	0
Black Separatist Support (very high)	3	—	3	—	5	—	8	0	—	—	6	8

TABLE 4.1 (continued)

(All entries are percents except where noted.)

Sample Attributes	General Residents	All Leaders	Black Leaders	White Leaders	Black Polit. Elite	White Polit. Elite	Neighborhood Radicals	Respectable Militants	Neighborhood Establishment	Uninvolved	Edler Elites	Missing Data
F. Political World View												
Describe 3 Community Problems	18	49	51	40	62	64	69	77	38	54	30	0
See Discr./Oppression as Cause Poverty	21	25	28	19	29	25	42	27	16	0	17	5
Politicization (high)	22	29	32	23	25	23	47	49	22	4	26	2
See Need for Fundamental Change in Gov't.	19	29	36	21	40	21	46	49	4	20	13	2
Evaluate Local Institutions (low)	56	59	64	48	72	48	67	68	25	50	54	1
Political Demands (high)	50	59	64	49	69	39	82	68	41	57	45	5
Faith Direct Action (high)	37	33	39	26	48	44	38	37	19	30	15	2
Believe Picketing would Help	64	65	77	47	88	64	76	74	30	61	41	3
G. Alienation from Government												
Angry at Things in Neighborhood	78	77	86	65	94	79	93	91	47	42	67	2

TABLE 4.1 (continued)

(All entries are percents except where noted.)

Sample / Attributes	General Residents	All Leaders	Black Leaders	White Leaders	Black Polit. Elite	White Polit. Elite	Neighborhood Radicals	Respectable Militants	Neighborhood Establishment	Uninvolved	Elder Elites	Missing Data
Attributes												
Believe Major Changes in Country Needed	50	64	70	56	86	72	82	91	67	48	50	2
Disaffection from National Govt. (high)	48	42	48	33	43	24	61	45	31	33	49	1
Alienation from Local Govt. (high)	18	13	17	.8	10	0	22	2	0	0	36	2
Alienation from Local Govt. (some)	61	40	42	34	38	21	52	18	19	25	63	2
Propensity to Violent Political Act. (some)	24	—	29	—	41	—	54	45	—	—	9	1
Propensity to Violent Political Act. (high)	5	—	7	—	10	—	14	10	—	—	6	1
H. Political Action												
Political Action (good deal)	10	50	57	38	80	56	71	76	28	20	5	1
Protest Political Action (mod. amount)	21	48	58	32	75	52	78	74	14	9	20	6
Talk Local Officials (11-100/Year)	—	30	27	33	48	50	39	48	41	8	7	47
Vote Every Chance	—	77	81	71	96	100	81	84	75	65	65	48
Have Picketed	19	35	45	19	56	22	53	56	3	13	20	5

TABLE 4.2 DEFINING CHARACTERISTICS OF LEADERSHIP TYPES

(Entries are percents)

Leader Types	% Who Belong to Action Groups	% Who Belong to Traditional Groups	% Very Angry at the Local Situation	Alienation from Local Government, % Some	Propensity to Violent Political Activity, % Some	Propensity to Violent Political Activity, % Very High	Protest Political Action, % High	Conventional Political Action, % High
Neighborhood Radicals	88	1	64	53	54	14	78	71
Respectable Militants	98	100	56	18	45	10	74	76
Neighborhood Establishment	0	100	19	19	*	*	14	28
The Uninvolved	96	26	7	25	*	*	9	20
Elder Elites	1	0	29	63	9	6	20	5

Characteristics

*N's too low for accurate percent.

5 The New Group Life of the Poor

In America, membership organizations breed like rabbits. Some look at the resulting population and see only overcrowding—a people tricked by the desperate need to believe that meetings, ceremonies and outings return friendship and progress for energy invested. In a political system, however, where groups provide critical links between rulers and ruled, such cynicism is something of a luxury.

Unlike the European democracies, where political parties set out early to mobilize the lower classes, and unlike the Third World nations, where governments themselves assume this responsibility, America is a country where voluntary organization has been uniquely tied to social class.[1] Here, there is a vicious circle which runs—no leadership and organizational skills locally, therefore no decentralization of power and resources to the local level, therefore no leadership and organizational skills. . . . In this chapter, we look at developments in poor neighborhoods to see if there are the makings of a revitalized organizational life.

We will look first at how many and what kinds of group memberships are found in poor neighborhoods, and how this varies between white and black areas. The kinds of persons that lead different groups will be examined as will group specialization in issue-areas. Churches, political parties, community social action and militant ethnic groups will be singled out for analysis as political subcultures. Popular conceptions of their nature—

held by friends and enemies—will be matched against Local Change data concerning values and activities of members themselves.

HOW MANY BELONG?

It is generally believed that the group life of the poor is impoverished. "When we look at the culture of poverty on the local community level, we find . . . above all a minimum of organization beyond the level of the nuclear and extended family. . . . Indeed it is the low level of organization which gives the culture of poverty its marginal and anachronistic quality . . . most primitive peoples have a higher level of socio-cultural organization than our modern slum dwellers."[2] The reasons cited are many.[3] Compared to the poor, economic and status elites inherit more social confidence, have more training in organizational skills, keep better informed of the variety of useful affiliations, and have more money to hire full-time group staff so their own part-time involvement will still be rewarded.[4]

Almond and Verba's figures concerning group involvement of Americans at large will provide a reference point for our figures concerning levels of involvement among the poor. They report that about 57 percent of Americans belong to some type of organization.[5] Local Change data indicate that membership in poor areas is not this frequent. When we asked the 4,000 persons in the Hundred City general sample "Have you had anything to do with any neighborhood or community organizations?" only 21 percent said yes. In another question, the Five City general residents sample was asked to list "the most important groups or organizations that people in this neighborhood belong to," and then to indicate the ones in which they held memberships.[6] By this criterion, only 16 percent of the poor belonged to a community group.[7] This figure is undoubtedly somewhat low, especially regarding church membership.[8] Nevertheless, the true figure is surely less than half of the 57 percent for Americans generally. If this is something more than a minimum of organization beyond the family level, it still falls short of the organization characteristic of society as a whole.

Local Change data, however, suggest two important qualifications to this bleak picture. First, among neighborhood *leadership* there is a very active group life indeed, and second, there is a remarkable *political cast* to all forms of association in poor neighborhoods. For instance, of the people who were nominated as a leader by even one resident among the 40 we interviewed in each neighborhood, 68 percent belonged to at least one community group and the figure rises to 74 percent for a cross section of all leadership. The typical leader belongs to 1.9 different community groups. By any standards this is an active group life. Our picture of the culture of poverty must be broadened to include, for most neighborhoods, an indigenous leadership strata on easy terms with the full variety of organizational life.

Of equal importance is the intensely political nature of groups found in poor neighborhoods. Figure 5.1, (see column 4), presents, for comparison, the kinds of groups to which the typical American belongs. Over half of memberships are in social and religious

FIGURE 5.1 KINDS OF GROUP MEMBERSHIPS IN POOR NEIGHBORHOODS AND IN THE COUNTRY AT LARGE*

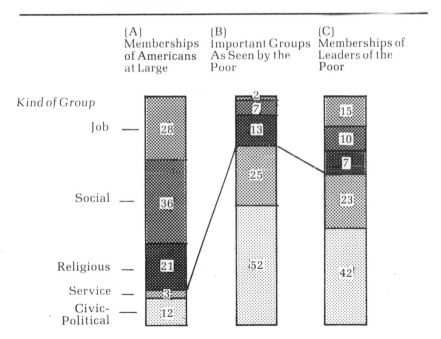

*Percentages based on total memberships for each group. See Appendix C-15 for details.

groups, one quarter are job related: unions, professional societies, business groups and the like. Only a relatively small proportion are political or service oriented. The picture is dramatically different in poor neighborhoods. When general residents of the Five City sample were asked to name important groups in their neighborhoods, only 2 percent named job related organizations. Adding social and religious groups brings the proportion accounted for to one in five. For Americans at large, these three categories make up not 20 percent but 85 percent of memberships. Over half of groups the poor indicate as important in their neighborhoods are civic or political in nature; another quarter are service oriented. These two categories make up only 15 percent of the memberships of Americans at large.

The Local Change Study provides precise information concerning group memberships of local leaders in poor neighborhoods. As might be expected, political groups dominate the picture (see Figure 5.1, column C). Only one in ten is social, even fewer religious. Veterans societies, business groups and political party organizations, three of the mainstays of group life in the larger society, play only a limited role here. Civil rights groups are overshadowed by a congerie of block, tenant and neighborhood issue groups to be discussed in detail later. Militant ethnic groups are a small proportion of total memberships but already outnumber attachments to political party organs.

A threefold breakdown of group membership will be used in much of the analysis to follow (see Appendix B, "Group Membership" for details). Church, social, fraternal, veterans and nationality organizations are combined into a *friendship* group category. Older community organizations are placed into a single category of *traditional* groups. The final category, *action groups,* includes government sponsored poverty organizations (mostly Community Action and Model Cities groups), welfare rights, civil rights and militant ethnic groups, and neighborhood community social action groups of all kinds.[9]

RACE AND GROUP MEMBERSHIP

Black neighborhoods have received the greatest attention from observers of lower class politics, but it is not black areas alone that are taking part in new political developments. Figure 5.2 presents membership profiles for the leadership of white, black and chicano communities respectively. Leaders of all race groups

**FIGURE 5.2 VARIETIES OF GROUP MEMBERSHIP
AMONG LEADERS BY RACE***

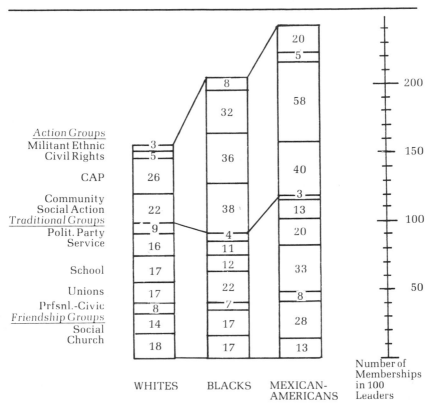

*Entries are number of memberships per hundred leaders.

have about the same number of friendship group memberships. White leaders add to this a relatively full spectrum of traditional group memberships including more political party, service, school, and professional-civic associations than blacks. The difference comes in action group memberships, held only half as frequently by white as black leaders.

Federal anti-poverty groups are unusually important in white areas. If these were discontinued, whites would lose nearly half of action group memberships. The figure for blacks is closer to a third. There is some evidence of political evolution in poor white areas. Action group memberships make up only about a third of all memberships for whites, but this proportion falls only slightly short of equalling all traditional group memberships taken together.

For black leaders, the overall balance has shifted strongly toward action groups, now comprising a majority of all group memberships. In 100 black leaders there are typically 114 action group memberships equally divided between community social action groups, civil rights organizations, and government sponsored poverty groups. Militant ethnic group memberships outnumber those in political parties two to one.

Poor black communities now have highly politicized group infrastructures. A full 73 percent of their group memberships are in organizations devoted to civic purposes. The figure for Americans generally, as we noted, is closer to 15 percent.[10]

We interviewed 52 chicano leaders across the country and found that they have the most highly evolved organizational life of any racial group, with an average of 241 memberships per hundred leaders. The chances are one in five that a chicano leader will belong to a militant ethnic group and 50–50 that he is affiliated with a government sponsored poverty organization. Even if government programs folded in these areas there would remain 65 other action group memberships per 100 persons.

OFFICE HOLDING AND LEADERSHIP DEVELOPMENT

If participation in group activities has strong potential for influencing one's political life, leadership and direction of these activities should have an even stronger impact. Few opportunities for leadership experience are open to the poor. The settlement houses, schools and public agencies of poor neighborhoods have traditionally been manned by outsiders. Most poor persons do not enjoy reliable employment and those who do, work in an economic system where worker control has never been seriously attempted. In this section we will look closely at officers of community groups to see if officership promotes personal confidence, political sophistication, and involvement in political action.

The poor do not obtain as much group leadership experience as other Americans. In the Five City general residents sample, only 1 in 40 said he was a "leader or officer" of one of the "important groups or organizations that people in this neighborhood belong to." The figure is conservative, focusing as it does on important community groups, but it comes nowhere close to the

26 percent of Americans reported by Almond and Verba who have held positions in voluntary associations.[11] The proportion of group members that have held leadership positions—what might be called the density of leadership opportunities—is low for the poor as well. Only 17 percent of those who indicate group membership say they have been officers of groups as well, far below the national average of 46 percent.[12] Assuming that all voluntary associations have roughly the same number of officer positions, this disparity can be taken as an indication of institutional oppression—discrimination against the poor in the distribution of leadership opportunities.

Officerships are much more common among community leaders. Even among those nominated as leader by only one person, 40 percent have held leadership positions in a local community group.[13] More striking than the amount of leadership experience is its deep politicization. About a quarter of positions held by leaders are in friendship groups, and another quarter in traditional groups, leaving almost half of local officership experience in action groups. Developments which have politicized poor areas in recent years have thus doubled the leadership opportunities open to local persons.[14]

Does holding an office in a local organization promote personal skills and self-confidence?[15] We asked each respondent if he felt he could change his life if he wanted to, expecting that confidence in this regard would accompany leadership of community organizations. This does not apply in two of the three types of groups studied. Only in action group officership does one find heightened self-confidence.[16] The same pattern is found in two central areas of hope for personal achievement—further education and improved job opportunities. Neither friendship nor traditional group officers have set their sights higher in either regard than non-members.[17] We found the leaders of the poor to be generally highly articulate but the differential that accompanies officership of action groups is twice that for other organizations.[18]

Any interpretation of these differences in skills and aspirations must mention the higher educational level of action group leaders. The impression persists, however, that action groups have escaped the cycle of dependencies in poor neighborhoods but that non-action groups are *part* of the problem—even leading them does not bring one closer to personal independence. Perhaps the power of action groups over values comes from their explicitly

political frame of reference—their insistence that some responsibility for frustrated personal hopes be nailed on society's door.

Does office holding contribute to political involvement? Figure
5.3 compares the political attitudes and involvement of non-members, members and leaders of specific local groups. Included are a
linked series of perspectives conducive to political mobilization;
generalized anger at the neighborhood situation, a capacity to see
the political dimension of social institutions, and a willingness
to translate these perceptions into demands on government.

An interesting pattern emerges. Officers of traditional groups
are behind both non-members and their own group constituency
on all indicators.[19] In action groups on the other hand, leaders
are consistently ahead of non-members and roughly at or above
the level of their constituents. A further clue is provided by the
hesitancy of officers in traditional groups to find fault with local
schools and the job situation in the city—just under half of this
group evaluates these negatively, whereas among the leaders of
action groups 69 percent (19 percent more than non-members)
do so. The close ties of traditional groups to the older service
nexus seems to keep them from the exacting evaluation of local
institutions characteristic of action group officers. One is forced
to the conclusion that leaders in this constellation of older community groups; civic and service, political and school, are
uniquely *unlikely* to press community demands in the political
sphere. Whatever other kinds of leadership they may provide,
they must be counted as a negative influence on community political mobilization.[20]

Only action group officers are distinguished by a heightened
sense of racial pride. One in five traditional group officers is
moderately high in racial identity, 9 percent *less* than non-members. Forty percent of action group officers score at the same level,
19 percent above non-members. Banfield has suggested that an
overemphasis on prejudice as a cause of black problems can
". . . lead to the adoption of futile and even destructive policies
. . .[21] The observation does not apply to officers of new political
groups in poor neighborhoods. On a scale measuring support for
race political objectives—getting black teachers and black enterprise into black neighborhoods and the imperative of block voting
—officers of action groups score *below* non-members. Fourteen
percent were very high on this scale compared with 35 percent
of non-members. It would appear that action group officers sup-

FIGURE 5.3 OFFICERS OF COMMUNITY GROUPS*

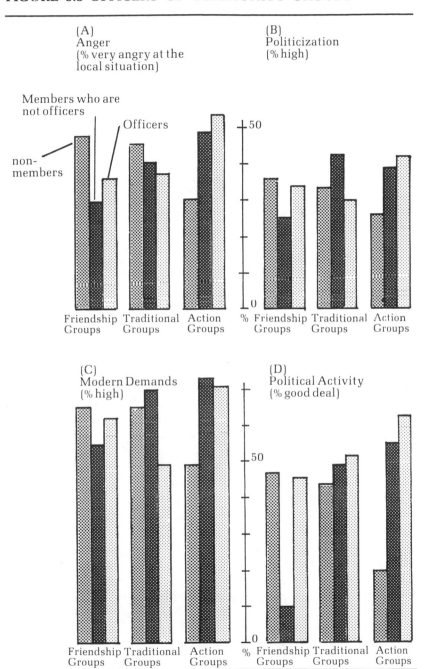

*See Appendix C-16 for exact percentages and N's.

port race pride as a path to personal dignity and organizational strength, but do not let this commitment dictate political goals and strategies.

Political action is somewhat more common among traditional group leaders than non-members, but the differences are nowhere near as large as those for action group leaders. Among non-members of action groups only one in five has undertaken a "good deal" of political activity. The figure rises threefold for leaders.

COMMUNITY GROUPS AS POLITICAL SUBCULTURES

In this section we focus in on churches, political parties, community social action groups, civil rights organizations, and militant ethnic groups. We hypothesize at the outset that each of these groups forms a political subculture, defined by the socio-economic status of its members, their attitudes toward the political world and the nature of their political activity.[22] All groups do not represent the interests of the poor equally well. Those concerned with poverty problems will be interested to know which kinds of community groups are most representative of poor communities and thus most likely to be closest to its felt needs. For those interested in radical change, evidence concerning the ideology and activities of various groups will be useful in assessing the balance of political forces at the local level.[23]

The unity of group subculture can be expected to vary from group to group. Some local organizations, poverty program affiliates and militant ethnic groups, for example, are difficult for members to approach with opinion defenses in full operation. While one need not be affected by the "culture" of the post office in mailing a letter, serving as a helper in Headstart or attending a rent control meeting is a different matter. Defining their own political world is itself an important task for some community groups. We are then presenting from one perspective a first reading on thousands of local efforts to define what the subcultures of community politics should be.[24]

Data is drawn from interviews with leaders of the poor in 50 of the 100 cities sampled.[25] Although our discussion will proceed group by group, data will be presented in figures giving information on all groups, a format designed to aid those who wish to test their own ideas about how groups differ. Most tables include data for 11 different groups although unions, service agencies, social, fraternal, educational, and civic-professional groups will not be given extended attention here. Before turning to the discussion of individual groups we will examine briefly two general characteristics of group members: the leadership roles they prefer, and the kinds of issues on which they have been active.

In the course of our interview, each leader was asked which of three leadership roles he preferred: getting people angry, organizing individuals into groups, or presenting demands to outsiders.[26] Figure 5.4 presents the roles chosen by members of six different groups. No group specializes exclusively in one role.

FIGURE 5.4 LEADERSHIP ROLES OF GROUP MEMBERS*

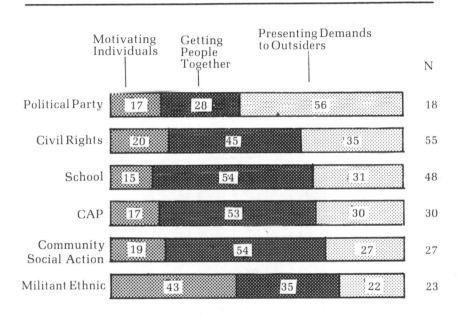

*Entries are percent of total group members holding different leadership roles.

Except in militant ethnic groups and political party organs, however, the balance tips toward community-oriented tasks, and within these, toward group rather than individually-oriented activities. Political party affiliates, as one might expect, emphasize their position as middle men; over half see their role in terms of carrying demands to those in government. Unfortunately, later examination of party affiliates will reveal how unsuited members are to this task. Persons emphasizing individual mobilization remain a constant one in five minority—except in militant ethnic groups where they comprise nearly half of members. Later we will examine one image suggested by these figures, that ethnic militancy is the ideological vanguard of local political action.

Figure 5.5 presents data concerning issue specialization for eight different groups. Each vertical bar represents all the mem-

FIGURE 5.5 ISSUE FOCUS OF GROUP MEMBERS*

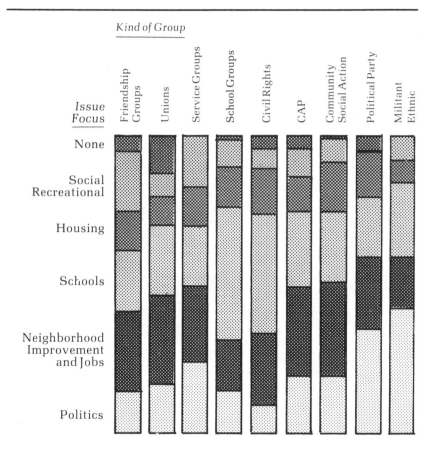

*Each column represents 100% of the members of a given group and is divided proportionately to the kinds of issues on which members indicated they were most active. See Appendix C-17 for exact figures and N's.

bers of a given group and is divided proportional to the primary issue focus of individual members. The general pattern is clear; no group is composed of members who specialize in only one kind of community issue. The distribution of focus within the large community social action category, for example, parallels precisely that of leaders at large. A similar issue diffuseness emerges in problems that group members say affect their communities. With minor exceptions, leaders in every kind of group cite the same kinds of problems in the same proportions.[27] Militant ethnic groups show the largest divergence from the norm in issue focus, with 42 percent of members mentioning political issues as a first concern. This fact suggests another image of these groups as "community political agents," that will also be investigated.

Relatively few leaders belong to organizations whose titles betray single issue concerns. Fifty-six of 834 memberships are in educational organizations, but for other issue specific groups, only 12 welfare rights, 2 civil liberties and 1 tenant organization could be found.[28] Welfare is mentioned by 22 different leaders as an issue on which they have been active, yet only 12 persons mentioned membership in welfare rights groups. Local civil rights groups are no longer concerned exclusively with racial discrimination. Only five percent of civil rights group members cite discrimination or oppression as an important community problem. Persons who do *not* belong to civil rights groups actually mention discrimination as their primary issue concern somewhat more often than those who do.

There are several interpretations of the issue diffuseness of local groups. Some of the homogeneity is due to the participatory ethic of community groups which pressures the agenda of each toward the will of the whole. Equally important, however, is the fact that many of the problems the poor face do in fact form a single political arena. In this respect, freedom from poverty is closer to the inter-related problems that colonized people faced in freeing themselves from imperialism, than the divisive regulatory and distributive issues which dominate upper class politics.[29] Progress in one area—increased representativeness of school administration—can often lead to progress in another—provision of summer job training programs. People brought to political consciousness by battling oppression in one area are the easiest to solicit for volunteers on another front.

Issue diffuseness, however, has a price. A high level of competitiveness is inevitable in a political system without ground rules for the division of political labor. The situation is most acute when new funds create distribution problems within the com- munity—who is selected to sponsor a housing project, who hands out community aide positions etc.. Having many community or- ganizations operating on similar issues places a high premium on peak associations like New Haven's black coalition which can co-ordinate demands, consolidate leadership and bargain in strength across issues.

CHURCHES, POLITICAL PARTIES, SOCIAL ACTION AND MILITANT ETHNIC GROUPS

In the remainder of the chapter we will discuss specific neighbor- hood organizations, beginning with churches. Figure 4.5 (at the end of the chapter) displays much of the original data to be dis- cussed. We have ranked a variety of organizations according to percentage scores of members on a number of attributes. Row C of the figure indicates, for example, that political party and profes- sional-civic group members tie for highest income (75 percent over $6,000); social group members are next, at 71 percent, etc.)

Churches

Whatever other institutions the poor lack, they have churches. Gans notes, for example, the many Irish, Polish and Catholic churches available to the Boston West Enders prior to the destruc- tion of their neighborhood for urban renewal.[30] Poverty stricken rural areas as well "are full of small struggling churches. In 1952, there were nearly twice as many churches per 1,000 population in the Southern Appalachians as in the country as a whole."[31] Few chicano households, no matter how destitute, are without their statuette and tinted print of the Virgin of Guadalupe or Jesus on the Cross. A full 96 percent of black Americans profess a religious faith; 40 to 50 percent attend church every week.[32] There is no doubt that the church has been involved to some extent in the recent political awakening of the poor, particularly in the black community. In the South, 35 percent of blacks who attend church report political discussions held there. One in five receives direct advice about the best candidate to vote for.[33] The homes of black clergymen have nurtured a fair share of radical political leaders: witness Malcolm X, James Farmer, Adam Clayton Powell, Elijah Muhammad.[34] As recently as the early sixties, studies indicated that nearly a quarter of top black leadership in Southern communities was drawn from the clergy.[35]

Occasionally ministers have pooled resources for political action. In Philadelphia, 450 ministers, led by Rev. Leon Sullivan, prosecuted a highly successful economic boycott in which groups of ministers approached local companies one at a time, requesting specific increases in jobs for black workers. Refusals were met with product boycotts preached from the pulpit. The technique has been copied elsewhere, although city-wide ministerial associations have never been as active in politics as non-sectarian organizations like the Southern Christian Leadership Conference (SCLC).[36] Recently, the call to become "revolutionaries in the pulpit" has begun to come from some quarters in the church hierarchy itself.[37]

The pre-eminence of the church among institutions supporting black liberation is based on its monopoly of local power resources. Although the church has been derided, states Wyatt Tee Walker of SCLC, ". . . the fact is, it's the most organized thing in the Negro's life. Whatever you want to do in the Negro community, whether it's selling Easter seals or organizing a non-violent campaign, you've got to do it through the Negro church or it doesn't get done. . . ."[38]

We emphasize the physical resources that the church has offered political movements because studies indicate clearly that, by and large, the church has not fostered *attitudes* conducive to political mobilization. A strong fatalism pervades the fundamentalist religions of the poor. Once a person has liturgized his acceptance of this-worldly troubles, the teachings of radicalism—that "trouble" is oppression, and salvation here or never—are a deep threat. In the words of churchgoers themselves: "In my religion we do not approve of anything except living like it says in the Bible. Demonstrating means calling attention to you, and it's sinful." "With God helping to fight our battle, I believe we can do with less demonstrations." "Praying *is* demonstrating."[39] The natural antagonism of religion and politics emerges clearly in Gary Marx's study of this phenomenon in a sample of about 1,000 blacks. Among those for whom religion is extremely important, only 22 percent were found to be militant, while the proportion rises to 62 percent among those for whom religion has no importance at all.[40]

It seems likely that churches are less important in white neighborhoods where a fuller range of community institutions has typically developed. Although in white communities, and particularly small towns, church and political elites can be virtually indistinguishable, it is rarer for whites to receive explicitly political advice from the pulpit.[41] The 18 percent of blacks who have received voting advice at church is matched by only five percent of whites.[42] The Catholicism of the poor is rarely a political faith. Italians, for example, concentrate on a worship of the virgin which has a matriarchal quality which corresponds to its avoidance of authoritative roles in community life.[43] Steiner reports that barely 10-15 percent of chicano men go to Mass. "Why go to church. God is in your deeds. He is not in the sermon of the priest. Let the women go and weep."[44] Chicanos understand that their priests might have some small influence with local officials but simply feel, in the words of a Rio Grande Valley man, "These priests are good and educated men and we must respect them. But they do not understand everything. Their learning comes from books. . . . A priest runs the machinery of the church. He does not see into the trouble of one's soul."[45] Sometimes churches actively contribute to anarchic tendencies in the community. We mentioned the great number of churches found in poor Appalachia. Ironically, the mountaineer uses this variety of churches to keep from making a substantial commitment to any one of them. Instead he will ". . . sample revivals and services in order to find one that meets his own felt needs." The individualism of the mountaineer keeps organized religion from becoming a training ground in cooperative endeavor. If a man doesn't like what his church is up to ". . . he may even form his own church, where he is the minister and "boss," perhaps erecting a building in his front yard and naming the church after his family." In Appalachia, concludes Weller, the church is, "beyond doubt, the most reactionary force in the mountains."[46]

Data of the Local Change Survey indicate that the church now contributes less to the political vitality of the poor than even this pessimistic review of the literature suggests. Of the 631 leaders we interviewed in poor neighborhoods, only 35 were clergymen. Church membership, tending so often among other groups to dominate organizational life, is relatively unimportant in the overall picture of memberships among leaders of the poor. Among white leaders, 12 percent of memberships are church affiliated.

Blacks, at eight percent, are even lower, and for chicanos the figure drops to five percent. Of the 630 leaders we interviewed, 55 indicated they belonged to church-affiliated organizations. Concerning nearly every dimension of political culture these persons resemble most closely members of fraternal, veterans and nationality organizations—groups of purely social intent. Members of both social and religious groups are somewhat older than their fellow leaders but differ little in income or education.[47] Neither category is distinguished by heightened sensitivity to local problems or strong connections to neighbors.

Members of religious groups have a modestly more benign view of the political world than fellow leaders. They are less alienated from government at all levels, and are more likely, when they have an opinion, to identify politics with conventional political institutions. Race pride is not pronounced among church members; only 20 percent feel that riots have contributed to progress compared to 36 percent of leaders at large.[48]

Will the church find a new political role? In neighborhoods which have been most heavily organized there is one possibility for evolution. Although politics and religion do not seem to mix, many of the day-to-day tasks of community building might very well be undertaken by the church. Training seminars, housing projects, cultural programs, educational activities, all need—and many require—affiliation with ongoing institutions. Both church and community would benefit if local congregations lent their strength to these activities. Whether ongoing political efforts will bring such a development in the next decade and whether churches will respond with an uncharacteristic public commitment remains to be seen.

Political Parties

Political parties are a pervasive modality of organization in American politics. Although they surface most visibly as the managers of countless competitions for public office, their influence goes far beyond this in depth and duration. Major issues are inevitably ground through the mill of party values. For better or worse, the fate of America's poor will be as well. We focus here on a small but important corner of the labyrinthine reality of the American party system, neighborhood-level party activists. We will test three perspectives on how parties *might* function against

Local Change data concerning the actual people who do affiliate with party groups in poor neighborhoods.

From one perspective, party organization at the neighborhood level is simply the most decentralized arm of the election system, the level of party organization capable of contacting voters where they live and work. We will not discuss this function of parties extensively because it plays the true potentials of local organization false. The most important dilutions of power in the election process occur not at the local party organization level, but higher up, where arbitrary limitations on the franchise are legislated and candidates indifferent to class issues are nominated by all "competing" factions. Local party group members undoubtedly perform special functions during elections; 91 percent of the ones we interviewed said they vote every time they get a chance, but they do not monopolize concern over voting. The same figure falls below 81 percent for no issue-oriented community organizations, from PTAs to militant ethnic groups. All black party group members support those of their race elected to office, but so do nine out of ten non-members.[49]

Ironically, persons strongly affiliated with a political party are in many ways least qualified as election counselors to the poor. Changing party loyalty, ticket splitting, or refusing to vote at all can be rational strategies for the poor; but their logic can never be admitted by party professionals.[50] Voting on the basis of race is a necessary election tactic of the black poor. A full 73 percent of black leaders we interviewed agree that "In deciding how to vote, you should pay more attention to a man's stand on the race issue than to what party he belongs."[51] Voting on color is inherently anti-party. Race-oriented political goals are strongly backed by about half of black leaders generally, but gain almost no support from black leaders belonging to party groups.[52]

A second perspective on parties comes from those periods when political machines ruled the largest American cities and the scope of political party functions widened to include tasks normally carried out by government itself. Party officials served then as free floating ombudsmen for their constituents, solving local disputes, helping the needy, lending influence to those whose problems brought them to the municipal bureaucracy.[53]

Some see signs of a renaissance of machine politics at the city level. If patronage is dead there are still many contracts, judgeships and municipal attorney positions. In 1971, after a term riddled with scandal, Richard Daley could win an unprecedented fifth term handily . . . with the help of a well-heeled ward organization. Renewed ethnic solidarity is seen by some as creating a favorable environment for modernized party machines. Blacks and Puerto Rican newcomers to the northern cities share with immigrant groups of earlier years the same problems of poverty, discrimination, political powerlessness, ethnic isolation, and inability to cope with life in the city. The result, argues Sorauf, is that "Many of the older political incentives and organizational styles 'work' in their neighborhoods."[54] The community building activities of classic political machines could contribute much to the struggle for unity in a modern day poor neighborhood.

Unfortunately, there is very little evidence that parties are actively engaged in community building in poor neighborhoods. First, they do not have the personnel to carry out major community activities. In white communities nine percent of leaders we interviewed belong to a political party group. In black communities, only four leaders in 100 belong to party groups, and these make up a tiny two percent of total group memberships. Among chicanos, the latter figure is one percent. Representativeness as well as numbers is required of community building cadres. Plunkitt could brag about Tammany chiefs: "Most of the leaders are plain American citizens, of the people and near to the people. . . . We've got bookworms. . . . We keep them for ornaments on parade days. . . . Every district leader is fitted to the district he runs and he wouldn't exactly fit any other district."[55] This is a far cry from the picture of party group members that emerged in the Local Change Study. Twenty-one of the 341 leaders in the Fifty City sample told us they belonged to party groups, usually local organs of the Democratic party.[56] These persons are older than leaders at large by four years and have lived in their locality an extraordinary 26 years longer than members of any other kind of association (see Figure 5.6). Unfortunately, in analysis not reported here, it was discovered that among the poor, long residence is a blunted sword, connoting inertia and fogeyism more than experience and familiarity with local problems.[57] High education and low income are characteristic of many progressive subgroups in poor communities. Party affiliates reverse the pattern, combining a relatively *low* level of schooling (only union members have less) with a high income mode ($8,300). This places them solidly in the middle class, $3,000 a year richer than their "constituents" and $2,000 ahead of the typical community leader. More than any other group, party members say they know a lot of people in the neighborhood, but there is no evidence that this contact goes to the heart of political needs. Party affiliates talk with their neighbors about community issues and have information about local political efforts in *fewer* numbers than members of community social action, civil rights, service, CAP, and militant ethnic groups. This second image seriously misses the mark as well, then: party affiliates are not sufficiently numerous or representative to lead the way in local community development activities.

The third perspective on party organization we will test makes more reasonable demands on party activists. Community mobilization requires a great deal of ongoing political work. Local bureaucracies must be kept honest, federal funds captured, demonstrations mounted, certain persons kept in, and others out, of appointive positions. In the early phases of local activism everyone has a great deal to learn. What better source than party activists for advice about allies and enemies, clues about effective kinds of pressure and practical suggestions for garnering support. From this third perspective then, parties are simply another political action group, but one whose experience and resources could be of special benefit to newer and less established community groups.

In testing this image we should keep in mind that political parties are a distinct minority of community political groups. We asked community leaders on what local issues they had been most active. Most mentioned employment problems, school issues, neighborhood improvement and so on, but about one third spoke of some form of neighborhood, city or national politics. Only 7 percent of those mentioning explicitly political issues belong to political party groups. The same is true of all forms of political activity. The half-a-dozen leaders we interviewed in each city told us they had contacted government officials together about a hundred times in the last year. Overall, only 17 percent of these contacts between community and government had been carried out by party affiliates. As might be expected, the salience of party personnel in more direct forms of political activity is even lower. About 7 percent of the picketing and boycott activity of poor neighborhoods has been carried out by party group members. Nine-tenths of the political activity in poor neighborhoods thus takes place outside the party framework.

In some ways, party affiliates do seem qualified to serve as community political agents, particularly if one thinks of them specializing in pressuring outsiders for change. As Figure 5.4 indicated, they volunteer "presenting demands to outsiders" as their most important leadership role twice as often as other group members. They are the least alienated of all issue-oriented groups from national and local governmental institutions. One third evidence high alienation from national government (15 percent less than average, and 35 percent less than the members of militant ethnic groups). Only one quarter show some alienation from local government (again, 15 percent less than average).

Further data, however, severely prejudices the image of party organs as political action groups. The political world view of party affiliates is not conducive to political involvement. Members, for example, do not see poverty as a political problem. More attribute poverty to personal failings and lack of education than to political or racial injustice.[58] Of all group members party affiliates are *least* angry at the local situation. They have less sympathy for the political demands of their neighbors than every kind of group except fraternal, civic-professional, unions, and service groups (see Figure 5.6 column D-G). Most devastatingly, the figures show that party affiliates are not, in fact, deeply involved in the every-day political activities of poor neighborhoods. Their commitment is more like that of fraternal, church and union group members than that of persons who belong to community political groups. It is difficult to avoid the conclusion that local party organs are pseudo-political agencies. Members might talk more to those in power, but what can they say—how impassioned is their plea—when they show so little sensitivity to the political dimensions of the struggle against poverty?

None of the images of party organizations we have investigated seems to fit. They are neither reliable election counselors, decentralized party-governments, or effective political action groups. In poor neighborhoods party organizations appear to be cultural "survivals," supported from the top down and staffed by the local establishment. All of the functions that parties might play are now being carried out with greater devotion and creativity by indigenous community groups. All this could be viewed with greater equanimity if the poor were not affected by the vitality of the American party system, but they are. Unfortunately, we have not shown that political parties are irrelevant to poverty issues, but that party organization on the local level is; not that the poor can ignore party politics but that party politics have ignored the poor.

We turn now to those organizations we labelled action groups, important numerically because 46 percent of all memberships are in action groups, and from the viewpoint of political innovation, as these are the newest associations of poor neighborhoods. Several types will be introduced briefly before we examine the distinctiveness of each group's political world view (how it diverges from opinion at large) and what contribution each makes to local political activity.

Civil rights groups, the oldest and most familiar of those under discussion, have been severely shaken by the new black political awareness.[59] Their primary goal, to end discrimination, and their primary tactic, to mobilize whites by an appeal to conscience, have both fallen on hard times. Priorities have shifted toward the demands of blacks as a collective nation: more black GNP, more black income, more black influence over local affairs. As James Farmer said after Watts, "Civil rights organizations have failed. No one had any roots in the ghetto." The monopoly of commitment to purposive organization which civil rights groups previously enjoyed among poor blacks is now over. In our sample of black leaders, about one in three belong to civil rights groups; fewer than belong to CAP affiliated organizations, or to community social action groups, or to the remaining miscellany of issue-oriented groups in the community. As Figure 5.5 indicated, the distribution of issue concern among civil rights group members parallels roughly that of other community groups.

Community social action groups are more difficult to describe. Something of their style is revealed in their names. Some betray a devout localism—Block Development Foundation, volunteers for pre-Headstart, United Block Committee Organization. Other names—Black Coalition, Kern County Liberation Movement—reveal attempts to co-ordinate a number of other organizations. Some announce a specific purpose—Welfare Rights Organization, Southeast Food Club, Community Ventures. Others emphasize ethnic makeup—Young Mexican-American Association, Indian-Mexican Alliance. Not a few bear the mark of the publicity director: Fight, Breakthrough, Peace and Freedom, Committee for Better Understanding.

Many community social action groups organize on a geographic basis—project, block, neighborhood—and concern themselves with ways of improving the local area. Getting people who live together to act together places an interesting bias on the kinds of action a group is likely to take. In the words of an Oakland organizer: "There is a strong pull for getting an issue or a project that everyone can agree on, and if someone in the group doesn't pull for this, the organizer does. That is his job. . . . Only a few people need jobs, not everyone has personal complaints about the school or trouble with his landlord. . . . Street cleaning or the need for a stop light are not the most pressing problems poor people face, but they are the ones that face everyone in the neighborhood: poor and non-poor alike. That is why the group turns to them as issues."[60] Some community groups serve as delegate agencies of centralized programs—Headstart, Day-Care or employment counseling, for example. Others are "social brokerage" groups which serve particular kinds of clients—welfare mothers, senior citizens, or victims of rent increases. Many are ad hoc groups formed to take action on temporary grievances—the absence of a street light, a freeway threatening the neighborhood.

As communities have begun to stand on their own feet, many groups that previously thought in terms of "area" or "community development" have moved toward the fullest expression of that goal, neighborhood government.[61] Although belief in decentralized political institutions is a pillar of American political ideals, those ideals have been carefully tailored to exclude the poor. While it is fine for suburbs and rural towns, school districts and watersheds, private corporations and professional societies, local rule does not apply to poor neighborhoods. There, it is said, local rule would preserve existing patterns of segregation, sacrifice honesty and professionalism to the popular will, prejudice metropolitan-wide solutions to social problems, and isolate the needy from revenues of the larger society.

The case seems strong, but it is based on a series of assumptions that many are beginning to question: that rational government is better than committed government; that the vast resources of the haves, if undisturbed, will flow naturally to the have nots; that segregation, not inequality, is the enemy; that local defense is less temperate than national defense; that the poor haven't the skills to compete for national resources with other interests.[62] Any movement in the direction of neighborhood government would see an enormous upsurge in the number and strength of community social action groups. Conversely, whatever vitality we find in these groups can be seen as evidence of leadership skills and habits of cooperation that would support larger responsibilities. If, as Kotler suggests, "The neighborhood is the last remaining unit, territorial unit of public confidence in our cities," then the leaders of these groups will bring that confidence to fulfillment.[63]

Community social action groups have been around long enough for the identification of some weaknesses as well as strengths. Decision making in such groups is often slow and reliant on administratively defined goals and the advice of "experts." In searching for an atmosphere of "sweet reasonableness," action groups can paper over important policy conflicts and stifle new ideas. The spontaneity destroying technicalities of Robert's Rules of Order often arbitrate meeting agendas. Active members are often those with middle-class ambitions, not those closest to the needs of the neighborhood. Staff skills are not always adequate to tasks. It is frequently difficult to interest the poor in political and organizational problems with collective benefits so distant and individual rewards so meager. "The poor do not want organization for its own sake, nor should anybody else. They want better housing, better schools, etc.—they want results. If organization gets them these things, they will buy it. If government gives them these things, as it should, the poor may not need to organize. Organization is only a means to an end."[64]

Militant ethnic groups, with names like Black Brothers Civil Rights Organization, Brown Berets, and New Black Society, form the third category under investigation here. Some Black Panthers are found in our sample, but they are underrepresented primarily because members have no patience with survey research. Among the individuals we did interview, some refused to name groups to which they belonged, indicating that this was information not available to strangers. While some 25 out of 341 leaders told us they belonged to militant ethnic organizations, it seems reasonable to assume that there is another group, somewhat more radical than this and of about the same size, that was missed by the study.[65]

These 25 individuals are, however, an important set of persons. There is much talk of ethnic militancy but little concrete evidence about the people who participate in it and the nature of their commitment. In our sample, one black leader in 13, one Mexican-American in five and one white in 30 said they belonged to a militant ethnic group. Although this is already a sizeable minority (except in the case of whites) the influence of these groups over policy and popular values is undoubtedly even larger than the figures suggest.

Although there is much disagreement concerning the nature of militant ethnic groups, three views predominate: one seeing them as lumpen revolutionary organizations, a second as an educated ideological vanguard, and a third as grass roots pressure groups. Data from the Local Change Survey can directly examine the relative validity of these points of view.

The first image, the organizational equivalent of the "rabble theory" of riots, predominates in the popular press and the musings of legislators. It perceives a movement filled with misfits and criminals manqué, dedicated to a violent assault on American institutions. Activities are sustained by roving revolutionaries who sow discontent in neighborhoods whose actual problems they have never experienced. Ideology is thus demagogic and negative. Adherents have little patience for finite problems with intricate solutions; energy is directed into violent forms of action which create obstacles to progress, not into constructive political activity which might move events slowly forward.

The second school of thought sees militant ethnic groups as an ideological wing of local activism. Support for this point of view comes from the autobiographies of militant ethnic leaders themselves, which often pivot on intellectual awakenings.[66]

From this perspective, the major contribution of militant ethnic groups to local mobilization is their ability to lay bare the complex underlife of capitalism—to present the subtleties of institutional oppression in a way that will move the poor to action. We have presented some evidence to support this perspective. As Figure 5.4 indicated, members of militant ethnic groups, more than those of any other organization, emphasize "getting people angry" in describing their own leadership roles.

The third point of view is the one most favored by partisans of ethnic militancy. It holds that radical ethnic groups are the natural manifestation of a community organizing to promote its political interests. Bobby Seale and Huey Newton split with the "cultural nationalists" of the Soul Students Advisory Council to form the Black Panthers because of their dedication to this interpretation of black power.[67] Violence, from this perspective, is not a preferred political tactic but one often requisite for community building. Its functions are to protect the local community against violence from outside, shock residents into an awareness of their own power, and to eliminate at least the unmotivated fringe of police brutality. Adherents of this image brag that ethnic militants are cut in the image of Stagolee, the ". . . bad nigger off the block [who] didn't take shit from nobody. All you had to do was organize him, like Malcolm X, make him politically conscious."[68]

At one time militant ethnic groups had so little popular support that their claim to leadership in the struggle for community development seemed hollow. This is no longer the case. In a *Time* poll, 41 percent of blacks countrywide agreed that "supporting militant organizations" is one way to help blacks make real progress.[69] General residents in our Five City sample support the increasing militancy of community groups two to one.

We turn now to Local Change evidence characterizing community social action, civil rights and militant ethnic groups as political subcultures (see Figure 5.6). One attribute common to all these groups can be noted at the outset: disproportionate contribution to neighborhood political work. The three rank first, second and third among groups in level of political activity of members. The importance of action groups to the political life of the community can be gauged from the proportion of total local activity carried out by members. If we include CAP sponsored organizations—similar in many regards to those under discussion—fully 80 percent of local activity by leaders is carried out by persons affiliated with action groups. The comparable figure for the entire collection of traditional groups is 35 percent.[70]

The fact that civil rights groups can be found contributing on a par with other action groups suggests a successful adaptation to the new modalities of local politics. It is interesting to note as well that militant ethnic group members participate extensively in *all* forms of political activity, including the most conventional. They vote, speak with governmental officials and confront local institutions in person as much as members of any other group.[71]

Differences between action groups begin to emerge when we look at the socio-economic status of members. Civil rights group members, predictably, come from a middle-class strata of community leadership. The modal income of members is $8,000, $1,600 above average. Sixty-five percent have attended some college, 24 percent more than average. Nearly a quarter have been to graduate school. Professional persons and full-time community service workers are over-represented among members.[72] This class bias probably accounts for the lackluster support members give demands for income maintenance and housing (civic and professional group members, with incomes averaging $8,700, show least support of all for these policies).

Community social action group members have a socio-economic status only moderately higher than leaders generally (15 percent more have attended college; earnings are $1,000 above average.) Members, at an average age of 39, are two years younger than other leaders.

Militant ethnic group members, however, show the greatest distinctiveness in socio-economic status—of all group members they have the highest educational attainment. For example, all those we interviewed had high school diplomas; a full 74 percent had attended some college. The facts seem to put to rest the Stagolee image of ethnic militancy, at least concerning community leaders who affiliate with the cause. Equally important, however, militant ethnic groups have, at $5,000, the *lowest* average income. Of the three kinds of groups under discussion here, they alone draw selectively from leaders with incomes approximating those of their constituents. With so much education, members have earning capacity far in excess of the poor generally, but for the time being, they seem uninterested in capitalizing on that potential. The poor are led in nearly every instance by persons of higher socio-economic status than themselves. Civil rights activists, with high education, high income, and no marked enthusiasm for class-oriented political demands, give the impression of being on their way out of the ghetto. Ethnic militants, with high education, low income, and dedication to class interests, seem more deeply committed to the needs of the poor.

We can go beyond evidence concerning socio-economic position in searching for sentitivity to the needs of the people. Surely those who know their neighbors and talk often with them about community issues—those familiar with neighborhood problems and community efforts to resolve them—have a special claim to representativeness. The three action groups under discussion here are in advance of leadership generally in all these respects. Among leaders at large, 68 percent talk often with neighbors about community issues; the figure for militant ethnic groups is 88 percent. Forty percent of community social action group members have a high level of information about local political events, 15 percent more than leaders at large.

Do members of any of these groups boast a distinctive political world view? For the large category of action groups the answer is no. Members represent rather precisely the prevailing consensus on poverty issues and local problems. Although those who belong to community social action groups would disagree at many points with middle Americans, they exert no independent force on their peers.[73]

Most interesting in the world view of civil rights group activists is the absence of race ideology. The movement that first brought the country to an awareness of racism has finally lost the initiative on race issues. Perhaps many believe their goals have already been achieved. Others undoubtedly feel that sensitivity to racism, once marked by calm strength, has now hardened to a turbulent and dangerous passion. For whatever reason, race pride is now not much stronger among civil rights group activists than among black leaders at large; support for race goals—black teachers, black stores, black voting—is actually weaker. Perhaps bitterness at the charges of Tomism which have emerged from the new ideological balance accounts for a negative cast to the world view of civil rights groups. When asked to define "political," 32 percent (10 percent more than average) use hostile imagery: "white folks lying to blacks to get their votes," ". . . racist methods and tactics used by whites . . . ," "the machine that runs this place." Although three out of four believe their neighbors can be trusted, this is the lowest figure for all action groups and 16 points behind participants in militant ethnic organizations.

The world view of militant ethnic groups is the most individualized of those under consideration here. It alone attains the status of a coherent ideology, distinguishable from the beliefs of ghetto leadership at large. It alone exerts a selective pressure on the belief structure of leaders generally. Its first aspect is an ardent localism, a trust in the people and their power to bring about change through united action. When asked why poor areas have received attention in recent years, twice as many militant ethnic group members cite factors originating within the community: "better organization of the community people," "riots," as cite factors external to the community: "more awareness of ghetto situation through media," "poverty programs assisted" and so forth.[74] While just over half of leaders at large described three different local problems to our interviewers, 76 percent of militant ethnic group members did.

A second aspect of this world view is a deep suspiciousness of traditional institutions, governmental and private. A third of leaders generally evaluate local institutions positively, only 16 percent of those who belong to militant ethnic groups do. Forty-one percent of leaders generally feel the community has a lot of say in the way the schools are run; other action groups are six percent lower, militant ethnic groups 17 percent lower. Alienation from local government is endemic among the poor. Leaders belonging to other action groups, however, differ in being *less* alienated than the average citizen—more willing to give mayors and councilmen the benefit of the doubt. Only militant ethnic group members show a heightened wariness of local government, with 64 percent (24 percent more than non-members) evidencing "some" alienation. In a similar vein, only ethnic group members are distinguished by heightened skepticism concerning national institutions.

There are other signs that ethnic militancy has a uniquely ideologized world view. When asked to define the word "political," about half of leaders mention something about traditional political institutions or say they have no idea at all. Among other action groups the proportion is about 40 percent, but among militant ethnic group members it falls to 16 percent with the rest giving answers indicating some political consciousness. This sophistication leads naturally to a tendency to see a broad range of social institutions as political. One-third of leaders at large, but a full 54 percent of those in militant ethnic groups, score high on our measure of politicization.

Finally, only militant ethnic groups provide a milieu in which race pride and race politics are looked on with special favor. We have already mentioned that civil rights groups no longer perform this function. Now we can note that none of the groups we are investigating show high race pride much above the 27 percent level for leaders at large. The figure for militant ethnic group members is 77 percent. The evidence suggests further that although militant ethnic groups use race issues, they are not captured by them. Support for specifically racial policies, like having black teachers in black schools, is higher in this group than among leaders at large but the differential is not great.[75] Support for race goals does not extend to plans which would have blacks go it completely alone. Black separatist sentiment is nowhere very strong—only three percent of black leaders at large give separatism more than "some" support—but the figure rises to only one in ten for militant ethnic group members.

There is a slight tendency for action group members to focus on specifically political issues, but militant ethnic group members are by far the most distinctive in this regard, with 42 percent mentioning some political issue as their highest priority. Some impression of activities undertaken by members can be gained from typical responses to our question concerning issues on which leaders had been most active: "organizing blacks who aren't scared to stand up for the right to get together," "education first, then employment," "voter registration; school involvement and control within the community; housing," "working with the strikers [farm workers in California], helping to raise money for them; model cities planning commission," "Helping young kids in the high school become more aware of police brutality," "education and the schools; welfare and job opportunities."

In introducing militant ethnic groups we outlined three competing viewpoints on their nature. The first, which we now see as furthest from the truth, holds them to be roving revolutionaries, blinded to the true and temperate needs of the poor. The image contains but one element of truth—members *are* more inclined to violent forms of political action. Nearly half of militant ethnic group members have a high propensity to violence, compared with seven percent of leaders at large. It should be noted, however, that increased openness to violence accompanies *all* forms of civic organization in poor communities, from the PTA to ethnic militancy. The image as a whole fails, however, because our evidence suggests that members *are* in touch with community needs and problems, *are* local persons and *do* participate in all forms of political activity, not only those that are more radical.

The remaining images contain more truth. Members are, as the second suggests, an ideological elite. They alone might move other leaders in the direction of a radical critique of governing institutions, heightened race pride, and sensitivity to institutional oppression. Also consistent with this image is the high educational attainment of members. Nearly 75 percent of leaders who belong to militant ethnic groups have attended institutions of higher education. What the image fails to capture, however, is the localism of members and their commitment to concrete political action.

The third viewpoint which sees militant ethnic groups as grass roots pressure organizations comes closest to the truth, even though its contention that members are a cross section of the poor is not fully correct. Adherents are local (the typical member has lived in the area for 16 years), and poor (their income of $5,800 places them midway between residents and leaders generally). Many have returned to the ghetto voluntarily after educational experience that would have equipped them for success in the larger society. Some told us they had dropped out of college and returned to the community to take on such jobs as "community organizer for Operation Bootstrap," "teacher," "groundsman at the University," "insurance agent," "newspaper reporter." Others went on to graduate school and found such jobs as "Project Director, Concentrated Employment Program," "Assistant Director, Headstart," and "cab driver and part-time poverty worker." This redeployment of educated persons into local militancy is a significant development for the political situation of the poor.

The image of ethnic militancy as grass roots organization alone does justice to the picture of political vitality revealed by this analysis. Adherents are more aware than any other subgroup of concrete local problems and, in spite of a healthy mistrust of all institutions, most inclined to say that people outside the area are more concerned about its problems now than five years ago. Rounding out the picture is the receptivity of members to all forms of political activity, conventional and direct, which might show promise in a given situation.

SUMMARY

In many ways the picture we have sketched supports the conventional view that group life among the poor is impoverished. Half of the general population we interviewed told us they did not even know if groups in their area had been getting more militant. People in poor neighborhoods have many local acquaintances—more, our data suggest, than middle-class persons—but interpersonal trust is depressingly low. Many read newspapers but few discuss community issues with their friends. Seventy-seven percent are angry at things around their neighborhoods, but half are openly pessimistic about getting people together for a common cause.[76]

A closer look at churches and political parties, two organizations with much potential for supporting community development, revealed two worn-out institutions. Other research has indicated that church membership saps militancy. Our data suggest the growing irrelevance of the church in two other areas: leadership development and the provision of political resources to secular movements. Now, only 6 percent of poor persons choose clergy as leaders and only five-eight percent of group memberships among leaders are church affiliated. Leaders who belong to church groups are more status quo oriented, complacent about community problems, and uninclined to take political action.

None of the images we tested concerning political parties fit well. Members are too few and too parochial to qualify as conscientious election counselors to the poor. Considering the paucity of problem solving resources available to members and their unrepresentativeness, the image of parties as neighborhood governments seems no more precise. Even the portrayal of parties as community political agents appeared severely flawed. Party group members are neither sympathetic to the·needs of the poor nor unusually active in the new politics.

Organizational life of the poor is not as highly ramified as that of the larger society. Other Americans are twice as likely to belong to some community group, four times as likely to have some experience as a group leader. These sobering facts must be kept in mind as we review signs of political awakening and organizational vitality in poor neighborhoods.

We can now appreciate more fully the special combination of community awareness and political concern that accompanies group involvement among chicanos. The average chicano leader belongs to two politically oriented organizations. One in five belongs to a militant ethnic group. Perhaps the most important sign of life in poor neighborhoods is the growing importance of what we called action groups. In almost every respect these represent an improvement over the values of traditional groups. Older community groups are tied directly to the local establishment and feed on elitism and satisfaction, not democracy and discontent. The impact of traditional groups is blunted by their officer-selection procedures which prove on a small scale the general rule of human association that the satisfied lead. Action groups, by contrast, respond to political and racial dimensions of cooperative impulse and are led by self-confident persons, angry at the local situation, sensitive to racial pride, and committed to acting on the basis of their convictions. This is a major new development. In black areas, fully half of memberships are in action groups. Group involvement may be weaker among the poor than in the society at large, but in recent times it has doubled—and doubled in the political dimension. For whites, the proportion of action group memberships is somewhat lower but at a third, still significant.

Within the category of action groups we find one subculture of great importance. Militant ethnic groups, although a minority of new organizations, set the highest standards of commitment to the needs of the poor and dedication to action on their behalf. There is some evidence that the depletion of community leadership resources is slowing down. Officers of action groups, and even more, those of militant ethnic groups, have high educational levels but seem frequently to have chosen community service employment which does not return much income.

It is particularly significant that we found a neighborhood leadership strata deeply committed to the political future of the poor and very active in neighborhood organizations.[77] Without these persons the picture would be a good deal bleaker. It is unlikely that the modest involvement of the poor generally could be sustained without the encouragement of local leadership. Only about one resident in four belongs to any group at all. The typical leader belongs to nearly two. Community leaders possess more of the prerequisites for active group life than the rank and file. They are more trusting of their neighbors, they talk more about local problems, and they are more familiar with local cooperative efforts. Although they have a higher socio-economic status than general residents, status is actually less important in promoting group membership among them than among the rank and file. Their participation seems less a protective consolidation of the local establishment and more a reaching out in friendship and concern to the neighborhood.

Understandably, group life in poor neighborhoods is not as lively as in American society at large. Our analysis, however, has revealed unmistakable signs of resources for further growth. Capable, committed leadership is now available for community endeavors. Rank and file are highly responsive to the organizational dimensions of political change. Policies based on *fear* of group action among the poor can now be seen as fantasies of the establishment, for it is precisely the most radical groups that provide a committed leadership, dedicated to responsible action for concrete progress. Poor communities with meagre resources cannot hope to go it alone, but the capacity to actualize decentralized control of social life does exist. It remains to the larger society to make use of it.

FIGURE 5.6
RANKINGS OF COMMUNITY GROUPS ACCORDING
TO SELECTED CRITERIA*

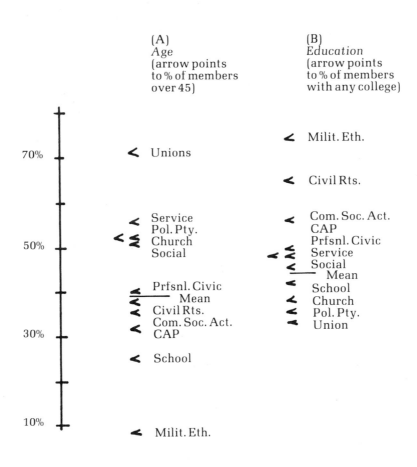

* Based on data from Leaders of the Poor in Fifty Cities. See Appendix B for scales, and Appendix C-18 for exact percentages and N's.

FIGURE 5.6 (cont.)

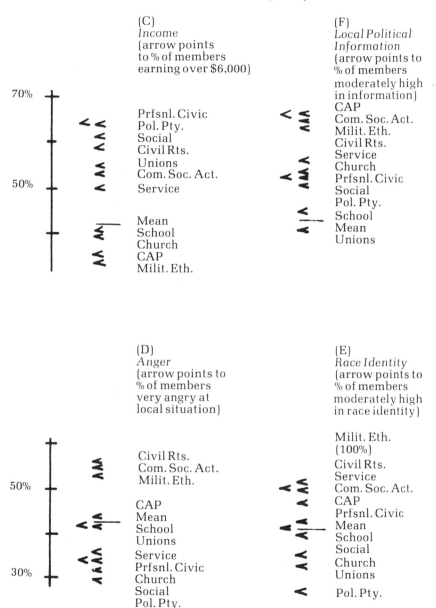

(C)
Income
(arrow points
to % of members
earning over $6,000)

70%

Prfsnl. Civic
Pol. Pty.
Social
Civil Rts.
Unions
Com. Soc. Act.
Service

50%

Mean
School
Church
CAP
Milit. Eth.

(F)
*Local Political
Information*
(arrow points to
% of members
moderately high
in information)

CAP
Com. Soc. Act.
Milit. Eth.
Civil Rts.
Service
Church
Prfsnl. Civic
Social
Pol. Pty.
School
Mean
Unions

(D)
Anger
(arrow points to
% of members
very angry at
local situation)

Civil Rts.
Com. Soc. Act.
Milit. Eth.

50%

CAP
Mean
School
Unions

Service
Prfsnl. Civic
Church
Social
Pol. Pty.

30%

(E)
Race Identity
(arrow points to
% of members
moderately high
in race identity)

Milit. Eth.
(100%)
Civil Rts.
Service
Com. Soc. Act.
CAP
Prfsnl. Civic
Mean
School
Social
Church
Unions

Pol. Pty.

FIGURE 5.6 (cont.)

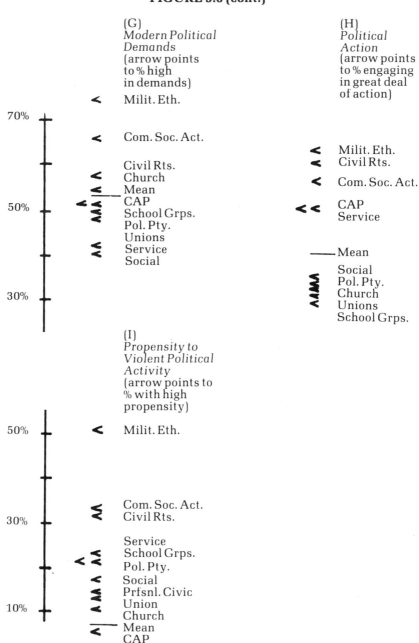

(G)
*Modern Political
Demands*
(arrow points
to % high
in demands)

(H)
*Political
Action*
(arrow points
to % engaging
in great deal
of action)

70%

< Milit. Eth.

< Com. Soc. Act.

Civil Rts.
Church
Mean
CAP
50%
School Grps.
Pol. Pty.
Unions
Service
Social

< Milit. Eth.
< Civil Rts.

< Com. Soc. Act.

CAP
Service

——Mean

Social
Pol. Pty.
Church
Unions
School Grps.

30%

(I)
*Propensity to
Violent Political
Activity*
(arrow points to
% with high
propensity)

50%   < Milit. Eth.

Com. Soc. Act.
30%   Civil Rts.

Service
School Grps.
Pol. Pty.
Social
Prfsnl. Civic
Union
10%   Church
Mean
CAP

6 The Political Status of Poor Women

Although women's issues have begun to enter strategic calcula
tions at all levels of American politics, women's liberation as a
movement remains one of the least intelligible trends of contemporary politics. Few have kept patience with a cause which
invades private lives with such resolution yet fails to offer a sat-
isfactorily precise manifesto of public goals. Understanding and
analysis are complicated by the smothering women's liberation
has received in the hands of the media.[1] Nine out of ten persons
in a recent Massachusetts poll had heard or read about the women's
liberation movement.[2] It is dangerous to turn to the movement
itself for facts. Political organizations must gear the divulgence
of information to overriding political imperatives: rounding up
support, converting support to action, and exacting maximum
concessions from those in power. Empirical analysis of women's
liberation as a social phenomenon is virtually non-existant.

The topic here is an important but little understood facet of the
movement: the political status of women in the newly awakened
poor neighborhoods of America. It is a sensitive issue. Women's
liberation can expect to have little national impact without the
support of poor and working class women. Until recently, however, its influence seems to have rarely spread beyond the ranks
of the educated and upper-middle class. There are many perspectives on the questions we will be dealing with—those of local
politicians, black male activists, committed feminists and, of

course, poor women themselves. We cannot hope to address such a variety of concerns directly. Our goal is rather to present some hard facts which should be of interest to all—hard facts concerning the attitudes, activities and political status of poor women nationwide. Of the 630 leaders interviewed in the Local Change Study in one hundred communities, 40 percent were women. In the five neighborhoods chosen for intensive study, 55 percent of the 1,114 general residents interviewed were women. Information gathered in these interviews will reveal with some precision whether or not the evolving political culture of poor neighborhoods has enabled new definitions of women's place in political life.

Following a brief look at the political status of American women generally, evidence from the Local Change Survey will be used to evaluate three hypotheses suggesting, optimistically, that the situation of poor women *is* more favorable than that of women in general. The first maintains that the political revitalization of poor neighborhoods has created a situation of *crisis egalitarianism* for women there. The second argues that *poor black women* are especially advantaged, vis-a-vis men, and can therefore be expected to be advanced politically. The third sees in the *women's liberation movement* a signficiant force for change in poor neighborhoods. Following these evaluations, a typology of women leaders, based on types actually found in poor areas, will be presented.

WOMEN IN AMERICAN POLITICS

The situation of American women as portrayed in the literature of political science can be summarized briefly. Women, it suggests, are uninvolved, moralistic and localist.

Lack of Involvement

Women's voting habits have often received tangential consideration in studies aimed at broader issues. *The American Voter*, a classic study of American voting, reports that although there are few differences between men and women in party identification and sense of citizen duty, when it comes time to vote, women turn out consistently ten percent less than men.[3] The disparity is affected by several factors. It rises to 28 percent, for example, in village and rural sections of the country. Less educated white women living in the South, where attitudes toward sex are more parochial, vote 19 percent less frequently than men. Among high school and college graduates in the North, however, education reduces the differential to three percent. Even at higher educational levels, however, women engage in such domesticated activism as letter writing less frequently than men.[4]

What explains the differential in voting between men and women?[5] Lane emphasizes the "limited orbits" of women and the prevailing media image of women in household roles. Others seek a clue in the gap between men and women in political efficacy— the feeling that one's opinions matter to those in power. Differences in this regard can be quite large. The proportion of college women outside the South "high" in political efficacy is 82 percent that of men.[6] For grade school educated women the figure falls to 41 percent.[7] Low political efficacy is sometimes traced to more general role prescriptions that make women the submissive partner in interpersonal relationships.[8]

Women by and large follow the political leads of their husbands. More husbands and wives (00 percent) share party identification than any other combination of persons in the immediate family. Given the class basis of marriage and politics in this country, it is usually unnecessary for either to change party affiliation, but when conflict arises, it is most often the wife who adjusts. There is evidence of enormous pressure for conformity in voting within the family as well. In one election panel study, only four percent stated they had voted differently than anyone in their family.[9] The political life of women is derivative. In early years, daughters more than sons remain loyal to parental political values. In marriage, allegiance is transferred from father to husband.

The "Moralism" and "Non-violence" of women

Many observers contend that women are more absolutist and emotional than men, more inclined to the feeling that "the values they are familiar with are the only values." This ethical emotionalism is attributed variously to physiological instability, the natural emotionalism of those most intimately responsible for bringing up children, and isolation from the virile outer world of competing moral orders.[10]

The most frequently cited evidence concerning ethical emotionalism is sex-related differences in attitudes toward war. Irrespective of the scale used, men are ". . . more certain nuclear weapons should be used . . . more likely to believe that the United States could achieve a meaningful victory . . . more confident that they personally would survive the war . . . (and) more optimistic about its outcome both in a personal and a social sense."[11] A simulation of the 1960 presidential election found at one point that Nixon had a slight popular margin due entirely to a 10 percent advantage among women who favored Nixon over Kennedy as capable of "avoiding war by negotiating with Russian leaders."[12] On a more local level, studies indicate that male-female juries favor underdogs (plaintiffs and litigants of inferior social status) more than all male juries.[13] The greater tolerance of men for violence is generally seen as an extension of the rough aggressiveness characteristic of the American ideal of manhood. Women, by contrast, are encouraged to ". . . express themselves as more compassionate and sympathetic, more timid, more fastidious and esthetically sensitive, more emotional in general."[14]

Emotionalism and non-violence are slippery concepts. Objectivity concerning them is frequently a cover for yet another level of sex-related prejudice. Is it a "non-violent" attitude which fears the most likely demise of the planet? Is it "emotionalism" which prefers government subsidy of pre-schools to that of big business? We will return to the issue again, suggesting that some sex-related attitude differences disappear altogether among individuals of similar power status.

The Localism of Women

There is broad public consensus that only certain issues are appropriate for the involvement of women. Lane presents two rankings of political issues in order of appropriateness for discussion by the League of Women Voters. The left column is the ordering by husbands, the right, that by their wives.[15]

	Rank by Husbands	Rank by Wives
Local Government	1	1
Education Policy	2	2
Civil Rights	3.5	3
Foreign Policy	3.5	4
Administrative Reform	5	5
Social Welfare Policy	6	6
Tax Policy	7	7
Labor Policy	8	8

Husbands and wives agree, local government and education are the most appropriate topics for women's groups to discuss, taxation and labor policy the least. Presumably the location of wifely responsibilities in the home and neighborhood qualifies women for greater responsibilities in the local policy area. In Lane's words, "Within the political sphere, a sexually differentiated role system makes appropriate a female interest and responsibility for local affairs, particularly as they relate to education, reserving labor and foreign relations more particularly for men." Later, we will present evidence suggesting that developments in poor neighborhoods have brought about major changes in this issue segregation of women.

As the brief literature we have just reviewed suggests, the topic of women and politics has not been a major concern of political scientists. Works on political parties tend to ignore the topic altogether.[16] It receives scant attention as well from students of political values and beliefs. Lane's sensitive exploration of American political beliefs, for example, treats without apology only the beliefs of men. It seems natural that his chapter on "Fathers and Sons" not be accompanied by one on "Mothers and Daughters."[17] The picture that political scientists have painted is one of a system in equilibrium. True, there is some disparity in inclination to vote, but with the ineluctable forces of education and urbanization on the side of progress, equality can not be far off. Women spend time on issues of special concern to them. So do men. The gracious non-violence of women helps keep the ship afloat when the passions of men threaten to capsize it. From a cross cultural perspective, some have even viewed the status of women in American democracy as one of its peculiar geniuses. Almond and Verba's elaborate study of political belief in the United States, Great Britain, Germany, France and Mexico, reports that in America, of all these countries, women are the least restricted to local issues, most equal to men in feelings of political competence and most "active and involved in their countries, both in an informal and in an organizational sense." It is because American women have closed the gap in political involvement, the authors contend, that the American family is such a powerful influence for democratic ideals.[18]

It is natural that few proposals for action have emerged from the political science literature. Although the gap in political involvement could be narrowed by a further politicization of the female role, this path, some note warily, has its price. ". . . It is too seldom remembered in the American society that working girls and career women, and women who insistently serve the community in volunteer capacities, and women with extra-curricular interests of an absorbing kind are often borrowing their time and attention and capacity for relaxed play and love from their children to whom it rightly belongs."[19] Adlai Stevenson lectured the '55 class of Smith College in a similar vein: "This assignment for you, as wives and mothers, you can do in the living room with a baby in your lap or in the kitchen with a can opener in your hand. If you're clever you may even practice your saving art on that unsuspecting husband while's he's watching television. I think there is much you can do about our crisis in the humble role of housewife. I could wish you no better vocation than that."[20]

The scientific study of the powerless has never flourished in the hands of the advantaged. There is, for example, Dr. Edward H. Clark's 1873 reply to feminist demands for more education: boys, he maintained, can study six hours a day, but if a girl applies herself for more than four, the "brain or special apparatus will suffer . . . leading to those grevious maladies which torture a woman's earthly existence, called leucorrhoea, amenorrhoea, dysmenorrhoea, chronic and acute ovaritis, prolapsus uteri, hysteria, neuralgia and the like."[21] Analysis of the political status of women has aimed at once too high and too low. The search for measurable attributes has abstracted the attention of analysts beyond the lived reality of powerlessness that fills the lives of women in the United States. When political scientists decided that discrimination by sex simply divided the political system down the middle without changing its policy output, that was all they wanted to know.[22] Only recently, through the writings of women on the issue, have the human consequences of powerlessness become clear. Attention to measurable behavior kept the same analysts from the powerful general observation that women are systematically denied positions of influence in all the institutions of power in American life.[23]

We turn briefly, then, to these two topics: lived powerlessness and exclusion from power.

Dependency and Political Resources

In American society women are systematically trained into dependency and denied a wide variety of resources, open to men, which could be converted to political power.[24] Because sex-roles are so integral to adult life, communication of the requirements of these roles begins at a very early age. By three or four, children have begun to choose "sex-appropriate" toys. For boys this means instruments of action—the guns, trucks, and kits which carry one's imagination to larger tasks. For girls, it means implements of service—playcookery, baby bottles and dressing-up. By age five or six, before formal education has begun, there is often strict learning of this segregation of objects into male and female.[25] A child's first contact with the printed word reinforces these images. A recent survey of five social studies texts for grades one to three revealed that men were described in over 100 job contexts, while women figured in only 30. With access to identical library facilities, girls quickly specialize in fiction and the recounting of domestic adventures while boys choose biography, history and non-fiction.[26] Girls tend to score lower than boys on standardized tests of analytical thinking because, some argue, there is a strong link between analytic capacity and "independence and mastery-training—whether and how soon a child is encouraged to assume initiative, to take responsibility for himself, and to solve problems by himself, rather than rely on others for the direction of his activity."[27]

This early training, in which men are cast as responsible agents and women as homemakers, has its impact on explicitly political attitudes. Greenstein's study of political values among students in grades four through eight in four New Haven schools confirmed this conclusion.[28] Girls have less political information, express less interest in news events, identify less with political figures, and score higher in "no opinion" categories than boys. Even more important for later political activity is a gradual lowering of self-expectation. In early school years, girls achieve higher levels than boys, but soon they fall behind. The shift is gradually internalized through a change in expectations. Boys are increasingly felt, by both boys and girls, to be *inherently* more capable of handling difficult tasks. The change comes at precisely the moment a child begins to sense the importance to society of his relations with the opposite sex. Girls learn quickly that "to achieve in life as an adult, females need to achieve in non-academic ways, that is, attaining the social graces, achieving beauty in person and dress, finding a desirable social status, marrying the right man." Many of the rituals surrounding early sex relations are variations on this theme of mastery and dependence. He exercises his growing ego by making all the physical arrangements. She nurtures her femininity by carefully preparing her person for encounters, developing patience where initiative is denied, coyly guarding her major political resource, access to her person. The culture sings for her:

> "Every girl needs someone who
> she can always look up to.
> You know I love you of course
> Let me know that you're the boss."

and advises him "How to get and hold a woman."

> "By herself woman is all mixed up but
> superb as an auxiliary."

The language used by high school girls to describe their dating relationships is political to the core: your steady "Likes to be the boss. He's the man—he's supposed to know everything." "Let's face it, what girl doesn't love to hear her boyfriend tell her what to do." "Girls act different on dates. More phoney-cute, always agreeing."[29]

Throughout their early lives, women continue to avoid success and undervalue themselves. In a recent study male and female undergraduates were asked to complete a story beginning, "After first term finals, Ann (John for the men) finds herself at the top of her medical school class." Sixty-five percent of the women showed strong fears of rejection and emphasized barriers to happiness or future progress. Only ten percent of the men indicated such fears. In another study, 140 college women were asked to evaluate a series of articles in six fields. All were given identical articles, but for one half, the article was attributed to a man, for the other half, to a woman. In every field, from law and city planning through the female preserves of art history and dietetics, the women rated the female-titled articles lower. This self-devaluation takes a deadly toll in the confidence necessary for political assertion.[30]

Marriage would seem to provide a respite from this syndrome of powerlessness. Here, one would suppose, a woman can finally relax in the security of her power-by-proxy over the world and enjoy her rightful role as mother superior of the values of the young. Soon, however, the generational cycle comes full swing as children begin to participate in the devaluation of their mother's political status. Fifth grade girls, when asked who would be the best to go to for voting advice, check "father" over "mother" two to one. For boys the proportion is four to one. An intriguing glimpse of the political status of wives comes from some figures quoted by Lazarsfeld in a study of voting habits. Forty-five women in his sample reported having discussed an election with their husbands. In a matched sub-group of husbands, only four mentioned such conversations with their wives. It would appear that for husbands political discussion with their wives does not attain the status of serious conversation.[31]

There is political learning in this: ". . . wherever there exists the display of power there is politics, and in women's relations with men there is continual transfer of power. Women are natural guerillas. Scheming, we nestle in the enemy's bed, avoiding open warfare, watching the options, playing the odds." The battery of political skills that a girl learns to manipulate are those classically available to the victimized: sensitivity, fantasies of power, indirectness, ingratiation, petty revenge, sabotage, identification with the dominant group's norms, and passivity.[32] Politics is the interpersonal art par excellence. In it one is constantly at the mercy of the quality of one's interactions with people. The female hesitancy to take issue, while occasionally easing political tensions, keeps women from participating in the creative turning points of purposive action. Political executives, like business executives, are fully aware of the problems that women face in convincing others of their seriousness. Eloquent testimony to the exclusion of women from outreach roles in business is the completely male complexion of airline flights during business hours.

The power disparity between men and women continues to grow through middle age. Women are considered old ten to fifteen years before men. At the same age that a man enters his prime working years, a woman enters a period of self consciousness associated with loss of youth. Aging men are granted all benefit of the doubt in point of physical presence. "The male body lends credence to assertions, while the female takes it away." "In this context, only imagine Johnson, Nixon, or Humphrey as women. Who would put up with them for an instant."[33] The culture smiles knowingly on the whims of an old man with a young girl. The knowing old woman with the young boy is taboo.

Women do not generally have the power base of working in

important and financially rewarding occupations. The statistics speak for themselves. One third of working women are employed in seven occupations: secretary, saleswomen, general private household worker, teacher in elementary school, bookkeeper, waitress and nurse. Recent changes do not alter the picture much. Since 1950, seven occupations have been added to the list of those in which over 100,000 women are employed: baby-sitter, charwoman and cleaner, counter and fountain worker, file clerk, housekeeper (apart from private households), stewardess, musician and receptionist. Men anticipate that the women they meet will be employed in one of these professions. All professional interactions of the sexes, political or otherwise, must thus overcome an implicit devaluation of one partner. Political strategists do not relish adding this to their list of dilemmas.

While occupational discrimination keeps women from status resources, concomitant pay differentials mean, fewer women bring financial independence to political life. A woman needs a college degree to match what the average man earns with an 8th grade education. The average annual salary in 1968 of full-time, year-round white female workers was $4,580, for white men $7,870. Comparable figures for blacks are $3,487 and $5,314.

In a discussion of political resources it is interesting to consider for a moment if there are *advantages* that might accrue to women and be denied to men. In the business world, for example, there is what some call a "pretty girl prerogative." Advantages can come to vivacious women if they are willing to exploit their relationship with men as a political resource (the limitations of the strategy in the "rough and tumble" world of politics are manifest). The formal deference accorded women can occasionally be turned to advantage. Kempton tells us, for example, that the role of female journalist has a few saving graces, "For one thing she never has to pick up a tab. If she is even remotely serious, people praise her work much more than they would praise the work of a comparably talented man. . . . And finally, people tell her things they would not tell a man. Many men think the secrets they tell a woman are automatically off the record . . . often they confuse her attention with sexual interest."[34]

Exclusion from Power

Women are excluded from positions in organizations in direct proportion to the power vested in those positions.[35] "Men are not generally speaking anti-women," said Gerald Ford during debate on the Equal Rights Amendment, "it just seems to work out that way." Figure 6.1 presents four typical examples of just how it works out. Along each vertical axis are ranged positions of increasing influence within a given sphere. The shaded proportion represents the percent of persons at each level who are women.[36] The unshaded portion is accordingly the proportion of men found at the same level. The dominant pattern in these charts is "peak discrimination"—the closer a position is to the peak,

FIGURE 6.1 PEAK EXCLUSION OF WOMEN*

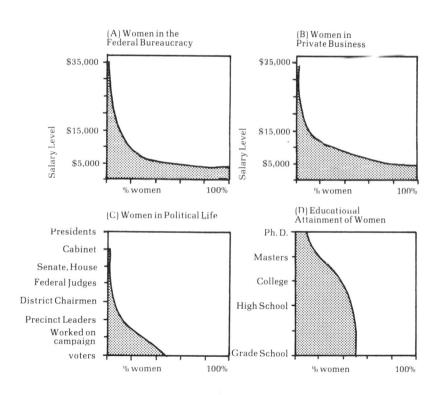

*See Appendix C-19 for references and exact figures.

the fewer women one finds in it. The implication of these figures for the distribution of power, as opposed to position, is even more radical, for in all organizations, power thins out rapidly downward in the ranks. To indicate no sex discrimination, the boundaries of the shaded areas would have to rise roughly in the center of each figure. Movement of the line to the right of center indicates a stratum of roles specializing women. These all occur at the bottom of the hierarchies as in 6.1, Part B, where the category of office workers earning less than $6,000 is 99 percent women. When the shaded portion *begins* to the left of center there are no levels where women hold a majority. There thus appears to be no form of political activity where women predominate. The nature of exclusion from educational attainment is clear in figure 6.1, Part D. Of equal interest is data indicating that at the higher levels, there has been no progress in equalizing attainment since 1900.[37]

The exclusion of women from influential work situations is well-documented. Figure 6.1, part B, contains employment data for one large financial institution. The figures at the peaks of all professions are similar: seven percent of doctors are women, four percent of lawyers, four percent of full professors, eight percent of scientists, two percent of business executives in general. Not revealed in the figure, however, is another phenomenon, the "helpmate" status which organizations often assign women. When a woman, low in the hierarchy, is discovered carrying unusually large responsibilities, she is often granted "Gal Friday" status—symbolic recognition without increased salary or title. Data concerning exclusion in private enterprise are included in Figure 6.1 for several reasons. First, to be excluded from private power in America, where government expenditures are only about a quarter of GNP, is to be excluded from a greal deal of power.[38] Second, the dynamics of exclusion from business and politics are quite similar. The reasons a corporation specializes women in secretarial roles are the same reasons a party turns to women for folders and stampers. Presidents of corporations with no women on their board would find easy commiseration with the nation's presidents, none of whom has appointed a woman to a cabinet post since 1955. Business leaders fear the inability of other businessmen to take a woman seriously; political dealers fear the 43 percent of the population who said in 1959 that they would not vote for a well-qualified woman from their own party for president.[39]

As Figure 6.1 indicates, patterns of exclusion in public bureaucracies are similar to those in private. Recent years have seen more progress in this area, however. Congress banned some forms of sex discrimination by employers in the Federal Equal Pay Act of 1963; and Executive Order 11375 requires that firms with federal contracts not discriminate on the basis of sex. In the two years between 1965 and 1967 the percentage of women enrolled in the federal management intern program rose from 14 to 29 percent.

Figure 6.1, part C, on peak discrimination in politics, puts our discussion of vote differentials on a new footing. Voting falls at the lower end of any continuum·of political participation. Up the scale of involvement, the proportion of women who fill political roles decreases religiously. Some of the figures probably underestimate the exclusion of women. Seven of the ten women senators in our history began their careers only after the death of their senator husbands. Two of their recent number, Eva Bowring and Hazel Abel both served Nebraska for several weeks after the nearly simultaneous deaths of their husbands. As one student of the Senate remarked, "No doubt their lack of office holding experience and political ambitions were among their major qualifications for the job."[40]

With this base line description of the political situation of American women in hand we can now proceed to the central question of this chapter: Is the political situation of women in poor neighborhoods different from that of women elsewhere? If so, how? and why?

WOMEN AND POLITICS IN POOR NEIGHBORHOODS

It would be possible to proceed by matching evidence from the Local Change Study against hypotheses derived from the conventional wisdom, suggesting that poor women are less involved, less politically aware, less influential, than women generally. We will take a different approach, however, and investigate hypotheses suggesting the opposite, that poor women are *more* politically advanced than middle and upper-class women. This strategy will keep analysis focused on progressive evolution, not on the status quo. Even negative findings can thus be of relevance to persons working for change in the political status of women. Three forces for change will be discussed: revolutionary equality, the "unnatural superiority" of black women; and the women's liberation

movement. Each discussion will be followed by empirical evaluations drawing on evidence from the Local Change Study.

Revolutionary Equality

A first source of optimism concerning the political liberation of
poor women is the generally progressive ideology concerning sex
role issues of radical social movements. Is it possible that there
are signs of a revolutionary sexual egalitarianism in poor neighborhoods? In this section we will investigate whether or not
some examples of the treatment of womens' issues by revolutionary regimes are relevant to an understanding of the situation of
poor women in America.

Radical movements are highly dependent on their ability to
mobilize large numbers of people for mass action. Especially during periods of military struggle, popular foces, unable to rely on
institutionalized conscription, must recruit personnel by all possible means. In the final action, devotion and courage, cowardice
and betrayal do not discriminate by sex. It is this, perhaps, that
explains the unusually strong position of women in the Provision-
al Revolutionary Government of South Vietnam. The struggle in
South Vietnam cannot afford the division of tasks into military
front and home front, male and female, that often characterizes
guerilla warfare. The PRG delegation to the Paris peace talks was
headed by a woman, Madame Binh, and several of those under her
were women as well.[41] In North Vietnam mobilization is geared
to increasing economic production. Laws outlawing polygamy
and giving women equal rights in divorce and property ownership
have been passed and Women make up 70 percent of the agricul-
tural work force and half of industrial labor.[42]

Mobilization need not be this total to affect the relative position
of women. The widely dispersed villages of traditional Africa have
never been highly organized, even at the height of struggles for
independence.[43] Sekou Touré, President of Guinea, is supported
enthusiastically by the village women of his country, however,
because he always made a special place for them in the struggle
for independence. Touré early realized that women formed an
untapped base of political support. Women played a critical role
in the 73 day general strike he called in 1953, and helped get party
candidates elected to influential French Assembly posts in the
middle 50's.[44]

When radical movements experiment with new forms of family life, they tend to foster progressive attitudes toward women. The strong All China Democratic Women's Federation led the early struggle for sexual equality in the Chinese revolution. Through the "Speak Bitterness" campaign in which groups of women denounced, sentenced and punished recalcitrant men, the Federation pressed for acceptance of monogamy, free choice of marriage partners, and protection of the interests of women and children. Since the Great Leap Forward, the Federation has concentrated its efforts on recruiting women to participate in the rural communes, in part because it felt that new social forms on the commune—collectivized housework and child rearing—would contribute directly to the emancipation of women.[45]

Finally, the logic of revolutionary ideology emphasizing social and class justice often broadens to include social justice for women. When women were excluded from the deliberation of the three Estates during the French Revolution, they organized groups to write *cahiers* of their own. Later, proletarian women led the march on Versailles over the "bread question" and at one point held control of the city government of Lyons for three days. Bourgeois women, under the leadership of Madame Etta Palm van Aelder pressed, during the revolutionary period, for their own egalitarian goals—education of girls, legal majority of women at age 21, the right to divorce and political freedom.[46]

Lenin saw clearly the implications of his political doctrines for the position of women. In a letter to Clara Zetkin, he wrote, "Our communist labors among the masses of women, our political work among them, involves a considerable effort to educate the men. We must root out the ancient outlook of lord and master to the last fiber. Every cook must learn to rule the state." Immediately following the revolution, a series of marriage laws realized the major hopes of the Russian feminist movement: abortions were made free and legal, children born out of wedlock were given full legal rights, and it was ruled that, in the concise words of the Marriage Law of 1917, "agreements by husband and wife intended to restrict property rights of either party are invalid and not binding."[47]

It is hard to be hopeful about finding revolutionary egalitarianism in America. The argument we have outlined linking radical movements and sexual equality (criticism of the argument's theory itself is left to the reader) is only tangentially relevant to the situation of America's poor. There has, for example, been little experimentation with new forms of family life in poor America. When family relations have become an issue, as they have with Black Muslims, for example, the goal is generally a *strengthening* of the family as traditionally conceived. As the announcement of a recent black cultural arts workshop on "black male/female relationships" explains, "It is crucial that the contempt and bitterness sisters and brothers regard each other in be resolved. A harmonious relationship is necessary between the sexes in order to form a strong family unit, the basic institution of any society."[48]

More centrally, as the Local Change Survey strongly indicates, rarely in America has the new activism of the poor achieved a revolutionary mobilization in word or deed. Less than a third of the poor strongly agree that things around their neighborhoods make them angry. Only a quarter speak of the need for radical changes in the way the government operates and about 45 percent rate the institutions that serve them in their neighborhoods moderately high. Less than one in ten has even a moderate amount of information about political developments in his community. Nor is there much support for moving to the kind of violent activity that would escalate the conflict to a true crisis level.

Examination of the Local Change data on poor women points to a clear, if gloomy conclusion: in poor American neighborhoods, themselves only partially mobilized, poor women are even *less* radical and active than poor men. Figure 6.2 compares men and women from the Five City sample of general residents on several dimensions of radicalism. As it indicates, women are consistently less angry, less inclined to large-scale criticism of society, less politcally involved than men.

A startling bit of evidence which casts even further doubt on the revolutionary egalitarianism theory comes from data concerning sex discrimination in neighborhood organizations. It is precisely in the most "radical" organizations that sexism is the most entrenched. Figure 6.3 shows the different kinds of community groups. Associated with each are two bars, the top one indicating the percent of a group's general membership comprised of women, the bottom one, the percent of officers that are women (data drawn from leaders of the poor).

As might be expected, women predominate among members and officers of groups working on educational problems. In no other

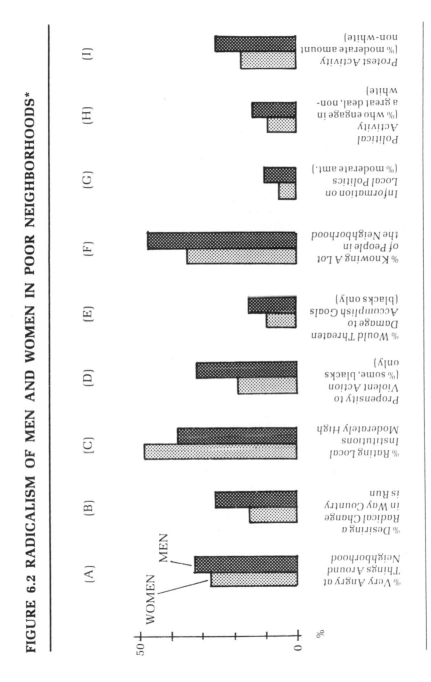

FIGURE 6.2 RADICALISM OF MEN AND WOMEN IN POOR NEIGHBORHOODS*

(A) % Very Angry at Things Around Neighborhood

(B) % Desiring a Radical Change in Way Country is Run

(C) % Rating Local Institutions Moderately High

(D) Propensity to Violent Action (% some, blacks only)

(E) % Would Threaten Damage to Accomplish Goals (blacks only)

(F) % Knowing A Lot of People in the Neighborhood

(G) Information on Local Politics (% moderate amt.)

(H) Political Activity (% who engage in a great deal, non-white)

(I) Protest Activity (% moderate amount non-white)

*See Appendix C-20 for exact figures and N's.

FIGURE 6.3 WOMEN IN COMMUNITY GROUPS*

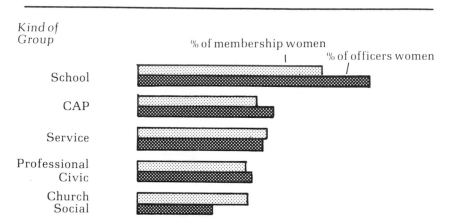

*Each bar represents the proportion of members (or officers) of a given group that are women. See Appendix C-21 for exact percentages and N's.

group does the proportion of women members or officers go above half. Of some interest is the fact that government sponsored community action groups are the only other category in which women claim a fair share of leadership positions. According to OEO, some 20 million women volunteers had participated in the war on poverty as of 1969.[49]

Perhaps the "public" nature of government sponsored organizations makes them particularly sensitive to demands for equal representation of women. Perhaps as well, public organizations can more easily distance themselves from existing social networks in which sexism is ingrained. The argument that women are able to receive equal treatment in local CAP agencies because these organizations exercise very little power is relevant as well.

In social systems which discriminate monolithically at their summit, women are often found concentrated in relatively powerless roles. The argument does not, however, account for the *relative* openness of government sponsored neighborhood organizations. Private community social action groups, civil rights organizations and militant ethnic groups all have fewer women in leadership positions than the Community Action Program.

At the bottom of Figure 6.3 is an interesting cluster of groups in which women play less salient roles—groups in which women are not only a minority of membership but in which their leadership role is even more reduced. Included are social and church groups, but also three of the nominally most progressive organizations in poor areas. The frequent complaint of women's liberationists that radical movements are among the worst discriminators seems grounded in fact. In Brownmiller's words, "Black power as practiced by black male leaders appeared to mean that black women would stand back while black men stepped forward."[50] At the very bottom of our cluster of "progressive" neighborhood organizations lie militant ethnic groups, with 40 percent of its members women but only 17 percent of its leadership female.

Is sex discrimination as pervasive in general neighborhood leadership as it is in group leadership? The data indicate a tentative no. When we asked 4,000 residents of poor neighborhoods who they considered as leaders, four out of ten persons named were women.[51] White leadership, at 49 percent women, was the most equally balanced, black, at 41 percent, next, and chicano, at 35 percent, least.[52] Nor are women excluded from local leadership "networks." Greenberg has analyzed the Five City sample by searching for leadership networks, defined as one leader, plus all those in the previous stage who mentioned him as a leader, and so on, through five stages of interviewing.[53] He found about half of leaders belonging to a network. None of the networks reported by Greenberg is without women. Their average female ratio (58 percent) is actually higher than the proportion of women in the sample at large.

The discovery of women among leaders generally and in leadership networks does not yet prove that they occupy positions of influence. Perhaps this is just another version of that domesticated localism which characterizes woman's place in American politics generally. Figure 6.4 addresses this question by asking if more or fewer women are found at the uppermost levels of the local influence hierarchy. The figure is in the form of a "peak exclusion graph," and "level of influence" is equated simply with

FIGURE 6.4 PROPORTIONS OF WOMEN IN
NEIGHBORHOOD POWER STRUCTURES*

(shaded portion indicates percent of women at various levels of the neighborhood power structure)

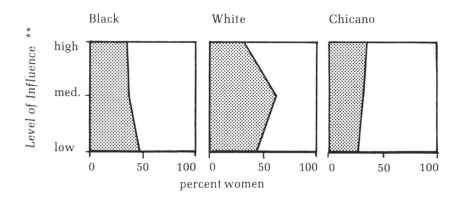

*Number of residents attributing persons with leadership
**See Appendix C-22 for exact figures.

the number of persons among the 40 questioned who mentioned an individual as a leader. The shaded section represents the proportion of leaders at each level who are women.

Although there are many white women in positions of leadership, they tend, as Figure 6.4 indicates, to be concentrated at intermediate, not upper levels of influence. The exclusion line for black women, on the other hand, is nearly vertical, indicating that they form the same proportion of leaders at all levels of influence tapped here. Among chicanos sampled by the Local Change Study, the proportion of women actually increases through successive influence levels.

We have found little evidence to support the argument that the radicalism of poor neighborhoods has promoted the liberation of women there. Women are not found more frequently among leaders of defiant or pragmatic militant communities than among those of the passive center.[54] Highly mobilized communities thus do not seem to be especially favorable places for women to make their mark. Poor women are not more radical and mobilized than poor men. Militant organizations are even more sexist than traditional and government sponsored groups.

Further important questions remain. While previous studies of local power structure found almost no women in positions of influence, our evidence indicates that almost half of local influentials in poor neighborhoods are women.[55] In black and chicano areas, if not white, these proportions do not decrease upward in the influence hierarchy. We must look more closely at the interplay of race and sex in the determination of the political status of poor women.

The Unnatural Superiority of Black Women

It has been argued that the black woman has special strengths which she could bring to the political arena. If black men were the machines of the slave factory, black women were in part the foremen. Men, presumed to be the active and therefore dangerous force in human affairs, were the most humiliated objects of the folk psychology of slavery. Women could be treated somewhat more benevolently as co-conspirators. It was they, after all, who insured the supply and good health of the race. Women were allowed greater access to the home of the slave master. Accepted as sex objects in the underlife of Southern manhood, black women could occasionally be saucy and escape. Some, as mammies, were entrusted with the children of the oppressor; others, often older women, became the wise "grannies" of the slave quarters. Some argue that because they were in a position to provide service to the institution, women were given a leverage for local concessions in the survival action. As intuited by the slave master, these concessions to womanhood were neatly exacted at the price of black manhood. The result, a last tribute to the folk psychology of slavery, was the "unnatural superiority of black women"—"The Negro man had to be destroyed as a man, to 'protect' the white world. Unwittingly, unintentionally, even against her will, the Negro woman participated in the process."[56]

Contemporary evidence of the effect of this special status can be found. Since 1910, the sex ratio (men per hundred women) in the black population has remained about 90. In 1962, the figure was higher generally (95.9) but lower in urban situations and in the critical years of marriageability, age 25 to 44. Some of the differential is due to accounting—surveys inevitably undercount black men—and to the greater number of men than women who pass into the white population, but an important interpretation as well is that the hazards of life are greater for black men than women.[57] Women in the black community have more education than men, 8.5 years versus 7.9 for men. The black woman has traditionally enjoyed certain advantages in employment. Domestic work, usually available even in the hardest times, took her into the world of middle-class values while the black man was more likely to spend his day in an employment ghetto. Black women report "housewife status" less often than white. Fifty-seven percent of black women in this study indicated they were housewives compared to 71 percent of white women.[58] Other studies report even larger disparities.

Although she rarely worked at jobs with much social status, the black woman's ability to get work at all contributed to her sense of self-worth. A Detroit study of black families discovered that "the relative power of the wife was low if she did not work and increased with her economic contribution to the family."[59] Black women are more often "heads of household" than whites and thus less subject to the housewife's intimate oppression described earlier. The percentage of black households headed by women rose from 24 to 27 percent between 1940 and 1960.[60] If the reverence which most women accord marriage is a mark of the internalization of oppression, lower-class black women seem to be liberated in at least this respect. There is strong evidence of incredible cynicism concerning marriage among lower-class black women. Sixty-three percent of married women of little education in one sample said that if they had to do it over again they would not get married. Six out of ten said that if it was their choice they wouldn't marry the same man. When forced to an exclusive choice between the passive status of wife and the active one of mother, one in ten chooses the former, seven in ten the latter. When they marry, black women, and not their husbands, are found more often in the role of chief decision maker within the family. Almost half of 116 black families in a Detroit study evidenced this pattern while only one in five indicated male dominance.[61]

Has the "unnatural superiority" of black women created a politically liberated status for them in poor neighborhoods? Two kinds of hypotheses can be tested. The first, concerning social and attitudinal foundations for action, posits that black women, compared to black men, have more education, better job situations, higher incomes, greater faith in their ability to affect the world, and higher interaction rates with their neighbors. The second, concerning the political attitudes and behavior built on this foundation, posits that, compared to black men, black women are more politically aware, have more information on politics, perceive community problems more clearly, and participate more in political activities.

As Figure 6.5 indicates, neither cluster of hypotheses is supported in any aspect. In poor neighborhoods, the unnatural superiority of black women appears to be a myth. Black women have lower education levels than men and report a median income of $4,600 compared to $5,700 for men. They do not hold jobs as often as men, but 46 percent experience some job insecurity (the figure for men is 35 percent). Black women know fewer people in the neighborhood than men, have less knowledge of political affairs and talk about community issues less. Finally, their involvement in political and protest activity is less frequent than that of men.

The doctrine of the unnatural superiority of black women has always been a thorn in the side of activist black women. To them it appears a cruel hoax, its kernel of truth pitifully small when measured against the self-recrimination it sets against political will.[62] The manifesto of a Poor Black Women's Study Group in Mount Vernon put it this way: "the class hierarchy as seen from the poor black woman's position is one of the white male in power, followed by the white female, then the black male and lastly the black female."[63] Or, from another observer: the black woman "must do more of everything than any other sexual group."[64] If there was ever a time when black women were superior to black men, that time appears past. If male dominance is not a part of black history, then the second class status of black women now is a vivid contemporary example of white cultural colonialism. "To be black and female is a double jeopardy, the slave of a slave," writes Frances Beale of SNCC's Black Women's Liberation Committee.

The Race Woman

Although the analysis just concluded suggests that black women are less active in politics generally than men, the possibility that they play an important role in *race* political mobilization remains live.[65] Black women can indeed be found at all levels of race movement politics. We have already noted that women make up 40 percent of black leadership cadres at the local level. Sheehy, in her study of New Haven Black Panthers, describes

FIGURE 6.5 POLITICAL RESOURCES AND ACTIVITIES OF BLACK WOMEN*

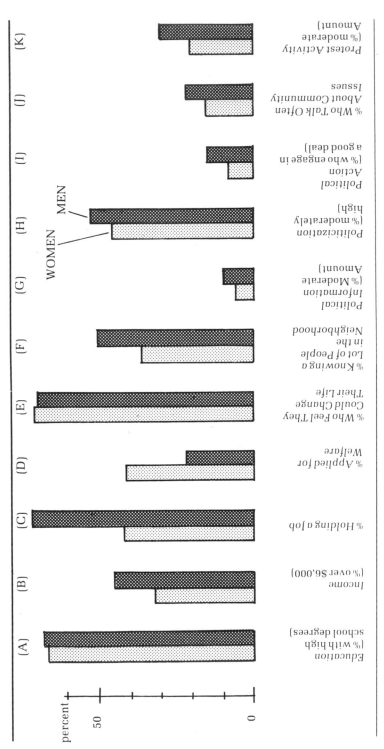

*See Appendix C-23 for exact figures.

two strong black women of radically different political styles: Betty Kimbro Osborne, "Forty, tense. A feet-on-the-ground realist. She is in the black middle as a Yale faculty wife and not about to apologize for it," and Ericka Huggins, highest ranking Black Panther in the state, about whom one black Yale student remarked: "We have had Erickas all our life. If it weren't for the toughness of black women, black men would be all like buffaloes, extinct."[66] Angela Davis, like Congresswoman Shirley Chisholm, completed a graduate degree before turning to politics. Her evolution from the world of ideas through group activism to revolutionary action, has marked a path followed by other black women at their own pace. Room was quickly made for her in the black pantheon when her action in the Soledad Brothers case made her a popular revolutionary hero.

The first hypothesis these instances of black female militance suggests is that black women generally are in the vanguard of the movement for race liberation. Figure 6.6 compares black men and black women on a series of race issues relevant to this proposition. There is no support in the Local Change data (as there has been little in other studies) for the contention that black women are more sensitive to race oppression and active in combating it than men.[67]

Our indicator of "race identity" includes the word a person uses to describe his race, and his opinions on black power and the possibility that blacks blame too many of their problems on whites. About one black woman in four scores "high" on this scale, eleven percent *fewer* than men. The picture of race relations held by black women is more benign than that of black men. Fewer black women than men favor policies seeking to redress racial imbalances in local institutions.

It is a conservative perspective which only matches the concern and involvement of black women against that of black men. In this section we will investigate hypotheses which explore another range of differences—those between black women and women of other races. The general hypothesis is that although black women are less politicized than black men, they are more involved in the political life of their communities than white women. Analysis will focus now on the large subset of community leadership comprised of women. These persons, selected by their neighbors as being active in or informed about local affairs, are particularly important in understanding the emergence of new political roles for women.[68]

FIGURE 6.6 VIEWS ON RACE OF BLACK MEN AND WOMEN IN POOR NEIGHBORHOODS*

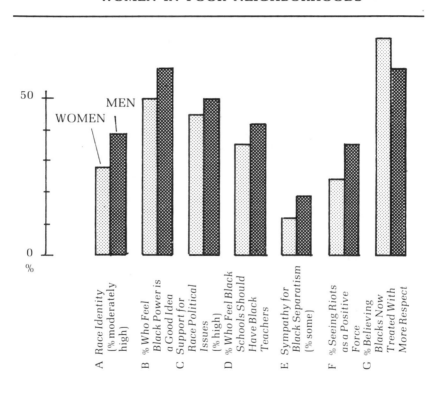

*See Appendix C-24 for exact figures and N's.

As might be anticipated, white women leaders lag behind black (and they behind chicanas) in community involvement, especially its more political forms. (See Figure 6.8) Forty-seven percent of black women leaders belong to two community groups; only 36 percent of white women do. Fifteen percent more black than white women have a moderately high level of political information. Among white women leaders interviewed, only 35 percent could give names of three other community leaders, 52 percent of black and 71 percent of chicanas leaders could. Disparities in political world view are even greater. Black women participate with black men in the major ideological dimensions of the black revolt. Compared to white women they are more alienated from government and more inclined to look warily upon local service institutions. One-half (twice as many as whites) have engaged in a moderate amount of protest activity.[69]

Black women leaders are twice as likely as white to have the increased responsibilities of being sole head of their households (a full 41 percent of black women leaders fall into this category). While more black women bear the burdens of poverty without support, they tend to take better advantage of the public resources open to the poor. Sixty-five percent have used a government-aided day care center, a public health clinic or received free legal service; only 44 percent of white women have. Twice as many have applied for public welfare. Perhaps as a result of this increased willingness to use poverty services, more black than white women leaders gain access to public sponsored employment.

In our description of women's place in American politics we noted the stereotyped segregation of political issues into domestic-local-feminine and national-fiscal-masculine. Figure 6.7 presents evidence that black, *but not white*, women leaders have transcended this bit of sexist legerdemain. Each horizontal bar of Figure 6.7 represents all the persons in our sample who described a particular community issue as the one on which they had been most active.

The shaded portion of the graph shows the proportion of activists in each issue group that are women. Women predominate among those focusing primarily on schools. Among whites, women also predominate on social and recreational issues and in the category of leaders that told us they don't work on any issues at all. Men outnumber women on the other hand, in housing, neighborhood and city politics, and jobs.

FIGURE 6.7 PERCENT OF LEADERS ACTIVE ON VARIOUS ISSUES THAT ARE WOMEN*

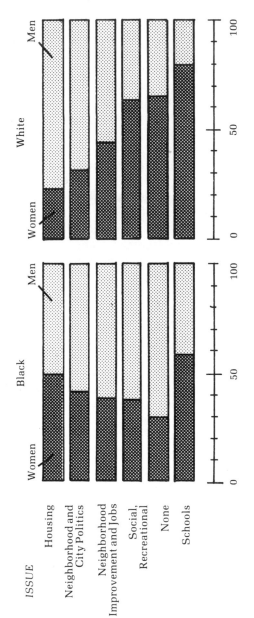

% of Those Active on an Issue that are Women

*See Appendix C-25 for exact percentages and N's.

Although black women are a minority of all issue activists (they form only 41 percent of leadership at large), they are *not* segregated into women's issue ghettoes. Almost half of black leaders who say they concentrate on job problems are women.[70] This, despite the unanimous opinion of husbands and wives that employment problems are the least appropriate topic for discussion by the League of Women Voters. Half of black activists involved in housing are women. Even education has been desegregated; the proportion of men active on school matters in the black community approaches 50 percent.

The question of role specialization by sex can be approached from another perspective in the Local Change data. We asked leaders which of three political "tasks" they considered most important. Two involved organizing people and presenting demands to local government. The third, "getting people angry about issues," was always chosen by a minority, but among white women the minority was particularly small (six percent). It is hard to imagine an activity less classically feminine than getting people angry. Most women do not take lightly the job of convincing a man he is not serious enough about a problem. Four times as many black women as white chose "getting people angry about issues" as their major political task. One black woman in four is thus willing to breach the masculine preserves of argument, speechifying and issue hustling.

The conclusion of this line of evaluation is clear: poor black women (and chicanas) are more politically evolved than poor white women. Their political views are more strident, they engage in more protest activity, and they have challenged more successfully the masculine-feminine division of political issues and roles. With this conclusion we can return to an analytic viewpoint which includes *both* sex and race as important determinants of the political status of poor women. We will now seek to define those realms in which sex differences are most important, those in which race differences predominate and those in which the two are combined.

Table 6.1 presents data in a format which will help distinguish between race and sex as influences on political culture. Aspects of political culture are listed across the table, each expressed as a percentage, for example the percent engaging in a "moderate amount" of protest activity. Figures for men and women—black, white and chicano—are listed in the table. Three patterns of differences between men and women will be distinguished. In the first,

TABLE 6.1 GAPS BETWEEN MEN AND WOMEN IN POLITICAL ATTRIBUTES*

	Samples Chicano Women	Men	Black Women	Men	White Women	Men
Political Attributes						
A. Sex more important than race as influence						
Income (%over $6,000)	29	46	33	63	38	71
Education (% with any college)	36	47	28	57	23	66
% with a Job	76	88	62	90	47	87
%Feeling They Could Change Their Lives	77	76	59	72	70	78
Politicization (% high)	25	49	25	35	13	32
Believe Threatening Damage Would Help Cause	12	24	15	29	6	20
B. Race more important than sex as influence						
Alienation from National Government	47	46	45	50	31	35
% Believing Police Rough People Up	38	60	67	71	28	38
Low Evaluation of Local Schools	46	63	54	61	28	43
% Desiring a Major Change In Way Country Is Run	58	63	71	70	52	61

The top of the bracket points to the percentage for men of a given race, the bottom to that for women ('s mark the occasional reversals). See Appendix C-26 for exact percentages and N's.

TABLE 6.1 (continued)

	Samples Chicano Women	Men	Black Women	Men	White Women	Men
C. Race and sex both important as influences						
% Who Talk Often About Community Issues	82	77	65	75	57	66
Political Information (% Moderately High)	71	80	58	63	43	54
% Belonging to 2 or more Community Groups	71	65	47	58	36	53
Faith in Political Action	29	29	34	42	18	34
Protest Activity (% Moderate Amount)	41	58	45	67	24	39

women of all races cluster together, distinct from men of all races. In the second, although slight differences exist between men and women of the same race, the most significant differences are found *between* races: all blacks versus all whites versus all chicanos. In the third, differences of both kinds are important.

Differences in socio-economic status fall primarily into the first type, differences attributable to sex, not race. The median income of women leaders of all races falls between $4,800 and $5,300. That for men is universally higher, varying between $5,800 for chicanos and $7,900 for whites. Among black and white female leaders about one in four has a white collar or professional job. Among men of both races the figure is twice as high. In education as well, women leaders of all races have fewer resources to call on than men. Only half as many black women as black men leaders have attended some college, and disparities are even greater for whites. American society does not place men and women on an equal foundation of social and economic resources. Women are disadvantaged by sex, irrespective of race, creed or color.

There is evidence that sex is more important than race in two areas of political values as well. Women of all races are behind men of all races in feeling that many areas of social life are "political." Perhaps it is one of the necessary defenses of womanhood to circumscribe the political realm, for as surely as an interaction is political, so it will surely be dominated by men. It is precisely to overcome this sex-linked hesitancy to take a stand in conflictual situations that women's liberation insists on the political nature of its task. The purported "non-violence" of women has already been mentioned. Evidence here that hesitancy to threaten violence for political ends is a sex-linked political value tends to support this theory (later we will discuss evidence placing the theory and this bit of support for it in doubt.)

There are some areas where race differences have eclipsed differences between the sexes. Black leaders of both sexes show a strong disaffection from national government, for example, an opinion shared by white leaders of neither sex. Irrespective of sex, black leaders are more sensitive to the problem of police brutality than white. Among whites, somewhat fewer women than men desire a "major change" in the way the country is run. Blacks of both sex are more strident in their demands for change.

By far the most prevalent pattern, however, is the third in which both sex and race play a role. Black leaders are generally more committed to community development than white, for example, but within each racial group, men are more active than women. Black women are on a par with white men in talking about community issues but 10 percent behind black men, just as white women are 10 percent behind white men. Roughly the same is true of membership in community groups and, most importantly, involvement in political activity. Black women engage in as much political activity as white men, but they are 20 percent behind men of their own race. In several important regards, then, race awakening can be said to have moved black women to levels of community and political involvement characteristic of white men but not to the level of black men. The black bus may be travelling faster than the white, but in both, men are drivers and women sit in the back.

The women's liberation movement

The women's liberation movement is the last force we will investigate for impact on the definition of new political roles for poor women. It will be useful to think of the movement as a set of issues and tactics aimed at changing the last two aspects of the political situation of American women outlined above: dependency (diminished political resources), and exclusion from power.

The target of the women's liberation movement is sex discrimination wherever it exists. Myths underwriting job exclusion are being attacked, beliefs, for example, that women don't want careers they want jobs; that women are interested in personal development not excellence, that absenteeism and turnover are higher among women, that women are "human oriented," naturally suited for tedious and repetitive tasks.[71]

Another focus of action is the Equal Rights Amendment, aimed at job discrimination itself, but also at beliefs supporting discrimination. Shirley Chisholm argues that this amendment will put pressure for change on "corporations, big insurance companies and so on—all those places where there is discrimination which can't be explained in any terms except sex—the essence of sex, not a stage of life or professional training or whether you are strong or weak."[72]

Institutionalization of subordinate roles forms a second set of women's issues. Day-care centers won't in themselves change a husband's attitude toward a working mother, but the absence of alternative daytime environments for children can severely restrict the enlargement of a woman's role. Abortion laws were likewise an institutionalized expression by men, that women are incompetent to make important decisions for themselves.

A wide variety of organizations are being formed to speak out and act on women's issues. A few, like the National Organization of Women with 35 chapters across the country, are national in scope. At the radical fringe is a shifting series of militant organizations. The New York Radical Women, formed in 1967, mobilized members to picket the 1968 Miss America Pageant and started the bra burning image which America so quickly took to its collective unconscious. It was soon followed by the October 17th Movement, The Feminists, Redstockings and local variants around the country.

None of these organizations is a mass movement in any sense of the word, yet the dream of adding an inch of political consciousness to every woman's shirt-tail remains. It occasionally even disturbs the slumber of the powerful. Representative Martha Griffiths of Michigan, chief architect of House action on the

Equal Rights Amendment, insists that certain Congressmen received so much mail on the topic they asked her to "call off the women." One of these, who remains anonymous in name if not sex, told an interviewer, "The amendment is of no great concern to me, one way or the other. But what you're dealing with here is some women with time on their hands, and nothing can be more dangerous than An Idle Woman. She loves a cause. She loves to ring doorbells. She loves to get on the telephone. And I don't want that kind of woman working against me."[73]

It is in the realm of changing private values, however, that the tactics of the movement have reached their greatest refinement. "Women's liberation is finally only personal," says Kempton. "It is hard to fight an enemy who has outposts in your head."[74] The core experience for most women in the movement is a series of meetings, one a week, with friends, talking. It is these personal encounter sessions that form the tactical genius of the movement. In "going around the room," each speaking informally from her own experience, the vital work of "consciousness raising" takes place. Simple concerns are aired: recurring patterns in encounters with men, the nature of relationships with other women, childhood remembrances. The format is typical for movements seeking changes in self as well as society. Early activists were familiar with the revival style of "testifying" that SNCC used so effectively and with the role of confessional meetings in Chinese communism—Mao's "Speak pain to recall pain." No authority is present to stifle enthusiasm. Voluntarism insures a personalized commitment. The exhilaration of being in a group of women taking each other seriously constantly affirms the validity of the search.

The approach is political to the core. "Whatever else we may do, consciousness raising is the ongoing political work," writes a member of Redstockings. "It cannot be overemphasized," writes Gottlieb, "how radical a technique this is, coming from creatures who, three years ago would have been damned, scorned, and shamed for 'subjectivism.' 'Consciousness raising' makes it possible to raze preexistent structures of thought, and then gradually to discover the form's potential in raw experience." Typical stages of politicization as described by one participant include: sensing the double standards that have been operative in one's own life, realizing that one's problem is social, not just personal; examination of significant persons in one's life, and elimination of a competitive attitude toward other women.[75]

Has women's liberation *as a movement* affected poor women? The answer is almost certainly no. Although some activists stress the need to organize in lower-class neighborhoods, particularly in conjunction with day care centers, few have actually done so.[76] A few women's liberation issues, abortion and day care, for example, are classless. The relevance of others—exclusion from peak positions in business, "discriminatory" laws protecting women from harsh working conditions, and the "no more alimony" plea, for example—are understandably lost on poor women. The consciousness raising phase of the movement has never caught on among lower-class mothers and wives. It is not difficult to intuit the disruption the technique could bring to personal relations in the more traditional context of lower-class life.

Many black women active in race liberation activities are unremittingly hostile to the women's liberation movement. "I think there are some women in the United States who need it," said Mrs. W. E. B. DuBois at a recent conference of black women, "but I don't think any black women need it." In the words of other activists, ". . . any attempt to analogize black oppression with the plight of the American white women has all the validity of comparing the neck of a hanged man with the rope-burned hands of an amateur mountain climber." "Women's liberation is only a tactic on the part of the white woman. Just as a small child throws a tantrum to gain attention, so the white woman pitches a nation-wide fit to alter her diminishing role in society."[77] There are many sources of hostility. Black women resent middle-class volunteers whose financial security and educational qualifications often see them promoted over others in community service organizations. Inter-racial marriage, when black men are already in short supply, is a sticking point. Black women sense a "cool, indifferent" attitude toward them on the part of white women and some feel that the white priority, "out of the home and into a job" is the reverse of that for black women. "The things white women are demanding liberation from are what we've never even experienced yet."[78]

Empirical studies of women in politics have generally looked at differences between men and women in absolute levels of belief and activity. A perspective taking into account the insights of women's liberation makes this now seem short-sighted. Outward similarities can mask different underlying processes. Mobilizing women to action might be quite a different task than mobilizing men. In this section we will be evaluating the relevance to poor women of the liberationist *analysis* of why and how women get involved in politics. In its general form, the hypothesis reads: while the political activity of men is based on social and economic status, the most important foundation of action for women is heightened political consciousness. Socio-economic *status* is not as important for women as socio-economic *independence:* having a job, being unmarried.

Multiple regression analysis, which sorts out the relative influences of a number of forces, will help test the hypothesis. Our goal is an explanation of the causes of political involvement among men and women of different races. Figure 6.8 presents some results of the investigation. (See Appendix C-29 for similar data on blacks and chicanos in the general residents sample.) Each stack of names is an attempt to explain political involvement for men or women of a given race. The higher a factor is on the list, the more important it is in explaining involvement, even when controlling for the influence of the others.[79] A large number of factors covering life situations, personal values and political attitudes were included to keep the explanatory framework broad.[80]

The major contentions of the hypothesis are upheld by the data. Socio-economic status is more important for men than for women in underwriting political involvement. Among black men, for example, education is the most important factor, although age, involvement in local groups and support of local government also play a role. For black women, the picture is quite different. For this group, being part of the world of work, (having a job, being off welfare) is important, but the presence of *low* income at the very top of the list indicates that this does not mean belonging to a local economic elite.[81] For white men, *high* income contributes to political involvement, for white women, it does not. The fact that group involvement is an important factor for black men but not for black women supports our earlier contention that established group life is more supportive of male than female needs.

Figure 6.8 is notable for a lack of ideological factors. A similar analysis of involvement in protest as opposed to conventional politics indicates that ideological factors are more important in this realm, but only for women, not men (See Appendix C-29). Personal anger at the local situation contributes to protest involvement among black and chicanas women, for example, but is not important for men of either race. The evidence thus supports

FIGURE 6.8 FACTORS CONTRIBUTING TO CONVENTIONAL POLITICAL ACTIVITY FOR MEN AND WOMEN IN POOR NEIGHBORHOODS*

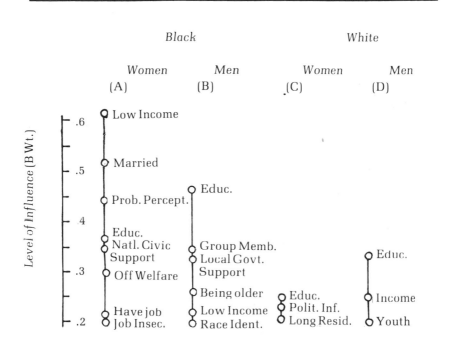

*See Appendix C-27 for details. N's and multiple r's for A-D are 69, .76; 93, .75; 57, .65; and 60, .65.

the theory that consciousness-raising is a particularly relevant tactic for prompting women to action.

It is interesting to note that job independence supports the political self-assertion of black women, but that quite the opposite is true concerning independence gained from being single. Being married is the second most important contributor to the political involvement of black women leaders. Marriage must be carefully distinguished from being a housewife—later analysis will show how few women activists fall into this latter category. The importance of marriage in sustaining political activity among black women is strong testimonial to the need for primary ties in an environment where permanent bonds are the exception, not the rule. Women's liberation must indeed take a different form among black and white women.

TYPES OF WOMEN LEADERS IN POOR NEIGHBORHOODS

It would simplify our concepts if many attributes converged to define a few distinctive types of women leaders. To investigate this possibility, data on 127 respondents was subjected to statistical tests to discover if there were groups of women leaders similar to each other along the following dimensions:

> Participation in traditional political activity
> Participation in protest activity
> Membership in traditional groups
> Membership in action groups
> Propensity to violent political actions
> Anger at the local situation
> Alienation from local government

These defining dimensions were selected on the basis of previous analysis. The typology itself, however—which reveals if any attributes are held in common by persons in the community—emerges directly from the data.[82] Profiles of each type were obtained along *all* the dimensions of our analysis, not just those listed above. On the basis of its profile, each type was given a name which hopefully captures some of its inner nature. All but twelve persons fell into the five types indicated on Figure 6.9. "Parochials" form the largest category of women. Two types of moderately active women were labelled "do gooders" and "hangers-

FIGURE 6.9 TYPES OF WOMEN LEADERS

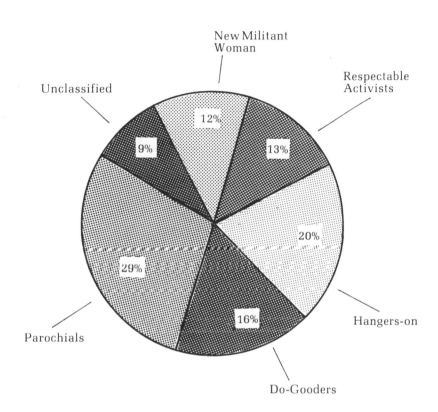

on". The most active women fell into two final types: "respectable activists" and "new militant women." Each of these types will be described briefly before we conclude with some interesting implications of the typology for the political mobilization of women.

The new militant woman is a political activist. She is the most active of all leaders in the newer forms of protest: picketing and boycotting. She is as well, however, a leader in traditional political activities such as voting and directing complaints to public officials. (See Table 6.2 for profiles of types along several major dimensions.) Members of this group are relatively young at a median age of 38. Although they have lived in their neighborhoods

TABLE 6.2 PROFILES OF TYPES OF WOMEN LEADERS*

(All entries are %'s.)

TYPE OF LEADER

ATTRIBUTE	New Militant Women	Respectable Activists	Hangers-On	Do-Gooders	Parochials
(A) *Protest Activity* (High)	100	59	35	11	14
(B) *Traditional Political Activity* (Great Deal)	100	77	42	10	3
(C) *Evaluation of Schools* (High)	7	12	27	50	16
(D) *Politicization* (Moderately High)	87	76	46	50	34
(E) *Propensity to Violent Action* (Some)	77	44	24	14	0
(F) *Anger* (Very angry at local situation)	67	77	54	35	30
(G) *Alienation from Local Government* (Some)	53	6	35	15	73

*See Appendix C-28 for N's.

for an average of 18 years, they appear relatively new to political involvement, belonging only to newer, action-oriented community organizations. More than any other, this group breaks through the stereotypes of women in politics. Members have, for example, a high propensity to violent activity. Thirty-one percent of their number would agree to threaten a local establishment with damage to induce it to stop discriminatory practices. This is, as well, the only group which sees poverty in a stridently political perspective: over half cite oppression, discrimination or the general political situation as the major cause of poverty. The new militant woman is angry and hostile to government. She is also the backbone of local political action. Eighty-six percent of her numbers have complained to heads of local establishments about community problems; three-quarters have marched on picket lines, all report having participated in a boycott. Almost all of the group was judged very articulate by our interviewers—and they make use of their verbal skills. Getting people angry about issues is seen by a full half as their primary leadership task.

A second group, respectable activists, is somewhat less active than the first, especially in the newer forms of protest activity. Interestingly, however, its members belong to both service-oriented community groups *and* newer organizations. They are the angriest of all leaders but are not so ready to translate anger into violent political action. A clue to their situation is a long residence in the area (25 years) and the fact that they have higher incomes and are somewhat older than new militant women. It seems likely that the respectable activists have been active in local affairs most of their lives. The new current of activism undoubtedly placed them in an awkward position by its radical questioning of the traditional forms of involvement open to poor women. But women in this group *did* adapt, adding new forms of group membership and political activity to old. Respectable activists are central in the constellation of political forces in poor areas. They have a strong resource base for activism, know a lot of people in the area, and belong to fully four community groups each on the average. Although they participate in a radical critique of existing institutions they still act in the belief that civic action on public issues will bring change. The best estimate of militance among women leaders in poor areas comes from the observation that one woman in four belongs to the two activist types just described.

Hangers-on form a third group, and like the new militant women, belong only to newer action organizations. Unlike this group, they do little else. The anger and alienation of this group matches that of the first two groups described, but their values are not translated into action. Because of this inactivity, and the fact that few are officers in the groups to which they belong, they were labelled hangers-on. It is difficult to know whether they are moving toward fuller participation in political life or are permanently stuck in this half-way house to activism.

The fourth group, women in the do-gooder category, belong only to the older, apolitical service organizations. Members operate from a resource base nearly as strong as that of respectable activists but show little evidence of political awareness or concern. Only 30 percent can describe three different community problems (the figures for the new militant women and respectable activists are 80 and 69 percent). Group members are anti-ideological. When asked to define "politics," a third mention only the Presidency, Congress, and other institutions while another third give definitions with no content at all. Most of these women fit the classical picture of the do-gooder, the housewife who fits a measure of status quo social activism into an otherwise domestic routine.

Parochials, the most numerous single category of women leaders, are the easiest to describe. Although they were all attributed influence by at least one person—or they would not have arrived in our sample—they are inactive in almost every regard. Members are the least angry, least violent and least engaged of all leadership types and are overwhelmingly status quo oriented. It is particularly interesting to note, then, that of all groups, parochials are the *most* alienated from local government. Their complacency thus appears on deeper examination to be a desperate complacency which includes little hope for responsiveness should problems arise. Perhaps this extreme cynicism (a proto-radicalism?) concerning government will provide a clue to those interested in mobilizing congenitally inactive community leaders to greater involvement.

Several interesting conclusions emerge in a comparison of types with each other. Most importantly, a definite series of conditions appear to support women in the more active roles described above. These are: not being a housewife, having a job, being employed in community work, being politicized, and finally, being black. On these points the data speak eloquently. Only three out of the 54 women in the three most active types are housewives while about half of remaining types are. Over 80 percent of women in these first three categories are employed. In the last two categories, the hangers-on and the parochials, the proportion falls to one-third. Again, we note the centrality of government sponsored social roles, with two out of three new militant women employed in public capacities (among respectable activists the figure is about one-half).

There is more support here for our earlier contention that consciousness raising is an appropriate mobilizing strategy for poor women. Activist types of women leaders uniformly told us they believe a great many areas of social life to be political. This "politicization" is actually a more distinctive characteristic of active women than their educational attainment. Parochials and hangers-on have almost as much schooling as new militant women but lag far behind in their perception of the political nature of their world.

The typology offers an interesting perspective on the putative non-violence of women. Conventional wisdom holds that non-violence is a central feminine perspective. The strongest outside evidence we reviewed on the matter concerned differential attitudes toward war, but our own data concerning the tactic of threatening violence pointed in the same direction. Our typology indicates that another hypothesis should be tested, one that relates non-violence more closely to powerlessness. It would hold that non-violence is a frivolity women grant themselves because they understand it is not their role to have responsible opinions. Evidence to support this hypothesis comes from two sources. First, although we have discovered several "non-violent" attitudes among women—a hesitance to threaten damage, a reduced belief in the efficacy of riots—there is one question on which differences were reversed. All respondents were asked "Do you personally feel that this country is worth fighting for, or not, and why." It is an interesting question because it forces women to a momentary "responsibility"—as if fighting were their business. And at this moment they say yes, their country is worth fighting for, in *greater* numbers than men. Thirty percent of men but only 16 percent of women indicate that there are circumstances in which they would not fight for their country. Stronger evidence comes from the typology. As Table 6.1 makes evident, political action and propensity to violence, even for women, go hand in hand. While there are no parochials with even "some" propensity to violence, 44 percent of the respectable activists and 77 percent of the new militant women fall into this category! The non-violence of women seems to disappear either when women take their attitudes seriously or when they participate actively in political life.

All of this adds poignancy to the private hope of the women's liberation movement, that women will make more gentle rulers than men. Particularly after high dosages of "save face," "back down," "no win," talk from high officials, one is inclined to agree with Steinem: "The old-fashioned idea that manhood depends on violence and victory is, after all, an important part of our troubles in the streets and Viet Nam." Her further remarks are equally pertinent, however: "I'm not saying that women leaders would eliminate violence. We are not more moral than men; we are only uncorrupted by power so far. When we do acquire power, we might turn out to have *an equal impulse* toward aggression."[83] Our evidence is sobering. Those seeking to preserve the empathy for the powerless that presently infuses women's spirit have chosen a difficult task. It seems distressingly likely that the final price man will exact from woman on the road to power is agreement with his competitive vision of political life.

Our typology allows us to investigate directly the importance of race to the political awakening of poor women. Figure 6.10 lists types of women leaders on the left and indicates the proportion of each type that are white.[84] Parochial and do-gooder types are found equally among women of all races. There are, however, many fewer white than black women in the remaining three categories. Few white women evidently choose to embrace the new militancy wholeheartedly or to add new forms of political awareness to more respectable kinds of involvement.

FIGURE 6.10 TYPES OF LEADERS AMONG BLACK AND WHITE WOMEN*

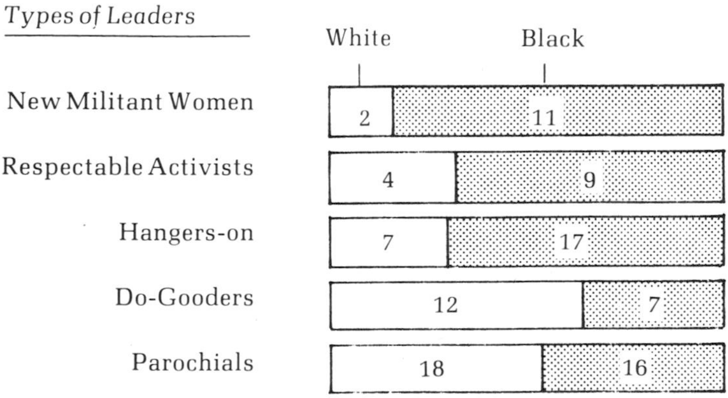

Types of Leaders	White	Black
New Militant Women	2	11
Respectable Activists	4	9
Hangers-on	7	17
Do-Gooders	12	7
Parochials	18	16

*Each bar represents 100% of women leaders in a category. Numbers are actual numbers of women falling into each category.

SUMMARY

We have touched on many issues in this analysis of roles for women in the political culture of poor neighborhoods. Some general conclusions merit emphasis.

There are many women in positions of leadership in poor neighborhoods. At this level, and in this context, exclusion is not as pervasive as that found in other areas of American life. Women leaders join groups nearly as frequently as men. And the groups they join are political. About a quarter of women leaders in poor neighborhoods are highly militant and must be described in terms classically reserved for males: angry, articulate, hostile to middleway institutions, likely to commit acts of violence.

A complete study of the politics of poor women would, of course, include substantial samples from other social strata for comparative purposes. The present study did include one smaller control sample, however. In a middle-class Detroit suburb, 117 persons, 48 of them women, were given an interview schedule identical to the one reported on here.[85] A comparison of these typical American women with women in the Five City general residents sample supports the hypothesis that these are novel developments. Nearly half of poor women report talking "some" about community issues. In the suburbs the proportion drops to 27 percent. Suburban women belong to "important community groups" less than their disadvantaged counterparts (15 percent versus 10 percent). Middle-class women have a less developed political consciousness than poor women. Twenty-eight percent of them ranked moderately high on our scale of politicization, 11 percent less than poor women. Middle-class women see poverty as a personal failing: 56 percent of them told us this was "the most important reason people in this city are poor." Poor women do not agree. Only 21 percent in our sample cite personal failings as the primary cause of poverty.

Progress is not distributed equally among all poor women, however. It is black women, not white, who have broken out of the stereotyped issue specializations of women. Even in the many areas where they lag behind black men, black women are often as active and aware as white men.

Political forces have not frequently overcome sex role differences. The most common pattern, and the one characterizing most political activities, is that of sex distinctions persisting within race differences. Militant ethnic groups seem to be among the worst sex discriminators. The dilemma this presents black women is acute. Although they express no sympathy for women's liberation as a movement, black women know best of all that sexism is a faithful camp follower of political activism. As one black woman states it:

> . . . now that the revolution needs numbers
> Motherhood got a new position
> Five steps behind manhood
>
> And I thought sittin' in the back of the bus
> Went out with Martin Luther King.[86]

Perhaps some new synthesis can emerge from the knowledge that conflict between the sexes only renders men and women "unable to bring the contradiction to its logical conclusions and synthesis —confrontation with *The Man*."[87] Because women *do* have potential for sacrifice and accomplishment equal to men, it is the movement that suffers when women are not allowed to participate to their fullest. "The cry of black women's liberation is a cry against changing a much needed labor force to a role that belongs to ". . . apolitical white women."[88]

Black women, as this study makes clear, have begun the work of creating new modes of political interaction which involve men and women as equals. It is also evident, however, that they are struggling at brief remove with the same powerful Victorianisms as white women. Will the youthful forces of ghetto activism prevail against habits of interaction passed on for generations? Our data only add empirical confirmation to the common truth that the pace of political progress matches the slow evolution of personal values.

PART III
LESSONS IN POLITICAL REVITALIZATION

7 Conclusion

With our survey of politics in poor neighborhoods completed we return to the three questions that began our investigation: how advanced and how successful is political revitalization among the poor; what lessons does it have to teach those interested in similar developments among other social groups in American society; and what are its implications for poverty policy.

SCOPE AND ACCOMPLISHMENTS OF MILITANCE

None of our data support the conclusion that political revitalization is a universal phenomenon in poor neighborhoods. Among general residents, nearly two-thirds can name no important local group; 78 percent rank very low in knowledge of local political events. Group membership among the poor was estimated at half that for other Americans, experience in officer positions even less. Political participation, although roughly on a par with that found elsewhere in American society, seemed low when matched against full activism. There is great belief in the efficacy of direct action tactics, but only 11 percent say they have complained to a public official, 16 percent that they have marched in a picket line. Similar conclusions came from other portions of the analysis. Analysis of data on leaders in 50 communities revealed that nearly half fall into status quo or apathetic types: the uninvolved, the neighborhood establishment or an elder elite. The picture among women leaders is even bleaker. Those fully involved in

189

the political revitalization of their communities fall into types —new militant women and respectable activists—that comprise but one woman leader in four. Information given by heads of organizations in each community indicates a similar pattern. On any given indicator of political mobilization, a third of neighborhoods show almost no activity whatsoever. In only a third was there marked vitality—functioning groups, inventive leadership, reasonable turnout for public presentations, close coordination among local organizations. Our typology of political systems in poor neighborhoods, based on yet further data, revealed a similar picture. A third of neighborhoods cluster in a group, the passive center, whose political involvement is low indeed. While over half of communities show some activism, there is a kind of specialization whereby only 13 percent (pragmatic militants) are highly active in protest *and* conventional activity with the remainder emphasizing one or the other kind of involvement.

From a slightly different perspective, however, these results give a strong impetus to our search for lessons in political revitalization. Although most communities are unmobilized, a few are highly so, and although most individuals are inactive, a few are deeply involved. It would have been much less encouraging to discover that beneath overblown media coverage, governmental panic, and strident rhetoric, poor neighborhoods were totally apathetic, without leadership or organizational life. Equally discouraging would have been a picture of moderate, but *homogeneous*, levels of involvement on an individual and a community basis. This result would have left no examples to turn to for special lessons. But we *did* discover several types of active people and communities. We can ask, with great profit, what makes new militant women and neighborhood radicals tick, what accounts for the success of pragmatic and defiant militant communities.

Militancy, involvement and membership are not to be valued in themselves. Without results, these only parody community control, compromise the proto-radicalism of the poor, and consume the few political resources available to the disadvantaged. The Local Change Survey did not collect accurate statistics on the most important dimensions of poverty: employment, income and educational levels, although we have occasionally cited evidence of lack of progress according to these standards. We did present concrete evidence in one important area of results: how local institutions have changed over a five year period. On the whole, the picture, as outlined in Chapter 1, was grim. A third of the poor live in neighborhoods without *any* private welfare agency that has changed on a given criterion—by word of agency executives themselves, and on scales extremely generous in their definition of responsiveness. Change that has occurred in private agencies is concentrated in less costly areas of operation, like public relations techniques. Program innovation and hiring of poor persons in paid positions is less frequent. Schools in poor neighborhoods show little signs of movement toward the open school, freedom school, or community school pattern. Although almost all communities show increased parental involvement in schools affairs, in only 11 percent did all schools improve their resources in even two out of eight ways measured. Three quarters of local employers, on evidence of their personnel officers, have taken steps to recruit hard core unemployed. Yet the payrolls of these firms, major employers in areas 50 percent black, average only 17 percent black, and only one company in five has increased this figure by 3 percent over the five years prior to 1969. Overall, one-third of local institutions exhibit no change and another third, but subsistence change. Only in the remaining third is there something like responsiveness to the needs of the poor.

The critical question of Chapter 2 was that, although mobilization and change are the exception, do they occur together? Rigorous empirical testing answered affirmatively: in cities of all types nation-wide, political mobilization at the neighborhood level does bring about change in local institutions. It appears that we can consider the pattern of mobilization revealed by this analysis as a potent one for the accomplishment of real change.

DYNAMICS OF REVITALIZATION

Radicalism—disaffection from government, class awareness, support for fundamental changes in society—contributes to political revitalization, but only in certain contexts. A proto-radicalism (radical attitudes without strong ideological underpinning or systematic conversion to policy demands) was one of the few resources for political involvement generally found among the poor. Components of radicalism contribute to group membership for some populations. Pivotal subgroups were found distinguished by radical attitudes: white youth, members of militant ethnic groups, and most significantly, political elites in black neighborhoods.

There is, however, a fundamental ambivalence in the interplay of radicalism and political revitalization. Radical attitudes were found characteristic of two quite different community types for example, defiant militants and idle radicals. In the first context, when it is allied with aggressive protest action, radicalism is part of a syndrome which is highly effective in bringing about change. In the second, acting alone, it leads nowhere.

Emerging repeatedly in our analysis was the conclusion that support for local government is a contributor to political involvement. Members of action groups are less alienated from local government than non-members, for example. For welfare mothers, elder and uneducated blacks, and black men generally, local civic support makes a strong, independent contribution to political activity (support for *national* government does not play such an important role).

A similar conclusion emerged in our analysis of ideologies of local change. The greater mobilization of blacks gives their attitude toward local institutions (cynical discontent) precedence over that of whites (status quo dissatisfaction). Further analysis suggested, however, that positive elements of black political culture (youth, elites, community workers) pressure values away from cynical discontent and toward critical reformism—a position *more* critical of the present state of local institutions, but *less* critical of their efforts to reform.

The case for radicalism must account for evidence that its effect varies in different subgroups as well. Twenty-five percent of leaders in the uninvolved category show some alienation from local government; 52 percent of the much more active local radical group do. Equally intriguing, however, is the fact that apathetic elder elites top the scale at 63 percent! The same phenomenon among women leaders means that two highly divergent types, new militant women and parochials, show the strongest alienation from local government. It seems unlikely that inducing *more* hostility to local government among uninvolved subgroups is likely to get them more involved in political activities. Radicalism does support political revitalization, then, but only when it occurs among subgroups not withdrawn from the system, and only when it does not deny responsiveness in those who must act on demands for change.

Being informed of local problems and events was frequently found more important than ideological militance in supporting political mobilization. A majority of the poor state a problem when asked about conditions in the neighborhood, but only 17 percent describe three such problems. It seems important that this latter statistic rises to 27 percent among those affiliated with local leadership, to 49 percent among leaders as a whole, and to 63 percent among political elites. In analyses holding other aspects of political belief constant, knowledge of local political affairs frequently emerges as an important contributor to political activity. It seems best never to underestimate the power of getting the word out concerning grievances and efforts at their redress.

What role does cultural revitalization play in political mobilization? The failure of traditional cultural institutions among the poor is well documented by the Local Change data. Churches, for example, may once have nurtured black leadership and provided groups with vital organizational resources but this seems no longer to be the case. Only six percent of persons identified as leaders by the poor are now clergy, and less than eight percent of local group memberships are religious in nature.

Political parties may once have functioned as decentralized municipal bureaucracies, concerned with the daily social and economic needs of the people. Now, our analysis indicates, party organization in most poor neighborhoods is a cultural survival. Parties account for less than 20 percent of local contacts with government officials, less than 10 percent of neighborhood political work generally. Compared to non-members, leaders who belong to party groups are *less* angry at the neighborhood situation, *less* supportive of modern political demands, *less* involved in political activities. Our typologies of local leaders offered insight into the kinds of persons most strongly affiliated with traditional values in poor neighborhoods. Most benign are the elder elites, insensitive to local problems, unsympathetic to demands for change, inactive politically. More dangerous are members of the neighborhood establishment, equally unsympathetic to community mobilization but in frequent communication with city power brokers. Long-term local residents were investigated as a possible link between traditional society and the new activism. Unfortunately, long-term residents are a dispirited, apathetic group, marked by much social, but very little political, involvement.

Positive evidence concerning the contribution that cultural

renewal can make to political revitalization comes from the relatively advanced situation of blacks, and the part played by race consciousness in bringing about that development. Sixty-two percent of leaders nominated by residents in black areas fall into pro-change activist types; a full 39 percent qualify as neighborhood radicals. Among whites, the picture is quite different, with neighborhood establishment, elder elite and the uninvolved accounting for 65 percent of all leaders.

Group memberships differ markedly by race as well. One hundred black leaders have, on the average, 56 memberships in traditional groups, 11 *less* than whites. In the same black group, however, there will be 114 memberships in newer action groups, *twice as many* as for whites. Black women, although not on a par with black men, are significantly more evolved politically than white women. They are less prey, for example, to political divisions of labor specifying domestic issues and administrative busy work as women's special preserve. Poor blacks are more conscious of poverty problems, more politicized and more politically active than poor whites. Particularly significant is the fact that poor black neighborhoods now draw their political elites from a strata of leadership lower in socio-economic status and more militant than leadership generally. This is not the case in white neighborhoods.

All this points to a special vitality in black communities, and constitutes. an a priori argument for the powerful contribution that cultural awakening can make to political revitalization. That argument is furthered by the integral yet selective role that race values can be seen to play in black political culture. Race identification, for example, is part of a mobilization syndrome including politicization, perception of local problems, political information and involvement in political action. This syndrome, observable among blacks generally, is twice as marked among community leaders. Evidently, leaders are especially adept at converting group solidarity to political action. Support for specifically racial policies, on the other hand, although moderately prevalent among blacks at large, is not salient in the world view of black political elites. Flexibility in setting policy priorities is not sacrificed to group loyalty.

Militant ethnic groups emerged in the Local Change Survey as ideal vehicles for integrating cultural awakening and political revitalization. Members of these groups, high in education but *lower* than other leaders in income, are almost alone among leaders in having a distinctive political world view. Members are deeply involved in the day-to-day realities of their communities, having more local acquaintances than members of any other group. Finally, members are deeply practical when it comes to political tactics, accepting the deepest involvement in conventional, as well as protest political activities when that seems appropriate.

There is little need to recapitulate the many arguments of preceding chapters concerning the centrality of leadership, direct action and organization to successful political mobilization in poor neighborhoods. Without the leadership strata revealed by the Local Change Survey, poor neighborhoods would be disgruntled, apathetic communities, socially unorganized and politically benign.

It is important for the poor to be wary of manipulation by upper-status community elements, as our data concerning the neighborhood establishment indicates. This warning, however, does not compromise the general conclusion that strong, committed leadership is crucial to political revitalization. The institutionalization of protest in membership organizations is a central facet of mobilization as well. Nothing so consistently distinguishes activists from non-activists as participation in action groups. Evidence points to the need for militance on the part of individual organizations, but even more, to the need for coordinated effort between organizations. The most effective political strategy monitored in the Local Change data is the combination of protest and conventional action characteristic of pragmatic militant communities. Second place goes not to reformist communities, where conventional action is preferred to protest, but to defiant militant communities where protest predominates.

REVITALIZATION STRATEGIES FOR OTHER SOCIAL GROUPS

The following factors, our analysis suggests, have aided effective political mobilization among poor Americans. Few of the inclusions are novel, but all are backed by detailed evidence concerning the experience of poor neighborhoods nationwide.

- a radicalism, accompanied by political action, which does not deny all responsiveness in those responsible for change.

- cultural revitalization and group solidarity.

- dissemination of information on local grievances and political action.

- protest and direct action.

- committed leadership.

- aggressive membership organizations acting in concert.

None of these factors can set specific priorities for other groups seeking political revitalization, but together they form a strong framework for making decisions on strategy to be followed. We spoke earlier of the relatively limited impact women's liberation as a movement has had on poor women. Within the framework outlined here it would be possible to pose much broader questions concerning the status of women's liberation as a movement for political revitalization. It could be noted, for example, that the movement has had difficulty finding ways in which committed leadership can evolve without compromising the personalism of the movement. Women's membership organizations are few and weak. Strong coordination of efforts across groups is yet to come. Women's movement ideology, our framework would suggest, must retain its radical bent but also develop sensitivity to ways in which men might be responsive to its demands.

The framework would prompt those concerned with political revitalization of other social groups to ask similar questions. What does the need for group solidarity suggest in the context of mobilizing prisoners, for example? What would cultural revitalization look like in the prison context? In prisons, where protest and organization are difficult, perhaps the nominally more neutral political information function could be emphasized. If our analysis is correct, it is not as benign as it might appear to administrators. It would be irresponsible to issue a universal call to protest in the potentially deadly prison environment. Our analysis of experience in poor neighborhoods will not let us hesitate, however, before the conclusion that protest is indeed an effective tactic for bringing about institutional change.

Similar questions could be asked concerning political revitalization among dissident professionals, high school students, reformist clergy and many other groups. No questions of political strategy are simple. There are no panaceas. Hopefully, however, the experience of poor neighborhoods will give encouragement to those engaged in the difficult task of political revitalization elsewhere.

POLICY IMPLICATIONS

The implications of our analysis for governmental policy in poor neighborhoods is more direct. If government is interested in the political revitalization of poor neighborhoods and change in the institutional environment of poverty, it must support the new forces contributing to those developments described throughout this work. The irrationality of administrating funds along more traditional lines was clearly documented in the Local Change data. The two community subgroups most likely to attain control over conventional programs are the neighborhood establishment and political party affiliates. Yet it is precisely these persons, the data suggest, who are most hostile to political revitalization—most callous to poverty problems. More resources in the hands of these individuals would compromise, not enhance, the vitality of local political life.

Some federal programs have sought active involvement of the poor themselves in setting up and running local agencies. Others have, as a stated goal, the development of organizations capable of pushing for progressive change in neighborhood conditions. Our data document both the appropriateness of this strategy in principle and its failure in practice for want of resources. It would be generous to conclude that the Local Change Survey found even the beginnings of meaningful commitment to change in many institutions serving the poor. The task of political revitalization in poor neighborhoods has just begun; not, as government policy might suggest, just ended. If the pragmatic militant pattern is an appropriate goal in this regard, only one neighborhood in eight has achieved success. Although not significant in absolute terms, some government programs have aided political revitalization among the poor. A very large minority of persons that the poor nominate as leaders are employed by the government (23 percent) and the figure rises among politically relevant strata (to 27 percent for black political elites, 39 percent for white). The critical reformist attitude of these "community workers" toward local institutions, noted in Chapter 1, marks them as a positive influence on political values in their communities. There is evidence that more government programs along these lines would meet with even more success. Most important are indications of the vitality of neighborhood leadership, its localism, its political engagement, its practical, nonideological approach to problems. Poor neighborhoods do have leadership cadres capable of competent involvement in the full range of anti-poverty programs.

There are many explanations for the inadequacy of government commitment to political revitalization of the poor. We are told that a backlash among middle Americans would ultimately revoke any progress made. Others say that there is no longer a constituency among the "haves" for resource-hungry "have not" programs. Americans have little patience with problems that do not capitulate to D-Day like policy landings. Welfare chiseling, race mixing in the schools, exclusive zoning, are the issues with national constituencies, not minimum incomes, integration and adequate housing. Because these explanations of failed poverty policy concern attitudes of mainstream Americans, the Local Change Study cannot speak directly to their truth or falsity. We can insist, however, that failure should not be blamed on lack of readiness among the poor themselves—it is not social disorganization among the poor that has frustrated poverty policy, but the failure of a timid country to act.

Appendix A
Survey Methodology

Because this study relies so heavily on empirical evidence, it is important to be explicit concerning methodology. At issue are more than problems of respondent, survey instrument, and interview technique. The authenticity of evidence on poverty is a *political* question. Just who are "the poor" reported on here? Even more delicately, Who are the persons we grant the title "leaders of the poor"? A brief historical summary of the persons and institutions behind the data gathering of the Local Change Study will begin to place these questions in perspective. Particularly hazardous sample biases concerning general residents, leaders and institutional informants will be discussed and the specific steps taken to guard against them outlined. A concluding section will discuss the attitude of the Local Change Study toward analysis based on communities as opposed to individuals.

Data Collection

Throughout its life, the Office of Economic Opportunity has sought feedback concerning its programs and their success. One early move in Nixon's anti-OEO strategy parodied this worthwhile impulse by suggesting that OEO be stripped of all its programs except research and evaluation. The early "gray areas" projects were the subject of case studies commissioned by OEO. Yankellovich Associates were asked to write extensive studies of the early years of poverty agencies in a large number of cities. The strategy of citizen participation was the subject of a special analysis mounted by researchers at Brandeis University.[1]

In August, 1967, OEO's evaluation division approached Barss-Reitzel and Associates with their concern that piecemeal research was failing to address one of the central issues of the war on poverty: Does the collection of agencies and activities known as the Community Action Program bring about actual change in the institutional environment of poor Americans? With a resolve characteristic of those priding themselves on "systems analytic research," a number of agencies waded into the data gathering and analysis that marked the start of the Local Change Study. Attention was directed to three questions: How much change has taken place in institutions dealing with the poor? What role has CAP played in bringing about these changes? and, What characteristics of community structure might account for the changes and/or CAP's role in fostering them?

National Opinion Research Center, Kirshner Associates and U.S. Research and Development Corporation collected the first data of the study between August and September, 1968. In each of 48 communities, teams of "knowledgeable informants" (most often political scientists from a local university) were asked to fill out some 300 pages of semistructured case study material covering everything from percentage voting Republican in the last three mayoralty races to histories of power struggles on CAP Advisory Boards. Public and private welfare agencies, public employment services and education were the institutions chosen for analysis. The research was not conspicuously successful (later sections will discuss analytic strategies in detail), but it did provide some lessons which helped place subsequent data gathering on more stable ground.[2]

The next research strategy emphasized the collection of precise empirical data concerning local institutions, focusing this time on private welfare, public education and major employers of local people. The National Opinion Research Center was contracted to draw up, pre-test, and administer questionnaires appropriate to each area. Between August, 1968, and January, 1969, these questionnaires were administered in 100 communities selected from communities over 50,000 in population with OEO agencies. Interviewing of institutional heads was done by NORC's trained field staff, generally middle-aged women. Race appropriateness was preserved in most instances.

In the private welfare sector interviewers sought information from *private welfare agency heads*, executive directors or chief administrative officers of private service agencies which served the neighborhood.[3] In each neighborhood the three largest agencies, as determined by staff and/or budget, were covered, with an eye to distribution among agency types: settlement houses, family services, psychiatric services, youth agencies, day care centers, job training centers, programs for the elderly, etc. If agencies could not be found within the target area, interviewers were instructed to search on the border (within a half mile), and, as final recourse, to turn to agencies in the city at large which served local persons. Branch offices located locally were to be preferred over main offices and between several local branches of the same agency only the largest was to be chosen.

The survey instrument administered to agency directors contained some 300 questions of which about 70 were open-ended (all open-ended questions were coded into categories for empirical analysis). Some questions were quite specific: "How many people used your services in 1968?" "What percentage of the people who used your services in 1964 were Mexican-Americans?" Major aspects of agency structure and programming were covered, "Do you canvass door to door?" "Are there any residents of the neighborhood who serve on your board of directors?" "How many people on your staff now are professionals, sub-professionals?" "How many referrals did you make in 1968? in 1964?" A few questions asked for personal judgments: "If you found yourself in an ideal situation . . . what one part of your current program would you expand?" "How do you account for changes in the way you are using your physical facilities since 1964?" To highlight change in institutions, almost every question about present reality was matched with one probing the same situation five years earlier.

Information on local schools was obtained from interviews with 286 *PTA presidents*. These, it was hoped, would be more in touch with local educational innovations, or their lack, and be more objective in evaluating them, than either school officials or teachers. PTA presidents, although by no means universally sympathetic to militant forms of parental involvement, were nevertheless felt to be familiar with such developments on the local scene. Three elementary schools were chosen in each area (elementary schools were felt to be a more integral part of neighborhood political systems than more regionalized junior and senior highs). In 13 areas it was necessary to use other than elementary schools or to interview more than one official in the same organization. Interviews, averaging an hour and a half, were conducted with PTA presidents in each school. Among topics covered were school politics: "Has the race of teachers ever been an issue in this school community?" "When did this occur?" "Who raised the issue?" General improvements: "What is the current teacher student ratio in your school?" "What was it in 1964?" and innovations in minority programs: "Do any of your new textbooks use pictures and stories which show children and families of different nationalities and races?"

The third category of institutional leader surveyed was *local employers*. In each neighborhood, the personnel officers in charge of "setting employment policy and/or hiring employees" for the three largest local employers were interviewed.[4] Respondents were questioned at length concerning the minority composition of their work force, outreach and training programs, practices concerning hiring and promotions, etc.

In each community, three *organization heads,* directors of local membership organizations, were interviewed by NORC. Community political organizations were originally conceived as a fourth institutional sector which the Community Action Program might affect. We will use data from these interviews as evidence of structural dimensions of local politics. Three organizations were selected from the following types in each community: "general purpose membership organizations," "specifically political organizations," and "single-purpose, semi-political organizations." One leader or officer in each was then interviewed (an elected official representing the neighborhood could be included as well).

Each of these organization leaders was asked in detail about local political events "Are residents of this neighborhood involved in welfare rights organizations? . . . in tenants' unions?" "Have there been any voter registration drives in this neighborhood?" "How many people participated in a recent public expression of demands concerning community control of schools?" Each respondent named two "organizations in the neighborhood which have the largest membership and in which the members are most active" and then described in detail the structure, activities, and effectiveness of each: "Does the (organization) have a source of income other than dues?" "Which kinds (of the 12 groups listed) does (organization) work with on any issues?" "Since 1964, has (organization) conducted any Sit Ins? Boycotts? Demonstrations? Mass Marches?"

A cross section of *CAP personnel* was interviewed in each city as well. The CAA Executive Director, the Director of the Neighborhood Center Program, the Employment Program Director, five members of the CAA Board (the President and representatives from the Mayor's office, the business community, and the poor), and the local Neighborhood Center Director. Five extensive survey instruments were constructed for these categories of respondents plumbing all aspects of CAP organization, strategic priorities and program effectiveness.

Simultaneous with the interviewing of institutional leaders, plans were made to sample general residents of poor neighborhoods and their leaders. It was felt important to place formal community action in the context of community mobilization generally and to match the views of institutional leaders concerning change against those of persons pressing for such change. A questionnaire was devised covering a wide variety of beliefs and behaviors (the best introduction to it would be a glance at the questions and scales described in Appendix B). Included, for example, were questions concerning local events: "Are community groups more or less successful in getting what they want than they were five years ago?" On social involvement: "To what groups do you belong?" On political loyalties: "Do you personally feel this country is worth fighting for?" On political attitudes: "What do you think when you hear the word 'political'?" On race: "Would black people do better if they voted only for blacks?" On political behavior: "Have you ever picketed?" "Would you agree to threaten a manager with damage to his store?"

The team that constructed the interview for Barss Reitzel and Associates was headed by Stan Greenberg. Others who contributed to its development were Joan Laurence, David Sears, and Warren Tenhouten of the Survey Research Center at UCLA and Diana Tenhouten and Jonathan Lane, the Project Managers for OEO. It was at this stage of the evaluation process that I began work on the project. My own involvement touched instrument construction, survey, design, interviewer training, data analysis and project reporting.

Two sampling strategies were employed. In the full *One Hundred City Sample,* only "Leaders of the Poor" were interviewed. In order to identify these leaders, 40 general residents in each neighborhood were asked to name persons active on local problems or familiar with local events. Respondents were then selected from this list (details of the process are covered in the next section). Persons interviewed to obtain names of leaders were also given a reduced form of the full questionnaire. Where possible, data from this sample of 4,000 poor persons was incorporated into the analysis. The full questionnaire was administered to a total of 630 leaders (37 percent white, 54 percent black, 9 percent chicano) in 100 communities nationwide.

A second sampling strategy took a different tack. In order to comment with some certainty on the dynamics of community mobilization—a highly localized phenomenon—it was decided to investigate a small number of communities in great depth. A representative subset of five cities was selected for this purpose: black neighborhoods in Detroit, Philadelphia, and Atlanta, a white community in Hamilton, Ohio, and a chicano neighborhood in San Jose. A total of 1,114 general residents and 441 leaders, were given the full questionnaire in this phase of the research. This *Five City Sample* provides extensive data on the attitudes and behavior of general residents of poor neighborhoods. Even though it is a 1 in 20 subset of the hundred cities it will be used whenever the attitudes of the poor as a whole are in question. Unfortunately, extensive sampling of residents in each of the 100 cities was beyond the scope of the project.[5]

Several interpretations of those data have been submitted to OEO. The first, in July, 1969, was an interim analysis of the first 50 cities visited.[6] A second volume presented social and political profiles of persons affiliated with Community Action, and discussed the opinions of institutional leaders concerning change in their organizations and the role they felt CAP had played in those changes.[7] Stan Greenberg explored community political mobilization from several perspectives through the Five City data in *Mobilizing Poor Communities.*[8] The most comprehensive reporting of the data is contained in *Community Action and Urban Institutional Change* presented to OEO by Barss Reitzel and Associates, August, 1970.[9]

Survey Bias

At each level of sample selection there are biases which plague survey research on poverty problems. The following are potential biases in the selection of geographic areas to be surveyed:

- Toward middle-class communities
- Toward white communities
- Toward communities with high levels of social and political organization
- Toward poverty concentrations at the expense of semi-rural poor and poor persons living in more affluent neighborhoods.

We deal with areal sample biases first because the definition of poverty for sampling purposes selected by the Local Change Study was geographic, not personal. The problem of finding consistently poor areas is not a trivial one. Most of the studies to which one must turn for precedents are unsatisfactory. Matthews and Prothro, the Lemberg Study, and the Supplemental Studies for the Riot Commission all sample exclusively by race, and not poverty level, for example.[10] The approach is dangerous. Senator Prouty discovered, for example, that his geographic sampling of poverty in Washington, D.C. yielded a 42 percent "minority" of persons with incomes over $7,500.[11]

There are many reasons for the poor slipping through nets cast by data surveys. Middle-class field workers are out of their element in the ghetto. They make mistakes in judgment (could anyone live in this place?) and hedge on standards (one interview attempt is enough on *that* street.) Transient populations and persons not directly affiliated with a household—the poor are often both—go undersampled. The result, as Greenberg points out, is that even "the most rigorous sample of the United States population (ostensibly exhaustive) under-counted Negroes in 1960 by 1,178,000, a deficiency of 5.9 percent"[12] The problem is especially acute among young, male blacks. Bogue reports that at age 33 nearly one in five of this group went uncounted in the 1960 census.[13] Among persons earning under $5,000, 22 percent report having been interviewed at some point in their lives. The figure rises to 65 percent for those earning over $15,000.[14] Evidence that the transient nature of ghetto populations can lead to sample bias is provided by studies of characteristics of persons interviewed on callbacks. Campbell et al., in their study of urban riots, write: "those interviewed on later calls were more often males, more often employed, and more often in their 20's and 30's."[15] Given these difficulties in accurate enumeration of the poor, it was decided to sample, not poor individuals, but poor places.

The procedure involved several steps, some practical responses to OEO's needs, others hedges against the biases noted above. A list of 100 cities over 50,000 in population was drawn at random from NORC's Permanent Communities Sample.[16] A few communities were discarded from the list because they lacked a Community Action Program. In each city one neighborhood was selected from target areas (T.A.'s) as defined by the citywide CAA agency. One T.A. was selected at random from all those in the city. Although T.A.'s vary a great deal in size from city to city, they are of roughly comparable populations within a given city. Within each T.A., all the blocks with over 50% deteriorating or dilapidated houses, as recorded in the 1960 census, were marked on a map. Interviews were then taken in a random sample of ten of these blocks. Probably to avoid jurisdictional conflict, most CAA's seem to have drawn T.A. boundaries quite generously. It was thus necessary to hedge against the possibility of sampling middle-class areas "inadvertently" included in a T.A.. The study also fell at an awkward time in the census cycle. It had to rely on eight year old statistics in a time of rapid change for many central city areas. For these reasons, field workers were asked to phone in reports of any blocks on their sampling lists which did not fit the sampling criteria or were not public housing.

The areal sampling procedure outlined here is by no means a perfect solution to the biases outlined above. Indians and poor persons in rural areas and small towns are excluded outright. The T.A. approach biases the sample modestly toward areas of concentrated poverty, although the inclusiveness of T.A. boundaries mitigates this problem. It is difficult to make a definitive judgement on the poverty level of persons sampled. The median income of general residents in the Five City Sample is $5,200, that of leaders in the One Hundred City Sample, $6,200.[17]

Poverty research is prone to many sampling biases at the individual level as well:

- Toward women
- Toward those without jobs
- Toward more articulate, upwardly mobile elements of the community
- Toward the residentially stable
- Toward political moderates

On each of the blocks selected by the procedure outlined above, two or four persons were chosen to be interviewed. To save time and money, dwelling units were used as the sampling unit, not individuals or households. A more equal stratification by sex was promoted by specifying that a man should be interviewed at the nth unit to the right of a corner, and a woman the same distance to the left.

Most of the biases in sampling poor individuals result from the tendency of field personnel to prefer visiting *homes* in the *daytime*. Unfortunately, ᵫis is precisely the place and location avoided by a large minority of the poor population. As a middle aged Harlem man told a HARYOU interviewer one summer, "We can't go back in the house because we almost suffocate. So we sit down on the curb, or stand on the sidewalk, on the steps, things like that, til the wee hours of the morning, especially in the summer when it's too hot to go up."[18]

It seemed imperative to include representatives of street corner society in the sample, so it was determined to stratify day-night and commercial-residential. The first task of field personnel upon arriving in a neighborhood was thus to list all the local commercial places where people could be found and estimate usage of each. A typical list, this one from the Hansel Center neighborhood of South Bend reads as follows: Jelly's Bar, K and F Market, G and B Liquor Store, Deka's Bar, Sarah's Lounge, Nyikos Bar, St. Vincent DePaul Thrift Shop, Happy Days Bar, Al's Food Market, Hansel Center. A series of pretest questions probing usage of places like these set stratification quotas at 3/8 residential day, 3/8 residential night and 1/8 each commercial day and commercial night. The result of these measures in the Five City Sample was an evenly balanced sample, median age 36 (36 percent under 30), 55 percent female, with a median income of $5,200. Of the 1,114 persons interviewed, 16 percent were white, 70 percent black and 14 percent chicano.

There is concrete evidence that refusal rates, no answer rates, and questionnaire responses themselves are all affected by the race of the interviewer. In a classic instance, a 1942 Memphis poll asked black respondents "Would Negroes be treated better or worse here if the Japanese conquered the U.S.A.?" One in four responded "worse" to a black interviewer; 45 percent to a white.[19]

The amount of bias by race is related to differences in social class between interviewer and respondent as well. In questioning upper-status blacks concerning sit-ins, Williams found little difference in the answers given to white and black interviewers. When lower status blacks were faced by upper-status white interviewers, however, distortion of responses was marked. Only 56 percent as many would say they disapproved of sit-ins to a white interviewer as to a black.[20]

Bias is also related to the threat perceived in a question. Pettigrew found a 21 percent differential on the question "the trouble with most white people is that they think they are better than other people." Intelligence and information tests, filled with personal, if not political threats, show similar differentials. Only on the simplest factual items does the race of the interviewer seem to be of little importance (age, 4 percent; church attendance, 5 percent).[21]

The Local Change Study subcontracted interviewing to Trans-Century Corporation, a black-run, multi-ethnic survey research organization. Although local people were occasionally hired on the spot, the majority of interviews were carried out by young, educated, semi-professional interviewers.[22] For better or worse, interviewers on this project were not local activists. In politics they ranged from throughtful liberal to quiet radical. Over 90 percent of interviews were administered by persons of the same race as the respondent.

An important question that haunted designers of the Local Change survey was how much cooperativeness could be expected from respondents. Conversations with local activists, hired as consultants in pretest communities (Roxbury, Boston; Venice, Los Angeles), confirmed that residents of poverty areas were beginning to view surveys as expensive balm for white consciences. A round table with community leaders in Roxbury on survey methodology came up with only one suggestion—respondents should be paid: "the issue seems to be, without stipend, black folks are being exploited." "One feels better about cooperating with a con game if they pay you."[23] The round table reluctantly lowered its suggested compensation from $100 per interview to $25 and the meeting was adjourned. The matter was shelved. Worst expectations of forthcoming hostility were occasionally confirmed in the field. A community leader in Pasadena dictated slowly to one interviewer: "It's a fucked up questionnaire, simplistic, stupid and a waste of money. They should pay the interviewees if they are interested in doing anything about poverty. Social scientists that help design this piece of crap are cheap prostitutes," and here he must have paused with a politician's instinct to state specifics "for the Federal government, Barss Reitzel, and Trans-Century Corporation." Importantly, however, the widespread hostility to survey methods which it was feared might cripple the project did not materialize. Our experience was much closer to that of Kenneth Clark in the HARYOU research: "Among the HARYOU subjects, the posture of exaggeration, if not bombast, seemed more apparent than did inhibition."[24] People were not universally sympathetic to the research; interviewers rated six percent of the Hundred City Sample "hostile" to the research and another 20 percent more unfavorable than favorable. Actual uncooperativeness was remarkably low. Only two percent of persons were rated "not cooperative" by interviewers while 85 percent were judged "fairly" or "very" cooperative. Refusal rate varied between five percent and 20 percent in each city.[25]

Following are some biases often found in studies of leaders of the poor:

- Toward persons presumed by *outsiders* to be influential in poor areas
- Toward persons in formal positions of authority
- Toward any leadership when none exists
- Toward opinion versus issue leadership
- Toward city-wide versus neighborhood influentials.

It is simplisitic to think of obtaining an accurate sample of community leadership by simply eliminating "biases." There are many conceptions of leadership. Differences between some of them can be simply a matter of focus. There is nothing more or less valid about studying city-wide as opposed to neighborhood leadership, for example. There were very few precedents to help in tracking down the kind of individual the Local Change Study wanted to question: persons that the poor themselves consider influential in their communities.

Designation of leadership by *reputation* for power has important precedents, with Hunter's influential study of Atlanta serving as the prototype. In this technique, as traditionally applied, a number of persons felt to be knowledgeable about local politics are approached for lists of persons influential in local affairs. Different lists are cross checked against each other and often against the opinions of the influentials themselves until the names of "top leaders" of the city emerge.[26] For several reasons, this technique is inappropriate for research of the present sort. First, it is heavily biased toward high status elites. Grass roots leadership, no matter how vital, tends to be winnowed out in the upper reaches of reciprocal attributions of power. There is a dangerous inevitability in the technique as well. It is almost impossible for the technique *not* to reveal a pyramidal power structure. In addition to these problems, the technique was felt to be prohibitively costly for a survey focusing on one hundred different communities.

A second technique seeks persons who have been instrumental in the resolution of specific *issues*. The method was refined by a series of writers reacting to the methodological and political biases of the reputational approach.[27] This strategy, which follows important public issues and notes the persons instrumental to their outcome, does indeed protect against some of the biases listed above. It is not taken in by empty, prescriptive authority or by persons who might influence attitudes but never seem to be where the action is. Unfortunately, the issue approach to leadership designation offered little help to the Local Change Study. Like the reputational approach, it tends to define leadership at a city-wide, not a neighborhood level. While few issues are resolved by forces operating exclusively at the neighborhood level, it seemed crucial not to accept a technique biased so strongly against local politics. It is hazardous, furthermore, to conceptualize politics in poor neighborhoods as issue-specific. If, during the civil rights movement, race could be thought of as a single issue, it no longer seems prudent to do so. Block groups, ethnic organizations and general purpose membership groups rarely restrict their mandates to the economic, social, political or cultural realm. It would have been dangerous to base data collection on a hypothesis which should be tested in data gathered through a more neutral procedure. The issue approach was unrealistic from a practical viewpoint as well, the historical research it requires being prohibitively expensive in a study of 100 different communities.

The *prescriptive* approach looks to power positions with formal authority.[28] It was, however, precisely the identification of community leadership with formal position holding that the Local Change Study was seeking to avoid.

The technique finally selected for leadership identification was a composite of several of these approaches. Once the careful delineation of poverty areas had been accomplished, interviewers approached 40 different persons in the neighborhood and asked them who they considered to be their leaders. Two separate questions were utilized. In a variation on the issue approach, respondents were first asked, "What kinds of problems are people in this neighborhood concerned about?" After listing up to three problems, the interviewer continued, "Who do you know around here who is doing anything about these problems?" A second question emphasized familiarity with community life and events: "Can you think of anyone around here who seems to know a lot of people in the area, someone who talks to a lot of people and gets in on things that are going on? (and, if this drew a blank) someone who usually knows things like who is moving in and out of the neighborhood, who has jobs, who needs jobs, and how people can get help for their problems." The first question resulted in 1,480 attributions (71 percent of respondents gave no names, 22 percent only one) the second in 1,137 attributions (78 percent gave no names, 17 percent only one). Names from both questions were combined (distinctions between leaders would be based on data collected from the leaders themselves). Blacks tended to name a few more leaders on the first question than whites, but all other demographic characteristics of persons giving names on the two questions were quite similar. In the typical community, the 40 persons gave 26 names of 12 different persons (seven on the first question, five on the 2nd). Six out of 10 persons gave no names on either question.

When the list of leader numbers had been compiled for each community, a cross section of leaders was chosen from three types: those named once, those named twice, and those named three or more times. Proportions falling into these categories were 60 percent, 20 percent, and 20 percent (proportions actually interviewed in each were 20 percent, 38 percent, 42 percent).

Methodological Problems in Defining the Neighborhood as a Unit of Analysis

Rigorously empirical studies rarely move to a level of abstraction that considers geographical entities as units of analysis. Survey costs are determined by two basic parameters: number of persons interviewed and number of locations visited. Given the expense of coordinating nation-wide studies and the common availability of a wide range of demographic types in any given locality, the decision is generally made to interview a large number of persons in a small number of locations. Bolstering the decision is the assumption, sometimes tacit, sometimes explicit, that personal variation is more important than group variation —the "behavioral persuasion" of social science. Too many of the work-horses of behavioral analysis must be abandoned in aggregate analysis. Especially vulnerable to "homogenization" are the most personal attributes of individuals, the nature of their personalities, the quality of their primary group relations and the like.

Closely related is a complex methodological problem: how does one measure attributes of collectivities? The initial goal of the Local Change Study was a precise evaluation of the Community Action Program's success in bringing about change in local institutions. It was obvious to both government sponsors and the private researchers given responsibility for the project that "community-as-unit" analysis would have to be attempted. A brief history of the project's experiences with this problem will be interesting from a methodological point of view. It will also give some sense of the kind and quality of data reported on in chapters taking neighborhoods as units of analysis.

An early decision was taken to measure not just the quality and number of CAP programs but "output" variables as well. Equally as fundamental was the decision to focus on change in institutions, not change in persons. It was no secret that the war on poverty had done little to improve the economic status or opportunities of poor persons as a whole. Measuring individual change would have required extended purposive sampling in each community to find a number of persons actually affected by the Community Action Program. Once the influence of larger forces had been accounted for (nation-wide trends in employment, pre-CAP individual potentials, etc.), it seemed inevitable that CAP's contribution to personal progress would be less than the margin of error produced by the measuring strategy.

If people were not to be the unit of analysis, the following collectivities and characteristics would have to be investigated and measured:

- City-wide Community Action Agencies and local Neighborhood Centers (internal structure, overall strategies, and level of activity).

- Neighborhoods (level of political mobilization, demographic characteristics).
- Neighborhood Service Institutions (internal structure, program parameters, change over the last five years).
- Cities (demographic and political characteristics).

A frequent approach to problems of this sort the case study, was briefly considered.[29] In the case study approach, however, many forces work to reduce the number of relevant instances from which conclusions can be drawn (the statistician's "N"). Because the analyst's personal values and insight are so important to the quality of a case study, there is an argument for considering "N" to be the number of authors writing, not the number of communities studied. In addition, the best case studies will frequently be those most marked by the idiosyncracies of their authors. Unfortunately, this means that the best analyses will be those least amenable to summary evaluations which demand comparisons across cases. Generalizing from a number of case studies is inevitably difficult. Each case merges into the next as the endless demographic statistics, acronyms, and personages pass by. One feels a constant reliance on the abilities of the individual analysts and is likely to long for a private word with the best of them. This methodological *politique des auteurs* means that the sponsoring agency would probably do as well to fund the private musings of the best commentator on the topic and leave it at that.

The first effort of the Local Change research team was a half-way house between case study and aggregate analysis via surveys.[30] It was a disaster. Between June and August of 1968, representatives of three separate research firms visited 50 cities. In some cases work was carried out by small journalistic teams which visited several cities, in others local academics were subcontracted to do the work. In every city an extensive survey instrument was filled in by the observer. It contained questions of great breadth and specificity covering all the different collectivities listed above and estimates of causal interactions as well: "How much was CAP responsible for the adoption of new programs by local schools?" "Was a certain change in welfare practices due more to efforts by the local Executive Director of the CAP, the extent of participation of the poor in CAP programs, or to the local political situation?" The result was the worst attributes of case studies and survey analysis. The presence of 50 cases with nominally similar data for each was just sufficient to submerge the identities of individual communities. On the other hand, once the sample had been discounted for errors due to the sheer impossibility of the assignment, the effective N for aggregate analysis was pushed far below the original 50. Special contributions by persons of unusual insight were frustrated by the questionnaire format. "Personal" comments and analysis were possible, but in the nature of things did not make their way into the statistical analysis. A clue to the overall problem was the presence of extensive response sets. About the only consistency in the data was in answers to questions adjacent on the questionnaire. Interviewers were capable of establishing a few gross parameters of CAP programs with some precision—estimates of overall funding agreed generally with figures derived later from budget reports ($r = .88$). Concerning more subjective matters, however, agreement with the observations of participants themselves was much less common (Phase I estimates of "community organization emphasis" of local CAP's correlated with later judgments of CAP personnel at the .22 level.)[31] The judgments of Phase I observers concerning amounts of change in local institutions bore no relationship whatsoever to the estimates of institution heads interviewed later. In the private welfare area the correlation was .01; concerning local schools it was .09.[32]

Out of these experiences grew the final plan for evaluation. Because funds were available to carry out a design of great complexity, it was decided to move in the direction of survey analysis and away from the case study plan. Sights were set on an N of 100 cities. The National Opinion Research Center was contracted to write the survey instruments and carry out the field work in two stages of 50 cities each (to allow for revision of priorities and techniques half-way). The most important change from previous plans was the decision to go to "experts" —local informants—to learn about local events and institutions. The kinds of persons interviewed through the strategy were described above.

The idea was to find a few highly informed persons and get precise information from them about local events within their sphere of knowledge. Information so gathered would then be treated as "facts" in later empirical analysis seeking factors associated with institutional change. Judgments concerning causes of events were treated somewhat differently. It was felt that such opinions had a certain face validity as estimates of CAP impact by knowledgeable observers.

This research strategy is at once highly efficient and very risky. Information is gathered only from categories of persons believed to be precisely informed about local affairs. There is no opportunity for cross-checking of data, however, as each respondent is questioned about a different institution. The complete lack of correspondence between the views of these persons and the scholarly teams sent out in the preliminary investigation has already been mentioned. An effort, backed by the best of intentions, was made to cross-check these "expert" views with those of leaders of the poor, presumed to be more hard-headed in evaluating the amount of change that had actually occurred. It was discovered first, that leaders were not a great deal more pessimistic than the experts—neither reported very much change in local institutions. Second, local leadership was often quite willing to extend the benefit of the doubt to local agencies that tried to respond to needs of the poor. Finally, it was brought home that in a politicized context "objective" evaluations are in fact highly personalized. As Jacobs discovered when he attempted to use the opinions of local leadership to corroborate "expert" views on institutional change, there is virtually no relationship between the two. More important than community attributes in predicting the views of leaders on this topic were attributes of leaders themselves; education, participation in protest activity, and sense of political efficacy, for example.[33]

The three institutional sectors chosen—private welfare, public schools, and employment—by no means exhaust those relevant to poor neighborhoods. Commercial establishments and the whole area of governmental institutions (public welfare, police, housing policy), were avoided. Inclusion of these would have shifted analysis away from community political dynamics toward analysis of the political system itself. What the chosen sectors give is a representative sampling of neighborhood institutions intimately involved in the community political system.

The analysis of this data for the Office of Economic Opportunity took place in several stages. Those interested in the methodology of this analysis and its conclusions should consult *Community Action and Urban Institutional Change: a National Evaluation of the Community Action Program*, Barss Reitzel and Associates, Bruce Jacobs, Project Director, Cambridge, Mass. (August, 1970).

Below are listed the names of the 100 communities sampled in the Local Change Survey. "Community Type" refers to the typology of communities derived and analyzed in Chapter 2. The number code is pragmatic militants (1); defiant militants (2); reformist (3); passive center (4); idle radicals (5); unclassified (6).

City	Community Type	Neighborhood
A. Five Communities chosen for intensive analysis:		
Atlanta	(3)	Summerhill-Mechanicsville and Edgewood Neighborhood Service Centers
Detroit	(4)	CAP Target Area III
Hamilton, Ohio	(4)	Belmont Neighborhood Center
Philadelphia	(3)	Area C, Ridge Avenue
San Jose	(5)	South County

City	Community Type	Neighborhood

B. Remaining 95 communities:

City	Community Type	Neighborhood
Akron	(1)	TA—South Akron, Community Action Council
Albany	(2)	Southend—SENCAP
Amarillo	(5)	South End—Alama Neighborhood Center
Ann Arbor	(4)	(not available)
Austin	(2)	East 1st Street
Bakersfield	(6)	Lakeview South Center
Baltimore	(1)	Area #2, TA—Central City
Baton Rouge	(1)	South Baton Rouge
Bayonne, N.J.	(4)	Berger Point Area
Berkeley	(3)	South Berkeley CAP #1 Lincoln—NC
Birmingham	(4)	Smithfield
Boston	(1)	Dorchester
Buffalo	(1)	Master District Neighborhood Center
Cambridge	(3)	Riverside—Neighborhood #7
Charleston, W. V.	(5)	Kennedy Center
Charlotte, N.C.	(3)	Eastside Area B
Cincinnati	(4)	Eastend Neighborhood Services
Cleveland	(1)	Hough Neighborhood Opportunity Center
Columbus	(2)	Target Area #2
Denver	(2)	Westside Action Center
Duluth	(2)	Hillside Community Center
Erie	(4)	Central City Nato II
Fayetteville	(3)	Area A—Winston Street Center
Fort Worth	(2)	Como #7
Hammond-Gary	(3)	West Calumet
Hartford	(2)	Garden Area Neighborhood Center
Haywood, Cal.	(4)	(not available)
Houston	(4)	Area II Market Street Center
Indianapolis	(4)	Broadway Park

City	Community Type	Neighborhood
Jacksonville	(1)	TA #2 Eastside Center
Jersey City	(4)	Marion Center
Kansas City, K.	(3)	Crossline Coordination & Development Center
Kansas City, Mo.	(4)	Area III Center
Lancaster	(4)	Lancaster Multi-Service Center
Lansing	(4)	Eastside Action Center
Las Vegas	(2)	(not available)
Lincoln	(3)	Target Area III
Long Beach	(4)	Westside
Los Angeles	(4)	Florence Graham Neighborhood Adult Participation Center
Louisville	(1)	Manly Area
Lubbock, Texas	(2)	MAE-Simmons Multiple Service Center
Lynn	(4)	America Park
Malden	(5)	Malden Multi-Service Center
Manchester	(5)	Rock Rimmon
Memphis	(1)	South Memphis
Miami	(3)	Opa Locka
Milwaukee	(4)	Walker Square Center
Minneapolis	(4)	South-Citizen's Community Center
Mobile	(4)	Maysville Center, Areas 8-9
Montgomery	(4)	Cleveland Area Multi-Service Center
Nashville	(3)	District #3
Newark	(4)	Area Board #4, People in Progress
New Britain	(5)	Pinnacle Heights Neighborhood Center
New Haven	(2)	Newhallville
New Orleans	(1)	St. Bernard Area Community Development Center
Niagara Falls	(2)	Eastside Multi-Purpose Center
Oakland	(3)	Fruitvale Service Center
Oklahoma City	(4)	Southeast 15th Street
Pasadena	(2)	Area Council III

City	Community Type	Neighborhood
Passaic	(2)	First Ward—Community Center #2
Phoenix	(3)	LEAP—Edison Council
Pittsburgh	(1)	Northside Committee on Human Resources
Portland, Ore.	(4)	Brooklyn Action Center
Provo, Utah	(4)	(not available)
Racine	(4)	Project Break Thru
Rochester	(2)	N.S.I.C. #1
Sacramento	(3)	Del Paso Robla Neighborhood Council
Salt Lake City	(4)	Northwest Action Center
San Bernardino	(6)	Mt. Vernon Contact Station
Santa Anna	(5)	Logan Center
San Francisco	(2)	District #4 Western Addition
Schnectady	(5)	Friendship—Riverside
Seattle	(4)	Park Lake Center
Shreveport	(4)	Cedar Grove
Sioux City	(3)	Ida County Service Center
South Bend	(2)	West Washington Street—Hansel Center
Springfield, Ill.	(2)	(not available)
St. Joseph	(3)	Southside Service Center
St. Louis	(3)	Pruitt—Igoe
St. Paul	(4)	Eastside—Jackson Wheelock
St. Petersburgh	(5)	Palm Court Youth Center
Syracuse	(4)	East Side Area E
Tampa	(1)	West Tampa
Troy	(5)	Hoosick Street Center
Tucson	(3)	Safford Area Council
Tulsa	(2)	Guadaloupe Center
Utica	(5)	Inner City Opportunity Council
Waco	(3)	North Waco Neighborhood Center
Warren	(6)	Trumball Homes
Washington, D.C.	(1)	Chase
Waterbury, Conn.	(2)	Northeastern Heights Opportunity Center

City	Community Type	Neighborhood
Waukegan	(2)	McAlister Center
Wichita	(2)	Grove Center
Youngstown, O.	(3)	Eastside Community Action Council

The Pattern Analysis Program

The first step in the pattern analysis program used here (devised by Richard Barnes for Barss Reitzel and Associates) is the calculation of similarity coefficients between all pairs of units to be clustered. An "associative" coefficient is used which has as denominator the number of defining variables for which there is information and as numerator the number of defining variables on which the two units have identical (or partially similar) values. The primary tasks of the analyst are careful identification and weighting of defining variables and maintenance of a balance between the number of categories on each variable and the degree of overlap required to establish similarity.

During the clustering process, each unit is first paired with the other unit in the data with which it is most similar. These small groups form the first level of clustering. Next, a "similarity coefficient" is calculated between these first clusters and every other unit and cluster. This statistic can be calculated on several bases. "Single linkage" defines the distance between a cluster and another unit/cluster as the distance between that unit/cluster and the constituent unit of the first cluster most like it. This procedure tends to relate clusters by their tails, resulting in long strings whose defining attributes might shift from one end to the other. "Complete Linkage" defines the distance between a cluster and another unit/cluster as the distance between that unit/cluster and the constituent unit of the first cluster *least* like it. The result is a set of tight, homogeneous clusters. The option used here, "average linkage" is a cross between the two, defining the distance between a cluster and another unit/cluster as the distance between the "centers of gravity" of the two.

At the conclusion of the clustering process the analyst is given a dendogram or tree. At one side, all units are isolated. Across the graph, at precisely increasing "similarity levels," each is seen uniting with other units in larger and larger clusters until, at the other side, all units form a single group. The analyst must then determine the best "similarity level" to accept as a typology. At *high* levels of similarity there are many small, tightly defined clusters. It is generally difficult, however, to make coherent theory concerning a great number of aggressively different unit types. At *low* levels of similarity, a small number of loosely defined types emerge. Theorizing is thereby facilitated—dichotomies come easy—but there is a constant risk of making much of distinctions which are not substantial empirically. It is my belief that the most useful typologies are those which sort almost all units into a comprehensible number of types (3-6).

There are many ways in which typologies can contribute to understanding (I would not grant priority to any of them). Clusters may be investigated as causal nexuses—groups united, say, by common predispositions to action and common patterns of behavior; or as subcultures in which to look for variation in certain social processes. Categorization is an important form of understanding in itself. Typologizing on empirical grounds can be an important antidote to the pathological form of this understanding, stereotyping. When the intent is descriptive, I feel it is important for the analyst to give names to types which emerge from the data. It is better to risk false concreteness than to accept the inevitable confusion of half-a-dozen types "defined" by the hundred or so distinctions that could be drawn between them.

NOTES TO APPENDIX A

1. See Lilian B. Rubin, "Maximum Feasible Participation: The Origins, Implications, and Present Status," *Annals of the American Academy of Political and Social Science* (September, 1969), p. 22.

2. Barss Reitzel and Associates, *Community Action and Institutional* from this phase of analysis, the results are reported in Barss Reitzel and Associates, *A Final Report on Phase I Data Analysis* for OEO, Contract B 99-4730. (Cambridge, Mass.: February 3, 1969).

3. National Opinion Research Center, "Community Political Leaders, Parent-Teacher Association, Employer, and Social Service Agency Director Assignment," Survey 5026, January 1969 9pp.

4. Ibid., p. 1.

5. See n. 30 below for a discussion of the comparability of the two samples.

6. Barss Reitzel and Associates, *Community Action and Institutional Change*, Prepared for Office of Economic Opportunity, Bruce Jacobs, Project Director, (Cambridge, Mass.: July, 1969).

7. Barss Reitzel and Associates, *National Evaluation of Community Action Programs*, Report No. 2 (Cambridge, Mass.: May, 1970).

8. Stanley B. Greenberg, Project Director, *Mobilizing Poor Communities*, Prepared for the Office of Economic Opportunity, by Barss Reitzel and Associates, Inc., (Cambridge, Mass.: August, 1970).

9. Bruce Jacobs, Project Director, *Community Action and Urban Institutional Change*, A National Evaluation of the Community Action Program Prepared for the Office of Economic Opportunity by Barss Reitzel and Associates, Inc., (Cambridge, Mass.: August, 1970).

10. The National Advisory Commission on Civil Disorders, Otto Kerner, Chairman, *Supplemental Studies for the National Advisory Commission on Civil Disorders* (Washington: U.S. Government Printing Office, 1968); William Brink and Louis Harris, *The Negro Revolution in America* (New York: Simon and Schuster, 1963); William Brink and Louis Harris, *Black and White* (New York: Simon and Schuster, 1966); Gary T. Marx, *Protest and Prejudice: A Study of Belief in the Black Community* (New York: Harper and Row, 1967); Lemberg Center for the Study of Violence "Six Cities Study—A Survey of Racial Attitudes in 6 Northern Cities—Preliminary Findings," Exhibit 273 Hearings before the Subcommittee on Executive Reorganization of the Committee on Government Operations, U.S. Senate, 90th Congress, 1st Session (June 28, 1967) pp. 4309-4317. Other studies using a similar sampling technique are Editors, "Black America 1970" *Time* special Issue (April 6, 1970) pp. 13ff. and William McCord and John Howard, "Negro Opinions," in William McCord, John Howard, Bernard Friedberg, Edwin Harwood, *Life Styles in the Black Ghetto* (New York: W. W. Norton & Co., June, 1969) pp. 78-104.

11. Jerry Finrow, "Community Involvement, Pros and Cons," in Walter McQuade, ed., *Cities Fit to Live In* (New York, Collier-Macmillan, 1971), pp. 51-52.

12. Quoted in Donald Bogue, J. Bhasker, D. Misra and D. P. Dandekar, "A New Estimate of the Negro Population and Negro Vital Rates in the United States, 1930-1960," *Demography*, Vol. I, No. 1, 1964, p. 7. The Los Angeles Riot study took an areal definition of sample, viz., the "curfew area" established by police during the riot. T. M. Tomlinson, and Diana T. Tenhouten, *Los Angeles Riot Study Method: Negro Reaction Survey* (Los Angeles: Institute of Government and Public Affairs, 1967).

13. Donald Bogue, "A New Estimate" p. 37. This section is based in large part on this excellent review of survey methodology relevant to poverty research. See also Staff Report, "The Census—What's Wrong With It, What Can Be Done," *Trans-Action* 5, 6 (May, 1968), pp. 49-56; and Jean M. White, "Census Missed One in Ten Negroes: Federal Planning Seen Periled," *Washington Post*, (June 23, 1967).

14. Elizabeth L. Hartman, H. Lawrence Isaacson, Cynthia M. Turgell, "Public Reaction to Public Opinion Surveying," *Public Opinion Quarterly*, Vol. 32, No. 2, (Summer, 1968), p. 296.

15. Angus Campbell and Howard Schuman, *Racial Attitudes in 15 American Cities* (Ann Arbor, Michigan: The Survey Research Center, The University of Michigan, 1968), p. 66. Quoted in Donald Bogue, p. 39.

16. See Peter H. Rossi and Robert Crain, "The NORC Permanent Community Sample," *Public Opinion Quarterly*, 32, 2 (1968).

17. The actual question asked was "What is the take-home pay for you and your family?" The phrasing excludes welfare payments, but includes income from both husband and wife. Response rates were not good, 71% for the two samples mentioned above.

18. Quoted in Donald Bogue, "A New Estimate" p. 41.

19. Quoted in Donald Bogue, "A New Estimate" p. 39.

20. J. Allen Williams, Jr., "Interviewer Role Performance: A Further Note on Bias in the Information Interview," *Public Opinion Quarterly*, 32, 2, (Summer, 1968) p. 60.

21. Gene F. Summers and Andre D. Hammonds, "Effect of Racial Characteristics of Investigator on Self Enumeration Responses to Negro Prejudice Scale," *Social Forces* 44, 4 (June, 1966): p. 517 and Thomas F. Pettigrew, *A Profile of the Negro American* (New York: D. Van Nostrand Co., Inc., 1964), p. 51.

22. See T. M. Tomlinson and Diana L. Tenhouten, *Los Angeles Riot Study Method: Negro Reaction Survey* (Los Angeles: Institute of Government and Public Affairs, 1967), p. 10; Richard Hill and Nason E. Hall, "A Note on Rapport and the Quality of Interview Data," *Southwest Social Science Quarterly* 44, 3 (December, 1963), p. 25; and J. Allen Williams, "Interviewer Role Performance," p. 291.

23. Quoted in Donald Bogue, "A New Estimate" p. 54.

24. Quoted in Donald Bogue, "A New Estimate" p. 55.

25. Further comment on these problems is available in Lee N. Robins, "The Reluctant Respondent," *Public Opinion Quarterly* 27, 2 (Summer, 1963); Kenneth Clark, *Dark Ghetto* (New York: Harper and Row, 1967).

26. Floyd Hunter, *Community Power Structure* (Chapel Hill: University of North Carolina Press, 1953). The techniques have been applied to Negro sub-communities in James Q. Wilson, *Negro Politics* (New York: The Free Press, 1960) and Ernest A. T. Barth and Baha Abu-Laban "Power Structure and the Negro Sub-community," *American Sociological Review* 24, 1 (1959). Most of the national surveys of black leadership have used a variant of this approach more heavily weighted toward those prominent in the media.

27. See Robert Dahl, *Who Governs* (New Haven: Yale University Press, 1961); Nelson Polsby, *Community Power and Political Theory* (New Haven: Yale University Press, 1963); and Edward C. Banfield, *Political Influence* (New York: The Free Press, 1961).

28. Kent Jennings, *Community Influentials* (New York: The Free Press of Glencoe, 1964) and James Wilson, *Negro Politics*, use this approach, in conjunction with others.

29. One major contract, undertaken by Yankelovich Associates, sought to evaluate the participation of the poor in CAP through a series of case studies of individual cities.

30. This was called "Phase I" of the research. Its major documentation is Barss Reitzel and Associates, *A Final Report on Phase I Data Analysis.* John D. Spence, *Phase I versus Phase II: A Comparison of Survey Methodologies Utilized in the 50 City Evaluation,* in Barss Reitzel and Associates, *National Evaluation of Community Action Programs, Report No. 2,* Cambridge, Mass.: May, 1970.

31. John Spence, *Phase I versus Phase II,* p. 5.

32. Ibid., p. 8.

33. Bruce Jacobs, "The Poverty Programs and Institutional Change: Opinions of Leaders of the Poor" in Barss Reitzel and Associates, *Community Action and Urban Institutional Change, A National Evaluation of the Community Action Program.* Prepared for the Office of Economic Opportunity (Cambridge, Mass.: August, 1970) found the Gamma between a composite measure of leadership perception of institutional change and change in local institutions to be -.06. A multiple regression analysis solving for perception of change by 9 variables (sex, education, age, employment status, group membership, protest participation, political dissatisfaction, self efficacy and politicization) found education and high self efficacy to be significant contributors to perception of change for whites; and high employment status, high self efficacy, low protest participation, low political dissatisfaction and low politicization for blacks.

Appendix B
Scales

Information on samples of individuals and communities can be found in Appendix A. In this Appendix are listed, in alphabetical order, the scales and variables utilized in the analysis with the questionnaire items on which they are based.

Where relevant, descriptions of scales below include "gamma range" (the largest and smallest gammas between scale items), "mean gamma" (the average absolute gamma between scale items), weighting principles, and scale groupings with names. Missing data (on up to one-third of scale items) was handled by substituting mean values on existing variables for missing scores. Scaling tests were carried out on the sample of leaders of the poor. "Don't knows" were sometimes placed in a mid-position between "yes" and "no," sometimes excluded altogether. The former treatment was more likely if a) the question was one of opinion, not fact, b) there were few "don't knows" and c) the "don't knows" did not overlap with "no answer" responses on other, similar questions.

ALIENATION FROM LOCAL GOVERNMENT

A scale composed of 3 items. "How much say do you think people in this neighborhood have about the decisions made by the city government?" (a lot = 0 points; some say = 1; very little, don't know = 2; no say = 3); "Do you think black people/Mexican-Americans/Puerto-Ricans/poor whites have more or less say in what goes on in (name of city) than they did 5 years ago?" (more = 0; same = 1; don't know = 2; less = 3); "Are there any government officials in this city who really care a lot about what people in this neighborhood want?" (yes = 0; no, don't know = 3). Gamma Range = .20 to .57. Mean Gamma = .40. Grouping: 0-1 point = none; 2-4 = little; 5-6 = some; 7-9 = great deal.

ANGER AT THE LOCAL SITUATION

Response to statement: "There are a lot of things around here which make a person angry." disagree strongly, disagree, agree, agree strongly.

ARTICULATENESS

At the conclusion of each interview respondents were rated very, fairly, slightly, or not at all articulate by the interviewer.

ATTITUDE TOWARD RIOTS

A scale composed of 2 items.

"Even if you didn't join a disturbance (like the ones that occurred after the assassination of Martin Luther King) would you feel in sympathy with people who did join?" (no = 0 points; don't know = 1; yes = 2); "On the whole do you think the disturbances have helped or hurt the cause of rights for black people, or would you say they haven't made much difference?" (hurt = 0; haven't made much difference = 1; helped = 2). Grouping: 0 = against riots; 1-3 mixed opinion; 4 = favorable to riots.

BELIEF IN PLANNING

Response to statement: "The wise person lives for today and lets tomorrow take care of itself." strongly disagree, disagree, agree, agree strongly.

BELIEF IN SELF

Response to statement: "I feel like I could change my life if I wanted to." strongly disagree, disagree, agree, agree strongly.

BLACK SEPARATIST SENTIMENT

A scale composed of three questions: "Some black leaders have suggested setting up a separate nation inside America run by black people only. Do you think this is a good idea?" (no = 0 points; don't know = 1; yes = 2);

"Do you personally feel that this country is worth fighting for, or not?" (yes = 0; conditional, not sure = 1; no = 2);

"What nationality are you?" (Negro, American = 0; Black, Afro-American = 2). Gamma Range = .31 to .62. Mean Gamma = .48. Grouping: 0-1 point = none; 2-3 = very little; 4-5 = some; 6 = very high.

BREADTH OF LOCAL ORGANIZATION

A community attribute based on data collected from the three organization heads in each community. Respondents were asked "Which of these types of groups are residents of this neighborhood involved in: welfare rights organizations; civil rights groups; nationality organizations; tenants' unions; PTA?" Scale score is proportion of positive responses over responses given. Grouping 0-.39 = low; .40-.50 = moderate; .51-1.00 = moderately high. Scale devised by John Mollenkopf for Barss Reitzel and Associates (titles mine).

CHANGE IN EMPLOYERS

A community attribute based on data gathered from three local employers in each community. Each of the eight categories listed below is itself a scale composed of questions concerning aspects of that dimension of change. Change in any aspect was counted as change in that category. 1) change in policy toward hiring blacks and some change in percentage of black employees, 2) change in on-the-job training efforts, 3) change in percentage of black foremen, 4) change in summer programs, 5) employer-CAP referral coordination, 6) regular attendance at business-man's meetings where poverty issues are discussed, 7) change in recruitment of the hard-core unemployed, 8) change in community involvement. In each instance, change was measured from a base line five years previous to the Local Change survey, 1968-69. Communities were scored by the average score of their employers on the statistic: number of categories in which employer changed/number of categories of possible change (the final five categories were weighted one-half). Grouping: under .36 = lowest third; .37-.50 = middle third; and over .50 = upper third. Scale devised by Dan Linger for Barss Reitzel and Associates.

CHANGE IN LOCAL INSTITUTIONS

A community attribute summarizing the indicators "Change in Private Welfare Agencies," "Change in Schools," and "Change in Employers." Each indicator was standardized (mean = 0, Sd = 1.0) and the 3 added together for each city. Grouping: below -.36 = lowest third; -.36 to .10 = middle third; above .10 = upper third. Scale devised by Bruce Jacobs for Barss Reitzel and Associates.

CHANGE IN PRIVATE WELFARE AGENCIES

A community attribute based on data gathered from the three private welfare agency heads in each community. Each of the nine categories listed below is itself a scale composed of questions concerning aspects of that dimension of change. Change in any aspect was counted as change in that category. 1) Change in number of people served, 2) Change in number of minority group members served, 3) Adjustment of type of service toward needs of the poor, 4) Adjustment in type of staff toward needs of the poor, 5) Change in participation of the poor in agency operations, 6) Change in number of people served, 7) Change in publicity methods, 8) Change in overall amount of service, 9) Change in interagency cooperation. In each instance change was measured from a base line of five years previous to the Local Change Survey, 1968-69. Communities were scored by the average score of their agencies on the statistic: number of categories in which agency changed/number of categories of possible change (the final 4 categories were weighted one half). Grouping: 0-.25 = lowest third; .26-.42 = middle third; over .42 = highest third. Scale devised by Emily Starr for Barss Reitzel and Associates.

CHANGE IN SCHOOLS

A community attribute based on data gathered from 3 PTA Presidents in each community. Five categories of change were measured, each with several aspects: 1) Personnel: addition of school-community representative, librarian, social worker, counselor, nurse, teacher aides, lunchroom supervisor, music teacher, or remedial reading teacher: 2) Innovations: adoption of nongraded instruction, a kindergarten program, team teaching, Afro-American history, or text-books with integrated pictures: 3) Competency: college counseling in the high school, vigorous leadership by principal, better teacher understanding of children, or higher quality teaching; 4) Communications: availability of school facilities to the PTA and the community, better relations between parents and administration, better relations between school board and parents, responsiveness to parent grievances, support for community cooperation by school, solicitation of parental opinions by school, greater consideration of parental opinions, increased availability of school phone number, or addition of a school-community representative. 5) Resources: reduction in number of temporary classrooms, reduction in double shifts, reduction in student teacher ratio (by 25 percent), reduction in number of students enrolled (by 25 percent), increase in physical space per student, increase in number of male teachers (by 25 percent), or increase in number of black teachers (by 25 percent). In each instance change was measured from a base line of five years previous to the Local Change Survey in 1968-69. Change in any of the aspects of the categories listed was counted as change in that category. Communities were scored by the average score of their schools on the statistic: number of categories in which school changed/number of categories with responses. Grouping: 0-.5 = lowest third, .51-.74 = middle third; over .74 = upper third. Scale devised by Jeff Raffel for Barss Reitzel and Associates.

CONVENTIONAL POLITICAL ACTION

This scale could be formed only for respondents in the second fifty cities surveyed. It is composed of 4 items: "How often do you vote in city government and national elections, every time there is one, most of the time, sometimes, seldom or never?" (Every time = 1 point, other = 0). "Have you talked to a government official or elected representative during the last year?" (Up to 2 times in the year = 0; 3 or more times = 1); One point was assigned for each of two items in the Political Action scale: having talked to a manager and having talked to a public official. Grouping: 0-1 point = low; 2 = moderate; 3-4 = high.

DAILY ACCESSABILITY

A scale composed of two questions: "Suppose I had tried to interview you yesterday about this time. Were you in (name of neighborhood)?" "Suppose I had tried to interview you last night/during the day. Were you in (name of neighborhood)?" Grouping: yes to both questions=high.

DEFINITION OF "POLITICAL"

An open ended question, "The word 'political' means different things to different people. What do you think of when you hear the word 'political'? Grouping: no content; reference to American political institutions; process oriented definition; definition emphasizing negative aspect of politics.

DISAFFECTION FROM NATIONAL GOVERNMENT

A scale composed of 3 items. "How do you think the United States government feels about poor people? Would you say it is trying to help poor people, or is it doing very little to help poor people, or is it trying to keep poor people down?" (help poor people = 0 points; doing very little = 1; trying to keep poor people down = 2); "All in all I'm pretty satisfied with the way this country is run." (strongly agree, agree = 0 points; disagree = 1; strongly disagree = 2). "People like me don't have any say in what the government does." (strongly disagree, disagree = 1; agree = 2; strongly agree = 3). Gamma range = .30-.54. Mean gamma = .41. Grouping: 0-1 point = little; 2 = moderate; 3-4 = high; 5-6 = very high.

EVALUATION OF RECENT CHANGE IN LOCAL INSTITUTIONS

A scale composed of 4 items: "Do you think the schools around here have gotten better or worse in the last 3 or 4 years?" (worse = 0 points; no change = 1; better = 2); "Do you think the schools pay more attention to the parents than they did 5 years ago?" (less = 0; not much change = 1; more = 2); "How about the employers themselves, the places that hire people from here. Do you think they are doing more or less than they did 5 years ago to help people get jobs or better jobs?" (less = 0; about the same = 1; more = 2); "Do you think the chances of getting a job at all or of changing jobs are better or worse now than they were 5 years ago?" (much worse, worse = 0; same, better = 1; better, much better = 2). Range of pairwise pearsonian r's: .16 to .38. Mean r = .28. Grouping: 0-2 points = very low; 3-4 = low; 5-6 = moderately high; 7-8 = very high.

FAITH IN DIRECT POLITICAL ACTION

A scale composed of 4 questions concerning a hypothetical situation. "Now getting back to what goes on in (city name), suppose a friend of yours told you that a big supermarket in this area would not hire Black/ Mexican American/Puerto Rican people and that he and others were going to try to get them to hire some. He wanted to know what you thought about different ways of doing this." (for white respondents: "suppose a friend of yours told you that a local merchant in this area was cheating his customers out of money"). "First he suggested complaining to the manager. Do you think this would help? How about complaining to a public official—do you think it would help? How about picketing the market—do you think this would help? Do you think it would help if you stopped shopping there and told all your friends not to shop there— like a boycott?" (on each item, no = 0 points; don't know = 1; yes = 2). Grouping: 0-3 points = very low; 4-5 = low; 6-7 = moderately high; 8 = very high.

GROUP MEMBERSHIP

In the first 50 cities sampled, respondents were asked "What are the most important groups or organizations that people in this neighborhood belong to? Do you belong to any of them? Which?" Group membership score was the number of groups named (up to three) on this question. Respondents in the second 50 cities were asked a different question: "Do you belong to any clubs, organizations, councils or committees? Which ones (up to 5 were listed)?" Fraternal organizations were not counted and responses were grouped (0 = 0; 1-2 = 1; 3-4 = 2; 5= 3) to align the distribution of responses on the 2 questions. Wherever possible, the more complete data of the 2nd question was used to describe subpopulations of the leadership sample.

KINDS OF GROUP MEMBERSHIPS AMONG
LEADERS OF THE POOR[1]

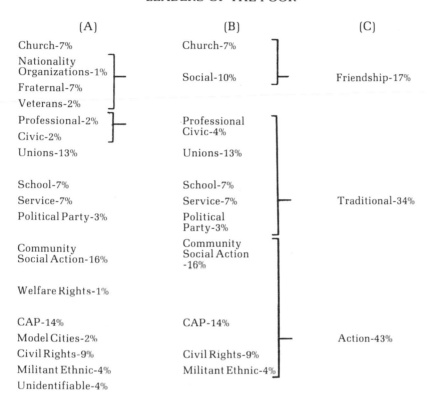

(A)	(B)	(C)
Church-7%	Church-7%	
Nationality Organizations-1%	Social-10%	Friendship-17%
Fraternal-7%		
Veterans-2%		
Professional-2%	Professional Civic-4%	
Civic-2%		
Unions-13%	Unions-13%	
School-7%	School-7%	
Service-7%	Service-7%	Traditional-34%
Political Party-3%	Political Party-3%	
Community Social Action-16%	Community Social Action-16%	
Welfare Rights-1%		
CAP-14%	CAP-14%	
Model Cities-2%		Action-43%
Civil Rights-9%	Civil Rights-9%	
Militant Ethnic-4%	Militant Ethnic-4%	
Unidentifiable-4%		

[1]based on listing of up to 5 memberships for 341 leaders in 50 cities.

HIERARCHY OF NEIGHBORHOOD LEADERSHIP STRUCTURE

A community attribute based on the number of times the average leader in a community was mentioned by the 40 general residents.
Grouped into thirds: 1.0–1.32 mentions per leader = lowest third; 1.33–2.13 = middle third; over 2.13 = upper third.

INTERGROUP ALLIANCES

A community attribute based on data collected from the 3 organization heads in each community. Respondents were asked to name the "organizations in the neighborhood which have the largest memberships and in which the members are most active." Concerning each he was then asked, "Which of the kinds of groups or organizations listed on this card does the organization work with on any issues? good government or reform groups; business groups; labor groups; private welfare groups; local foundations devoted to community organization; religious groups; the press; the mayor or manager; other government officials; other political leaders; The Neighborhood Center Advisory Board; The Neighborhood Center." Grouping: Less than 4 alliances per organization = low, 4 to 5 = moderate; over 5 = high. Scale devised by John Mollenkopf for Barss Reitzel and Associates (titles mine).

ISSUE FOCUS

An open-ended question asked of leaders only: "On what kinds of community issues have you been most active?" Responses grouped into "none; social; housing; schools; jobs; neighborhood improvement; neighborhood or city politics; party politics; civil rights-discrimination."

JOB INSECURITY

A scale composed of 4 items. One point for yes to any of the following questions, "Have you ever applied for unemployment insurance?" "Have you ever applied for public assistance or welfare?" "Have you ever gone to the state employment service?" Two points if presently unemployed. Gamma range: .51 to .78. Mean gamma: .67. Grouping: 0 points = none; 1 = little; 2 = some; 3-5 = great deal.

LEADERSHIP ROLE

Question asked of leaders only: "Which of the following do you consider your most important task as a member of this community, which second, and which third? Getting people angry about issues; organizing or talking before local community groups; presenting demands of local people and groups to government officials and elected representatives?"

LOCAL CIVIC SUPPORT

This scale is the negative of Alienation from Local Government.

LOCAL POLITICAL INFORMATION

A scale composed of 4 items. "What are the most important groups or organizations that people in this neighborhood belong to?" (1 point for each named, up to 3): "Do you know any particular employers who have gone out of their way to help people get jobs or better jobs?" (one point for each named, up to 3); "Do you know of any things the (name each of 3 local private welfare agencies) is doing to help people in this neighborhood?" (no = 0; yes = 1); "Do you know who is running the OEO Community Action Project in this area? (no = 0; correct director's name given = 3). Gamma range: .20 to .36. Mean Gamma: .29. Grouping: 0-2 points = very low; 3-4 = moderately low; 5-7 = moderately high; 8-12 = very high.

MAJOR CHANGES NEEDED IN COUNTRY

Response to question: "Some people say that things will never really get better for poor people without major changes in the way the country is run. Do you think this is true? yes, no."

MILITANT ACTS

A community attribute based on data collected from the 3 Organization Heads in each community. Respondents were asked to name 2 "organizations in the neighborhood which have the largest membership and in which the members are most active." Concerning each he was then asked, "Since 1964, has this organization conducted any sit-ins, boycotts, demonstrations, or mass marches?" The number of militant acts was then averaged over the number of organizations named by the respondents. (Scale devised by John Mollenkopf for Barss Reitzel and Associates) Grouping: 0 = low; .01-.17 = moderate; .18-1.0 = moderately high. (titles mine)

MODERN POLITICAL DEMANDS

A scale composed of 2 questions. "Do you think all people have the right to have enough money to live on whether they are working or not?" (no = 0 points; don't know = 1; yes = 2); "Do you think that everyone in this country has a right to have a nice home even if he doesn't earn much money?" (no = 0; don't know 1; yes 2). Grouping: 0-1 point = low; 2-3 = moderate; 4 = high.

OCCUPATIONAL ASPIRATIONS

Respondents were asked, "What is your present job?" and "If you could have any job you wanted, what job would you really like to have?" If the hoped for job was up the scale (unemployed, unskilled, skilled, community worker, white collar, professional) from the job held, respondent was considered to have some occupational aspiration.

OVERALL EVALUATION OF LOCAL INSTITUTIONS

A scale composed of 4 items: "Do you think that children in the schools around here get a good education?" (no = 0 points; yes = 2); "Compared to other schools in the city, do you think the schools around here are better, worse, or about the same?" (worse = 0, about the same = 1; better = 2); "What are the major problems about jobs around here?" (1 or none described = 0, 2 = 1; 3 = 2); "In your opinion, does the community have a voice in decisions about the schools?" (no = 0, yes = 2). Mean Pearsonian correlation coefficient between items = .36. Grouping: 0-1 = very low; 2-3 = low; 4-5 = moderately high; 6-8 = high.

PERCEPTION OF LOCAL PROBLEMS

An open ended question, "What do you think are the most serious problems affecting the people in this neighborhood?" Scale score is number of different problems described.

POLITICAL ACTION

A scale composed of 5 items. After being presented the contextual situation of a local supermarket discriminating in hiring (cheating customers for whites), each respondent was asked if he had ever done the following: complain to a manager, complain to a public official, participate in a boycott, or participate in a picket line. (Two points for each yes answer). "Do you talk about community issues with other people around here often, sometimes, seldom, never?" (never = 0; seldom = 1; sometimes = 2; often = 3). Grouping 0-2 points = little; 3-4 = some; 5-6 = good deal; 7-11 = very much.

POLITICAL ACTION POTENTIAL

A scale composed of 4 items. Each respondent was presented the hypothetical situation of a supermarket owner who was discriminating in employment (cheating his customers for white respondents) and asked whether he "would agree to" and "had ever done" the following: complain to the manager, complain to a public official; picket; boycott. Political Action Potential is defined as the number of actions the respondent would agree to do but has not yet done. Grouping: 1 or more = some; 2 or more = high.

POLITICIZATION

A scale composed of 11 items. "I'm going to read you a few things which some people think are political and others don't. I just want to know what you think. A) The United States Congress, B) Presidents of the United States, C) Newspapers, D) The Courts, E) Welfare, F) Libraries, G) Job Opportunities, H) Garbage Collection, I) Movies, J) Hospitals, K) The Schools. Grouping: 0-4 answered yes = low; 5-6 = moderately low; 7-8 = moderately high; 9-11 = high.

PROPENSITY TO VIOLENT POLITICAL ACTIVITY

A scale composed of 4 questions. Only black respondents could be scaled on this variable. "Do you think that black people today can win their rights without using violence?" (yes = 0 points; don't know = 1; no = 2); "How about threatening the manager with damage to his store. . . . Would you agree to do it?" (See Faith in Direct Political Action for question). (no = 0; don't know = 1; yes = 2). "Some people say that things will never really get better for poor people without major changes in the way the country is run. What kinds of changes do you think are needed? Do you have any ideas how this can or will happen? For the most part do you think this will happen peacefully or will there be violence?" (peacefully = 0; both, other = 1; violently = 2). "If a disturbance like the ones that occurred after the assassination of Martin Luther King broke out here, do you think you would join in, or would you try to stop it, or would you stay away from it?" (avoid, stay away = 0; join = 2). Grouping: 0-1 point = none; 2-3 = very little; 4-6 = some; 7-8 = very high.

PROTEST POLITICAL ACTION

Protest Political Action is a subset of the Political Action scale with 1 point for talking "often" about local issues and one point each for having participated in a picket line or a boycott. The second two items were included definitionally, the first because it correlated more strongly with these items than with those measuring conventional political participation. Grouping: 0 = none; 1 = low; 2 = moderate; 3 = high.

RACE IDENTITY

A scale composed of 3 items: "What word do you use to describe your race?" (Afro-American, Black American, Chicano = 3 points; Mexican, Mexican-American = 2; other = 0.); "Do you think the idea of "Black Power" is a good idea or a bad idea?" (bad idea = 0; don't know = 1; good idea=3); Blacks, (Mexican Americans) blame too many of their problems on whites." (strongly agree = 0; agree = 1; disagree = 2; strongly disagree = 3). Gamma Range: .24 to .69. Mean Gamma: .44. Grouping: 0-2 points = none; 3-5 = little; 6-7 = moderately high; 8-9 = high.

RESIDENCE

"How long have you lived in (local name of neighborhood)?"

SOCIABILITY

Question: "Do you know a lot of people in this neighborhood, some, or a few?" ("a lot" = high.)

SUPPORT FOR RACE POLICIES

A scale composed of 4 items for blacks only. "Stores in a Black/Mexican-American/Puerto Rican neighborhood should be owned and run by B/MA/PR people." "B/MA/PR people would do better if they voted only for Blacks/MAs/PRs." "Black/MA/PR people will have very little say in the government unless they all decide to vote for the same candidate." (For first 3 questions; strongly disagree = 0 points; disagree = 1; agree = 2; strongly agree = 3); "Do you believe that schools with mostly Black/MA/PR children should have mostly B/MA/PR teachers?" (no = 0, yes = 3). Gamma Range: .25 to .59. Mean gamma = .49. Grouping: 0-3 points = low; 4-5 = moderately low; 6-8 = high; 9-12 = very high.

TALK ABOUT COMMUNITY ISSUES

"Do you talk about community issues with other people around here often, sometimes, seldom, never?"

USE OF MODERN COMMUNITY SERVICES

A scale composed of 3 items. A person's score is the number of yes answers to the following questions: "Have you ever used a government-aided day-care center?" "Have you ever used a public health clinic?" "Have you ever gotten free legal aid?"

VIEWS ON THE CAUSE OF POVERTY

An open ended question: "There's been a lot of talk lately about poverty in the United States. What do you think is the most important reason people in this city are poor?" Groupings: fate; attributes of persons; lack of education; the job situation; the political situation; discrimination/oppression.

VISITS TO CITY OFFICIALS

A community attribute based on data collected from the 3 organization heads in each community. Respondents were asked to name the 2 "organizations in the neighborhood which have the largest membership and in which the members are most active." Concerning each he was then asked, "Do leaders of (name of organization) go to see city officials about issues in this neighborhood often? sometimes? seldom? never?" Score is an average for all groups. Scale devised by John Mollenkopf for Barss Reitzel and Associates.

Appendix C
Table Details

C-1

N's for items 1-10 on a community basis = 94, 95, 95, 78, 94, 84, 77, 100, 100, 60. In each community 3 organization heads were questioned in detail about 2 organizations ("Thinking of the 3 or 4 organizations in the neighborhood which have the largest memberships, in which 2 are the members most active?"). The maximum number of organizations per city on which data is based is thus 6. The actual number was closer to 5. Entry 2) cutoff was .18 of 4 activities. Scale includes 4 separate questions. Entry 3) cutoff = 1.5 of 3 areas. Entry 5) cutoff = 2.2-3.0 where never = 0, seldom = 1, sometimes = 2, often = 3. Entry 6) cutoff = 2.5. Entry 8) cutoff was 5 or more. Scale includes 12 separate questions. Other possible allies include labor groups, private welfare, local foundations devoted to community organization, religious groups, the press, other government officials, other political leaders, Neighborhood Center Advisory Board. Entry 10) cutoff = 5 of 6 organizations.

C-2

Data taken in part from Emily Starr, "CAP Impact on Institutions," Barss Reitzel and Associates, *National Evaluation of Community Action Programs*, Report No. 2, (May, 1970), pp. 28-30.
N's in left column, based on neighborhoods, 98, 99, 97, 81, 100, 100, 98, 94, 94. N's in right column, based on 287 Private Welfare Agencies: 218, 245, n.a., 130, 284, 287, 269, 192, 196. Entry 4) cutoff was 3 points where 2 are given for the "adoption of" any of 5 techniques listed, 1 for "continued use" if agency served more people than in 1964, and 1 if agency director said publicity efforts led to more

238 Political Power in Poor Neighborhoods

clientele and clientele served increased. Scale includes 8 different questions. Entry 5) An agency received credit if an inter-agency council in operation before 1964 increased its meetings since that time by 15 percent. Entry 6): Actual cutoff was score of 4 or more where an agency receives 3 points for 15 percent increase in poor or target area residents on its Board, or a change in procedures to include poor on Boards or Planning Councils; 2 points for a change in procedures to include some volunteers or employees from the target area; 1 point for increase in pressures by neighborhood groups on the agency. Scale includes 6 questions. Entry 7) is a complex indicator including 13 questions. Change was evidenced in the following typical situations: an agency added a consumer services program and used its facilities in new ways in the 5 years prior to 1964; an agency added educational and employment services programs over 5 years; an agency added a legal services program and would continue a CAP funded program even if its government support were discontinued.

C-3

N's for left column = 100, for right = 284. The community change column is based on a slightly more stringent measure of school change. To be credited with change in the right hand column a school need only have changed on 1 of the typically 6 to 9 scale subcomponents. To be credited with change in the left hand column, a school had to change on 25% of scale subcomponents. Entry 1) is a very soft measure leaving much leeway for the projection of sympathies. Entry 2) scale includes 8 questions. Entry 5) includes, in addition to those mentioned in the table, "better administrative or Board relations with parents," school "responsiveness" to parental grievances, more "community participation in decision-making which governs local school policy," more "seeking of" and "consideration of" parents' comments, suggestions and criticisms, and "addition of a school-community representative." Entry 6) is another soft measure. A school met the criteria if PTA Presidents felt that there had been a "general increase in parent activity," an increase in parental involvement with local groups, a parental turn to "issues more vital to the life of the community," or an effort to remove the local principal.

C-4

N's for left column = 95, 95, 95, 93, 90, 82, 95. N's for right column = 242, n.a., 245, 206, 197, 167, 244. Entry concerning "Promoting Blacks" includes 4 questions on numbers of foremen and black foremen in 1964 and 1969.

C-5

Figures for white "all" based on one city only. Exact figures for % "moderately high" on Evaluation of Local Institutions, % "moderately high" on Eval. of Recent Change in Local Institutions, and N, for Black: All: 38%, 40%, 747; Youth: 36%, 56%, 283; Community Workers: 30%, 68%, 80; Political Elites: 28%, 59%, 81; White: All: 56%, 49%, 171; Youth: 38%, 46%, 56; Community Workers: 37%, 68%, 40; Political Elite: 52%, 76%, 25.

C-6

Data drawn from Opinion Research Corporation, *White and Negro Attitudes Towards Race Related Issues and Activities*, A CBS News Public Opinion Survey (Princeton: Opinion Research Corporation, 1968), p. 10. Actual question reads, "Which of the things on this list would you be in favor of? Choose as many as you wish and just read me the numbers." "Which of the items on this list, if any, are not such good ideas? Choose as many as you wish. Just read me the numbers."

C-7

Mean scores (Upper third = 2, middle third = 1, lower third = 0) and N's for each row are 1.46, 13; 1.25, 12; 1.10, 20; .81, 32; .58, 12. Table X^2 = 18.9 with 10 degrees of freedom, sig. @ .04 level.

C-8

Figures are from John Mollenkopf, "Community Political Activity and Institutional Change," in Bruce Jacobs, Project Director, *Community Action and Urban Institutional Change*. (Cambridge: Barss Reitzel and Associates, 1970), pp. 97-98. See Appendix B for scale descriptions. Gamma for top table = .28 (sig. = .05); for bottom table Gamma = .50 (sig. = .01). N's for rows, top to bottom: 28, 34, 32, 33, 40, 28.

C-9

Data is adapted from John Mollenkopf, "Community Political Activity and Institutional Change," in Bruce Jacobs, Project Director, *Community Action and Urban Institutional Change*, (Cambridge: Barss Reitzel and Associates, 1970), pp. 100-01. Entries in first column are zero order r's of variables 1-7 with Local Institutional Change. Entries in column 2 are beta weights of multiple regression on Local Institutional Change including variables 1-7. Significances apply to multiple partial r's.

C-10

Scores for Change in Social Service Agencies, Schools, and Employers and N's for community types left to right are: Pragmatic Militants: 1.15, 1.39, 1.15, 12; Defiant Militants: 1.35, 1.20, 1.00, 20; Reformist: .95, 1.05, 1.16, 20; Passive Center: .94, .94, .89, 32; Idle Radicals: .75, .58, .83, 13.

C-11

N's for communities top to bottom are 14, 20, 20, 32, 12. N's for individual respondents top to bottom are 71, 130, 123, 216, 52. N's for Action Group membership are 24, 93, 59, 129. "Race" and "% blacks in the neighborhood" are based on One Hundred City General Residents Sample.

APPENDIX C-12 THE INFLUENCE OF MILITANCE ON LOCAL INSTITUTIONAL CHANGE*

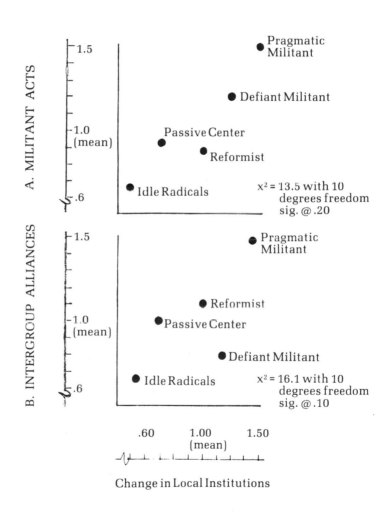

A. MILITANT ACTS

1.5 ● Pragmatic Militant

● Defiant Militant

1.0 (mean) Passive Center ●
● Reformist

.6 ● Idle Radicals

$x^2 = 13.5$ with 10 degrees freedom sig. @ .20

B. INTERGROUP ALLIANCES

1.5 ● Pragmatic Militant

● Reformist
● Passive Center

1.0 (mean)

● Defiant Militant

.6 ● Idle Radicals

$x^2 = 16.1$ with 10 degrees freedom sig. @ .10

.60   1.00   1.50
(mean)

Change in Local Institutions

APPENDIX C-12 THE INFLUENCE OF MILITANCE ON LOCAL INSTITUTIONAL CHANGE (cont.)

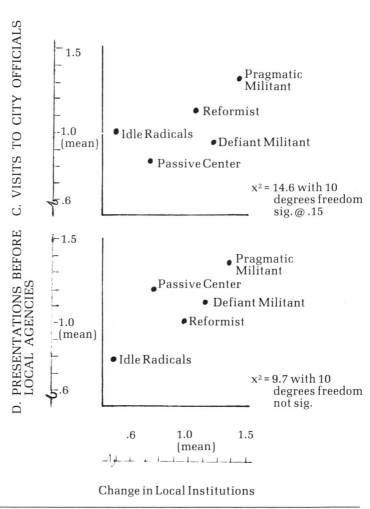

Change in Local Institutions

*See Appendix B for scales. Each community type is entered by its score on Change in Local Institutions and the appropriate Y Axis variable.

C-13

Percentage scores on Alienation from Local Government, Disaffection from National Government, and N's for samples are: Neighborhood Radicals: 52%, 61%, 93; Respectable Militants: 18%, 45%, 57; Elder Elites: 63%, 49%, 76; Uninvolved: 25%, 33%, 24; Neighborhood Establishment: 19%, 31%, 32.

C-14

Percentages for Overall Evaluation of Local Institutions (moderately high), Evaluation of Recent Change in Local Institutions (moderately high), and N's for Leader Types are: Neighborhood Radicals: 33%, 42%, 93; Respectable Militants: 32%, 63%, 57; Elder Elites: 46%, 44%, 76; The Uninvolved: 50%, 67%, 24; Neighborhood Establishment: 75%, 78%, 32.

C-15

Figures for Americans at large adapted from Gabriel A. Almond and Sidney Verba, *The Civic Culture* (Boston: Little Brown and Co., 1963), p. 247. "Other," (6% of total) and "co-operative" (6%) were left out and the rest regrouped as follows: trade unions (14%), business (4%), professional (4%) and farm (3%) = job; social (13%), veterans (6%), and fraternal (13%) = social; religion (19%) = religious; charitable (3%) = service; civic-political (11%) = civic political. (N = 970). Column C is a rearrangement of the data under "Group Membership" in Appendix B. Community Social Action, CAP and Model Cities groups have been allocated half to service, half to civic-political in recognition of the double nature of those programs. Based on 612 members in Five City data.

C-16

Percents and N's for the 9 columns, left to right are: Anger; 47, 226; 29, 53; 35, 46; 45, 213; 40, 48; 37, 62; 30, 132, 48, 91; 53, 104; Politicization; 36, 223, 25, 52, 34, 47; 33, 211; 42, 48, 29, 62; 26, 128; 38, 92; 41, 105; Modern Demands: 65, 216; 53, 49; 62, 47; 65, 204, 70, 46; 49, 61; 48, 121; 73, 90; 71, 103; Political Activity: 47, 227; 10, 52, 45, 47; 43, 214; 48, 48; 51, 63; 19, 131, 54, 92, 62, 106.

C-17

Percentages moving down each column, and N for the column are: Friendship Groups: 7, 19, 12, 21, 27, 14, N = 91; Unions: 13, 7, 10, 23, 30, 18, N = 61; Service: 0, 17, 14, 19, 26, 24, N = 44; School: 2, 8, 13,

46, 17, 15, N = 48; Civil Rights: 4, 7, 16, 40, 24, 9, N = 55; CAP: 4, 9, 13, 25, 29, 20, N = 163; Community Social Action: 1, 7, 18, 23, 31, 20, N = 102; Political Parties: 5, 0, 15, 20, 25, 34, N = 20; Militant Ethnic: 0, 8, 8, 25, 17, 42, N = 24.

C-18

Percentages and N's for each column of group names follow (for ties left and top come first), grand mean % and N included at appropriate place in list. (A): 71, 68; 56, 41; 52, 21; 52, 50; 51, 55; 40, 25; 39, 593; 38, 61; 36, 104; 32, 306; 25, 49; 8, 25, (B): 74, 23; 65, 58; 56, 94; 49, 107; 48, 23; 48, 42; 45, 53; 44, 579, 41, 46; 38, 50; 35, 20; 33, 67, (C): 75, 16; 75, 16; 71, 44; 69, 48; 64, 56; 63, 86; 60, 33; 52, 444; 51, 39; 50, 44; 47, 242; 45, 18, (D): 56, 59; 55, 101; 52, 25; 43, 320; 42, 354; 41, 49; 41, 70; 36, 42; 33, 24; 33, 54; 31, 55; 29, 21, (E): 100, 10; 53, 17; 52, 17; 52, 17; 49, 190; 45, 11; 44, 151; 44, 18; 43, 24; 37, 27; 35, 34; 29, 7, (F): 77, 359; 77, 104; 76, 25; 75, 61; 68, 43; 66, 55; 64, 55; 64, 25; 62, 21; 57, 49; 55, 323; 52, 71, (G): 84, 25; 75, 103; 67, 61; 64, 53; 63, 308; 61, 348; 61, 46; 60, 20; 58, 64; 52, 42; 50, 54; 17, 24, (H): 72, 25; 69, 61; 66, 104; 60, 359; 60, 43; 50, 619; 44, 55; 43, 21; 42, 55; 41, 7; 39, 49; 17, 24, (I): 48, 25; 31, 104; 30, 61; 21, 43; 19, 49; 19, 21; 15, 55; 12, 25; 11, 71; 9, 55; 7, 321; 6, 190.

C-19

Data for Women in the Federal Bureaucracy come from Robert Sherrill, "That Equal Rights Amendment," *New York Times Magazine* (September 20, 1970) pp. 25 ff; Marijean Suelzle, "Women in Labor," *Trans-Action*, 8: 1 & 2 (November-December, 1970) pp. 50-58. The actual figures are: at $35,000 salary, 1% women; $15,000, 7%; $6,500, 30%; $5,300, 72%.

Data for (B), Women in Private Business, come from an interview with Virginia Vockel, Personnel Manager, New England Mutual Life Insurance Company, (February 16, 1970). Figures are weighted averages of office grade categories (N = 1,779) for that firm: at $34,000, 1% women; at $15,500, 6%; at $10,300, 25%; at $6,000, 99%.

Data for (C), Women in Political Life, come from Robert E. Lane, *Political Life* (New York: The Free Press, 1959), p. 78, 55; Editors, "Who's come a Long Way Baby," *Time* (August 31, 1970), pp. 16-23; Samuel J. Eldersfeld, *Political Parties a Behavioral Analysis* (Chicago: Rand McNally and Co., 1964), pp. 50, 235; Donald R. Matthews, *U.S. Senators and Their World* (New York: Vintage Books, 1960) p. 13; Robert Sherrill, "That Equal Rights Amendment," p. 110. Actual figures are: Presidents, nil; Cabinet, 2%; Senate-House, 4%; Federal Judges, 3%; District Party Chairmen, 0%; Precinct Leaders, 19%; Worked on a congressional campaign, 34%; voters, 45%.

Data for (D), Educational Attainment of Women, come from Suelzle, "Women in Labor," Percentages of women in each category (the 1900 figure first then the 1968) Ph. D., 6, 11; Masters, 19, 32; College, 19, 41; High School, 60, 50; grade school estimated.

C-20

Percentages for women and men and N's for these percentages, left to right are: (A) 27, 32-564, 462; (B): 14, 26-534, 445; (C): 49, 38-580, 474; (D): 18, 32-396, 354; (E): 8, 14-389, 349; (F): 35, 47-577, 476; (G): 6, 10-591, 484; (H): 8, 13-483, 418; (I): 17, 25-473, 418.

C-21

Percentages of Membership then of leadership that are women, followed by N's for each group are: School: 63, 80; 49, 20; CAP: 41, 47; Service: 43, 42; 42, 31; Professional-Civic: 37, 40; 24, 10; Church, Social: 38, 27; 55, 26; Civil Rights: 33, 19; 61, 21; Militant Ethnic: 40, 17; 25, 12.

C-22

For blacks percent of women attributed power more than 3 times, 2 or 3 times and 1 time and associated N's are: 36%, N = 81; 37, 116; 47, 122; for Whites: 31, 26; 61, 84; 45, 112; for Mexican-Americans: 36, 14; 33, 27; 27, 11.

C-23

Percentages for women and men and N's for these percentages left to right are: (A): 66, 68-363, 311; (B): 32, 45-279, 224; (C): 42, 69-364, 312; (D): 41, 22-394, 353; (E): 68, 67-383, 346; (F): 36, 50-387, 346; (G): 6, 9-396, 353; (H): 45, 52-393, 351; (I): 8, 14-396, 354; (J): 15, 21-391, 349; (K): 20, 30-371, 339.

C-24

Percentages for women and men and N's for these percentages left to right are: (A): 28, 39-396, 354; (B): 50, 60-389, 353; (C): 45, 49-395, 354; (D): 35, 42-302, 271; (E): 12, 18-367, 331; (F): 24, 35-387, 352; (G): 70-60-394, 349.

C-25

The percentages of those working on a given issue that are women for blacks from housing to Schools and then for whites from housing to schools followed by all N's are: 50, 42, 39, 39, 30, 58; 23, 31, 45, 63, 64, 80; N's: 22, 25, 44, 18, 8, 25; 13, 16, 22, 19, 14, 20.

C-26

The 6 N's for each characteristic (chicano women, chicano men; black women, black men; white women, white men) are (A): 17, 26, 83, 130, 81, 85, (B) 14, 32, 130, 176, 101, 105, (C) 17, 33, 121, 180, 107, 108, (D) 17, 34, 122, 185, 105, 110; (E) 16, 35, 129, 191, 106, 113; (F) 17, 34, 130, 190, 105, 110; (G) 17, 35, 131, 190, 107, 113; (H) 16, 35, 130, 192, 109, 111, (i): 17, 35, 131, 192, 109, 113; (J) 17, 35, 129, 188, 107, 112; (K) 17, 35, 130, 192, 108, 112; (L) 17, 35, 131, 192, 110, 114, (M) 14, 26, 69, 94, 58, 60, (N) 17, 35, 130, 190, 105, 111, (O) 17, 33, 127, 189, 98, 101

C-27

All factors are directional, more education and more job insecurity contribute to Political Action for black men, for example. All the following factors were included in each multiple regression and can be presumed to have no effect if they do not appear on the lists: Education, Age, Residence, Having a Job, Being on Welfare, Job Insecurity, Belief in Self, Political Information, Local Civic Support, Anger, Politicization, Race Identity, Problem Perception. The actual β weights and significances reading down each column are:

(A): -.62, .001; .52, .001; .44, .001; .37, .003; .35, .005; -.30, .05; .21, .10; .20, .19; multiple r sig. = .001, (B): .47, .001; .35, .001; .33, .001; .26, .005; -.22, .02; .20, .02, multiple r sig. = .001, (C): .25, .14; .23, .21; .21, .26; multiple r sig. = .07, (D): .33, .10; .25, .18; -.20, .34; multiple r sig = .05.

C-28

N's for all except (E): 15, 17, 26, 20, 37; for (E): 9, 9, 17, 7, 16.

C-29

All factors are directional, more education and more job insecurity contribute to Political Action for black men for example. All the following factors were included in each multiple regression and can be presumed to have no effect if they do not appear on the lists: Education, Age, Residence, Having a Job, Being on Welfare, Job Insecurity, Belief in Self, Political Information, Local Civic Support, National Civic Support, Anger, Politicization, Race Identity, Problem Perception. The actual β weights and significances reading down each column are: (A): .18, .004; .17, .005; .12, .05; .35, .001; Multiple r sig. = .001, (B) .20, .001; .19, .02; .16, .006; .13, .02; .48, .001; multiple r sig. = .001, (C): .15, .01; .12, .02; .12, .03; .10, .07; multiple r sig. = .001, (D): .19, .002; .16, .01; .15, .01; .13, .02; -.13, .02; multiple r sig. = .001, (E): -:37, .003; .29, .02; .26, .03; .21, .05; multiple r sig. = .02, (F): .34, .01; .31, .08; -.21, .38; .20, .13; .20, .08; multiple r sig. = .002, (G): .31, .02, -.24, .05; .21, .10; multiple r sig. = .008, (H): .38, .20; .30, .05; .28, .06; .28, -19; .21, .18; multiple r sig. = .07.

APPENDIX C-29 FACTORS CONTRIBUTING TO POLITICAL ACTIVITY FOR MEN AND WOMEN IN POOR NEIGHBORHOODS*

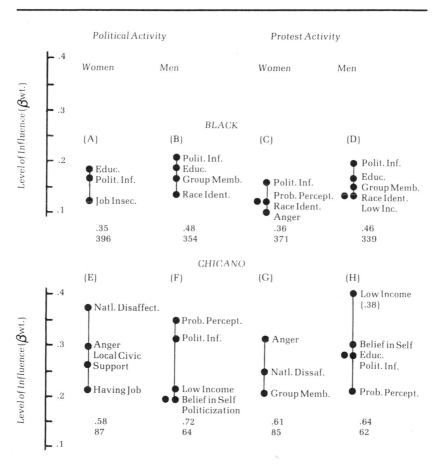

*Figures below each list are multiple r and N.

Notes to Introduction

1. From the conservative point of view, action challenging the system is an inherently defective instrument of social change, and it is the government's specific task to oppose it as destructive of a well ordered society in which all reasonable men can advance their interests. Those of the far left, on the other hand, believe that protest has been too mild, not too extreme; and that the government's support of militance is wrong because it necessarily stops short of the strongest insight and action.

2. See Bruce Jacobs, Project Director, *Community Action and Urban Institutional Change*, A National Evaluation of the Community Action Program, prepared for the Office of Economic Opportunity by Barss Reitzel and Associates, Inc. (Cambridge, Mass. August, 1970). Appendix A evaluates the ineffectiveness of the outlay from the government's viewpoint.

3. Opinion Research Corporation, *White and Negro Attitudes Towards Race Related Issues and Activities*, A CBS News Public Opinion Survey (Princeton: Opinion Research Corporation, 1968); William Brink and Louis Harris, *The Negro Revolution in America* (New York: Simon and Schuster, 1963); William Brink and Louis Harris, *Black and White* (New York: Simon and Schuster, 1966); The National Advisory Commission on Civil Disorders, Otto Kerner, Chairman, *Supplementary Studies for the National Advisory Commission on Civil Disorders* (Washington: U.S. Government Printing Office, 1968); Gary T. Marx, *Protest and Prejudice, A Study of Belief in the Black Community* (New York: Harper and Row, 1967).

4. John F. Kraft, "Attitudes of Negroes in Various Cities," in *Federal Role in Urban Affairs*, Hearings before the Subcommittee on Government Operations, U.S. Senate, 98th Congress, 2nd session, August 31, September 1, 1966. Part 6, pp. 1383-1408; Institute of Public Administration, Study Group on Housing and Neighborhood Improvement, City of New York, Edward J. Logue, Chairman, "Harlem Attitude Survey," *Federal Role in Urban Affairs*, Hearings before the Subcommittee on Executive Reorganization of the Committee on Government Operations, U.S. Senate, August 31, September 1, 1966, Part 6. Exhibit 125, pp. 1409-1423; William McCord and John Howard, "Negro Opinions," in *Life*

Styles in the Ghetto, eds. William McCord et al. (New York: W. W. Norton and Co., Inc., 1969) pp. 78-104; Winston Prouty, *Prouty Survey Report*, Part 11 (mimeographed).

5. Gabriel A. Almond and Sidney Verba, *The Civic Culture* (Boston: Little, Brown and Co., 1963); Daniel Lerner, *The Passing of Traditional Society* (Glencoe: The Free Press, 1958); Myron Weiner, "India's Two Political Cultures," in *Political Culture and Political Development*, eds. Lucien Pye and Sidney Verba (Princeton: Princeton University Press, 1965); Robert E. Ward, "Japan, the Continuity of Modernization," in *Political Culture*, eds. Pye and Verba, pp. 27-83.

6. Milton Kotler, *Neighborhood Government: The Local Foundations of Political Life* (Indianapolis: The Bobbs-Merrill Co., 1969), p. 50.

7. Charles A. Valentine, *Culture and Poverty* (Chicago: University of Chicago Press, 1968), p. 175, describes this point of view and questions it. On the need for studies pitched at the neighborhood level, see Richard W. Poston, "Comparative Community Organization," in *The Urban Condition*, ed. Leonard Duhl (New York: Simon and Schuster, 1969), p. 312; "Black America, 1970," *Time* special issue (April 6, 1970): 14.

8. Alan A. Altshuler, *Community Control: The Black Demand for Participation in large American Cities* (New York: Pegasus, 1970), p. 60, accords "top priority" to surveys comparing blacks and whites. Charles Valentine says, "Research must also be done among poverty stricken subsocieties that are not structured primarily in terms of ethnic identities." See Charles Valentine, *Culture and Poverty*, p. 127. See also Brink and Harris, *Black and White*, p. 138; "Here Come the Ethnics," *Newsweek* (April 3, 1972): 86.

9. Richard Bardolph, *The Negro Vanguard* (New York: Vintage Books, 1959), pp. 1-18; Opinion Research Corporation, *White and Negro Attitudes*, p. 12; Brink and Harris, *Black and White*, p. 244.

10. Everett Carll Ladd, Jr., *Negro Political Leadership in the South* (New York: Atheneum, 1969), p. 102; Lewis Killian and Charles Grigg, *Racial Crisis in America, Leadership in Conflict* (Englewood Cliffs: Prentice-Hall, 1964), p. 83; Daniel C. Thompson, *The Negro Leadership Class* (Englewood Cliffs: Prentice-Hall, 1963), pp. 13-27; James Q. Wilson, *Negro Politics* (New York: The Free Press, 1960), pp. 75-81; Ernest Barth and Baha Abu-Laban, "Power Structure and the Negro Sub-community," *American Sociological Review* 24, 1 (1959): 72.

11. Much of this study is a form of in-depth reporting. An attempt was made to let data speak in its natural voice before submitting it to more complex, analytic treatment. Finally, however, data never speaks for itself. I believe the empirical analyst has a responsibility to read as much meaning into his data as his creativity and conscience will allow. There is a great deal of lifeless data around—it is best left alone. Much exciting evidence, however, is suffocated because its guardians are concerned with professional, not public, standards of comprehension.

12. The several theoretical frameworks of the present research were selected for their interest to action personnel as much as for their elegance, comprehensivity, or face validity. Hopefully, a balance has been struck between theory scholars would consider simpleminded, and theory activists would consider trivial. It is a delicate equilibrium, particularly in areas like women's liberation where commitment is high and theoretical understanding limited.

13. Because the analysis would read so differently if my values were different, it seems important to indicate briefly at the outset what some of those values are. America, I believe, has two fundamental resources: productivity and resilience. Its productivity allows plans for human betterment to be mounted on a scale never before conceivable. Its resilience allows reformers to proceed free of the fear that this will be the prodding that destroys the system itself, and with it all hope for change. I believe that power belongs with the people, that the dimensions of our lives under our control are pitifully few, and that policies which redistribute wealth have an *a priori* moral validity. I feel traditional sex roles in this country are exploitive and inhuman. They cripple emotional development, self actualization and simple companionship. I believe we should move directly toward a society where work is undertaken for self-fulfillment and the needs of each are met as a matter of right.

NOTES TO CHAPTER 1

1. There are conflicts. Typically, the best way for an individual to get a better job is to do well in school, satisfy job interviewers, and impress superiors—in other words, make the powerful pleased with your behavior. Getting more jobs for the *community* can be quite a different task. People who are influential in the local job market must often be angered, not pleased. Push often comes to shove in negotiations for new hiring priorities and promotion practices.

2. His judgment is based on familiarity with the questionnaire and kinds of respondents chosen, personal acquaintance with the problems of community organization, and statistical analysis (including a factor analysis of the 10 indicators of Table 1.1).

3. Herbert Gans, *The Urban Villagers: Group and Class in the Life of Italian-Americans* (New York: The Free Press, 1962), p. 277. Gans favors dichotomization of the service professions, "assigning professionals to develop programs, and recruiting skilled nonprofessionals to adapt them to lower-class clients and carry them out. These nonprofessionals should be people who have themselves come out of lower-class culture,

and have successfully moved into a more stable way of life—either working or middle-class—but have not rejected their past."

4. The actual measure includes nine dimensions (change in people served, publicity methods, amount of service, inter-agency cooperation, poor served, minority served, service innovation, staffing, and participation of the poor) with the first four weighted half.

5. Ralph M. Kramer, *Participation of the Poor: Comparative Community Case Studies in the War on Poverty* (Englewood Cliffs: Prentice-Hall, 1969), p. 178. Kramer has described such cases, where "partisan political activity and social service projects resulted in the emergence of indigenous participants ready and able to promote minority interests . . ."

6. James S. Coleman et al., *Equality in Educational Opportunity* (U.S. Office of Education, 1966), p. 27.

7. The logic of this strategy from a methodological perspective is discussed in Appendix A.

8. Materials on the experiment in Great Britain are important to those looking for hope concerning similar developments in this country. For an excellent introduction to that experiment see the series of reports by Joseph Featherstone, "The Primary School Revolution in Britain," (Reprinted from the *New Republic*, August 10, September 2 and September 9, 1967 by Pitman Publishing Corp., New York).

9. There are several compelling introductions to the ideals of the free school movement, although none can substitute for observation of one of the experiments in action. See George Dennison, *The Lives of Children* (Westminster, Maryland: Random House, 1969); Herbert R. Kohl, *The Open Classroom* (Westminster, Maryland: Random House, 1969); John Holt, *How Children Learn* (New York: Pitman, 1967). For those interested in taking action to change educational systems toward the values of open education, the following are useful: Neil Postman and Charles Weingartner, *Teaching as a Subversive Activity* (New York: Delta Books, 1969); Portola Institute, *The Last Whole Earth Catalogue* (New York: Random House, 1971), The Educational Section, pp. 395-400; and Ellen Lurie, *How to Change the Schools* (Westminster, Maryland: Random House, 1970).

10. Paulo Freire, *Pedagogy of the Oppressed* (New York: Herder and Herder), pp. 13-69.

11. Alexander Moore, *Realities of the Urban Classroom* (New York: Doubleday, 1967), pp. 179-88, deals with the special problems of education in black ghettoes. Stephen M. Joseph, *The Me Nobody Knows* (New York: Avon, 1969), provides some "primary source" material for understanding the situation of black children.

12. They are twice as likely as other city-dwellers to feel that blacks are moving too slowly in their drive for equality, 51 percent versus 21 percent, and more inclined to see blacks as subject to racial discrimination, 70 percent versus 42 percent. See David Boesel, et al., "White

Institutions and Black Rage," *Trans-Action* 6, 5 (March, 1969): 24-31. Statistics in this section taken from The National Advisory Commission on Civil Disorders, Otto Kerner, Chairman, *Supplemental Studies for the National Advisory Commission on Civil Disorders* (Washington: U.S. Government Printing Office, 1968) pp. 133-138.

13. Parental concern with schools is seen in a generally positive light as well. Over 80 percent feel that they can communicate easily with parents, that parents generally see teachers as "on their side" and that teachers as a whole have the respect of parents.

14. Boesel et al., "White Institutions and Black Rage," p. 29.

15. For several approaches to the problem, see J. McVicker Hunt, "Black Genes—White Environment," *Trans-Action* 6, 7 (June, 1969): 19-20; Samuel Shepard, Jr., "The Disadvantaged Child," in *The Schoolhouse in the City*, ed. Alvin Toffler (New York: Praeger, 1968), pp. 77-78; William Brink and Louis Harris, *The Negro Revolution in America* (New York: Simon & Schuster, 1963), p. 58; and William Brink and Louis Harris, *Black and White* (New York: Simon & Schuster, 1966), pp. 32-37.

16. David Rogers, *Politics and Bureaucracy in the New York City School System* (New York: Vintage Books, 1969), p. 324. Kenneth Clark, "Alternatives to Urban Public Schools" in *The Schoolhouse*, ed. Toffler, p. 138, speaks of the disastrous effect that common promotion and advancement schemes have on competence and boldness.

17. See William McCord, "Taking the Pulse of the Ghetto: A Note on Methods" in *Life Styles in the Black Ghetto*, eds. William McCord et al., (New York: W. W. Norton & Co., Inc., 1969), pp. 141-142; Preston R. Wilcox, "The Community Centered School," in *The Schoolhouse*, ed. Toffler, pp. 100-101; Royal Institute of British Architects "Building for Education," *Royal Institute of British Architect Journal* (August, 1968): 349-368; Harold B. Gores, "The Demise of Magic Formulas," in *The Schoolhouse*, ed. Toffler, pp. 167-169; Robert J. Havighurst, "Differing Needs for Social Renewal," in *The Schoolhouse*, ed. Toffler, pp. 54-55.

18. Studies do not yet indicate that students in decentralized school districts perform better. The Coleman report found no association between PTA membership and student achievement; another study found no association between school district size and performance. See David Cohen, "The Price of Community Control," *Commentary* (July, 1969): 23-30; and Christopher Jencks, "Private Schools for Black Children," *New York Times Magazine* (November 3, 1968): 29 ff. Neither indicator, however, goes near the heart of the controversy. As Betsey Levin observes, "Whatever meaningful participation by ghetto parents may mean, it clearly does *not* mean membership in the PTA. What we need are new strategies of parental involvement, and new definitions and measures of parent participation. Until these are developed, tried, and evaluated, however, parental participation as a mechanism for affecting pupil achievement cannot be evaluated." Quoted in Alan A. Altshuler,

Community Control: The Black Demand for Participation in Large American Cities (New York: Pegasus, 1970), p. 54.

19. Three schools were surveyed in each community. The criteria described in the center column fits the right hand column most precisely (it is an abbreviated statement of a complex scaling procedure in any case). Change on any of the usually 6 to 9 scale subcomponents counts as change on the scale as a whole. Community percentages (the left hand column) are based on a slightly tighter requirement; to be credited with change here, a school had to change on 25 percent of scale sub-components.

20. Boesel et al., "White Institutions and Black Rage," p. 27.

21. Exact figures are 27 percent (N = 609) and 34 percent (N = 614).

22. Cited in Alan Altshuler, *Community Control*, p. 148.

23. Figures for 1959-1960, quoted in Altshuler, *Community Control*, pp. 148-149. A 1962 survey of 35 metropolitan areas revealed that expenditures per pupil were 35 percent higher in suburbs than in central cities.

24. Ben E. Graves, "The Decaying Schoolhouse," in *The Schoolhouse*, ed. Toffler, pp. 61-62.

25. Harold Howe II, "The City as Teacher," in *The Schoolhouse*, ed. Toffler, p. 11.

26. From an Office of Education Cooperative Research Report, 1967. Quoted in Harold Howe II, "The City as Teacher," in *The Schoolhouse*, ed. Toffler, p. 13.

27. See Table 1.3 and Appendix C-3 for scale construction.

28. Included also were additions of a school-community representative and a series of more general signs of school solicitation of, and responsiveness to, parental concerns.

29. Elliott Liebow, "No man can live with the terrible knowledge that he is not needed," *New York Times Magazine* (April 5, 1970): 129, summarizes some of these studies.

30. Herbert Hill, "Racial Inequality in Employment: The Patterns of Discrimination," in "The Negro Protest," special editor, Arnold M. Rose, *The Annals of the American Academy of Political and Social Science* 357 (January, 1965): 31. Arguments, such as Banfield's, that seek to partial out "non-race" factors such as socio-economic status miss the point that being black is defined by the aspects of being black. Edward C. Banfield, *The Unheavenly City: The Nature and Future of Our Urban Crisis* (Boston: Little, Brown, 1968) pp. 67-87.

31. Boesel et al., "White Institutions and Black Rage," p. 26. See also, Gary Marx, *Protest and Prejudice: A Study of Belief in the Black Community* (New York: Harper & Row, 1967), p. 220.

32. Quoted in John C. Donovan, *The Politics of Poverty* (New York: Western Publishing Co., Inc., 1967), p. 103.

33. Liebow, "No man can live with the terrible knowledge that he is not

needed," p. 130.

34. Liebow, *Tally's Corner* (Boston: Little, Brown and Co., 1967), pp. 34, 57.

35. John Howard and William McCord, "Watts: The Revolt and After," in *Life Styles in The Black Ghetto*, eds. William McCord et al., p. 53.

36. Quoted in John Donovan, *The Politics of Poverty*, p. 103.

37. Garth Magnum, "The Why, How, and Whence of Manpower Programs," *The Annals of the American Academy of Political and Social Science* 385 (September, 1969): 54. Quoted in Bruce Jacobs, Project Director, *Community Action and Urban Institutional Change: A National Evaluation of the Community Action Program*, prepared for the Office of Economic Opportunity by Barss Reitzel and Associates, Inc., Cambridge, Mass. (August, 1970), p. 202.

38. Figures in this section are from The National Advisory Commission on Civil Disorders, *Supplemental Studies*, pp. 115-123.

39. Brink and Harris reported in 1966 that since 1961, some 350 U.S. corporations have been enrolled in the White House's Plans for Progress, a voluntary program to provide job opportunities, and that "many of these firms have increased their Negro employment by 50 percent and more." Brink and Harris, *Black and White*, p. 30. A 1966 study of 47 major American companies by the National Industrial Conference Board, a nonprofit research organization, found a much wider gap between policy and practice. "Few of the companies studied are doing as well as they say they want to or as well as their top officers think they are doing." *Ibid.*, p. 32.

40. Emily S. Starr, "CAP Impact on Institutions: Reports from Institutional Leaders," in *National Evaluation of Community Action Programs*, Report #2, prepared by Barss Reitzel and Associates, Inc., (Cambridge, Mass., May, 1970), p. 10. Estimates of the average proportion of blacks in each neighborhood based on racial breakdowns of the 40 general residents interviewed in the 100 communities.

41. Community workers are defined as persons in service occupations sponsored by the government. See Appendix A for descriptions of Five City general residents and political elites. Youth are persons age 16 to 29. Groups are located in the matrices by their scores on the Overall Evaluation of Local Institutions and the Evaluation of Recent Change in Institutions scales (see Appendix B). Cutoffs are set here at 50 percent "moderately high" rating. Others may wish to adjust the threshold according to their own intuitions. Twenty percent has been left off the end of each scale to make existing differences more visible. Data for "all" and "youth" is drawn from the Five City Study of general residents and is thus not strictly comparable to the One Hundred City Sample from which "political elites" and "community workers" are drawn. The small N for general residents places this investigation in the realm of exploratory theorizing.

NOTES TO CHAPTER 2

1. Daniel P. Moynihan, ed., *On Understanding Poverty* (New York: Basic Books, 1968), p. 33.

2. For historical background on government action in this period, see Sar A. Levitan, *The Great Society's Poor Law* (Baltimore: The Johns Hopkins Press, 1969), and John C. Donovan, *The Politics of Poverty* (New York: Western Publishing Co., 1967).

3. There are many treatments of the period under question from a national perspective. See, for example, William Brink and Louis Harris, *Black and White* (New York: Simon & Schuster, 1966), pp. 24-44; Daniel Thompson, "The Rise of Negro Protest," in "The Negro Protest," special ed., Arnold M. Rose, *The Annals of the American Academy of Political and Social Science* 357 (January, 1965): 18-29; Lewis Killian, *The Impossible Revolution: Black Power and the American Dream* (New York: Random House, 1968).

4. Jerome H. Skolnick, *The Politics of Protest*, A Report Submitted by Jerome H. Skolnick, Director, Task Force on Violent Aspects of Protest and Confrontation of the National Commission on the Causes and Prevention of Violence (New York: Ballantine Books, 1969), pp. 25-176.

5. Milton Kotler, *Neighborhood Government: The Local Foundations of Political Life* (Indianapolis: The Bobbs-Merrill Co., 1969), pp. 15-19.

6. The major emphasis of this literature has been on the contribution of urbanization to national social and political participation. Although crosscultural studies deal in nations at various levels of urbanization and not cities of various sizes within a single state, their results are still suggestive of the importance of city life on individual attitudes and political culture. See Karl W. Deutsch, *Nationalism and Social Communication* (Cambridge, Mass.: The M.I.T. Press, 1953), Chapter 6, "National Assimilation or Differentiation: Some Quantitative Relationships," pp. 123-152; Daniel Lerner, *The Passing of Traditional Society* (Glencoe: The Free Press, 1958), Appendix C, "The Latent Structure Analysis," pp. 438-446; Norman H. Nie, G. Bingham Powell, and Kenneth Prewitt, "Social Structure and Political Parties: Developmental Relationships, Part I," *American Political Science Review* LXIII, 2 (June, 1969): 808-832; Robert A. Dahl, "The City in the Future of Democracy," *The American Political Science Review* 61 (December, 1967): 953-970.

7. Bruce Jacob's favorable experience in using city size, percentage black, and government expenditures per capita (among others) as attributes of city context were instrumental in the decision to emphasize them in the analysis reported here. Bruce Jacobs, Project Director, *Community Action and Urban Institutional Change: A National Evaluation of the Community Action Program*, Prepared for the Office of

Economic Opportunity by Barss Reitzel and Associates, Inc., (Cambridge, Mass: August, 1970), pp. 70-75; Robert Eyestone and Heinz Eulau, "City Councils and Policy Outcomes: Developmental Profiles," *City Politics and Public Policy*, ed. James Q. Wilson, (New York: John Wiley and Sons, Inc., 1968), pp. 50-53. Support for including differences between cities comes from the many studies of public opinion and attitudes toward race which find large differences between cities. The following studies all report data which indicate important inter-city differences: Stanley B. Greenberg, Project Director, *Mobilizing Poor Communities*, Prepared for the Office of Economic Opportunity by Barss Reitzel and Associates, Inc., (Cambridge, Mass.: August, 1970); William McCord and John Howard, "Negro Opinions," in *Life Styles in the Black Ghetto*, eds. William McCord et al., (New York: W. W. Norton & Co., Inc., 1969); chapter 5, "Negro Opinions," p. 78-104; Gary T. Marx, *Protest and Prejudice: A Study of Belief in the Black Community* (New York: Harper and Row, 1967), pp. 26-27.

8. Robert J. Havighurst, "Differing Needs for Social Renewal," in *The Schoolhouse in the City*, ed. Alvin Toffler, (New York: Praeger, 1968), pp. 47-55, speaks of the problems that face cities of different sizes.

9. Eyestone and Eulau found city size to be correlated with what they call "policy development." Eyestone and Eulau, "City Councils and Policy Outcomes," p. 51.

10. Greenstone, for example, has investigated the relative success of machine versus reform oriented cities in obtaining federal funds, concluding that while machines are better at obtaining funds and operating service programs, reform cities excel at community development oriented projects. "For the most part, the stronger the reform movement, the easier it was for neighborhood groups to gain influence but the harder for the city to inaugurate programs to alleviate the plight of the poor." J. David Greenstone and Paul E. Peterson, "Reformers, Machines and the War on Poverty," in *City Politics and Public Policy*, ed. James Q. Wilson, p. 290; Eyestone and Eulau have investigated the link between city political culture and public policy through the hypothesis that "differences in meeting common environmental challenges . . . are due to the fact that different cities are in different stages of urban development." Larger cities, they discovered, have a more vital and diverse group life, a factor which makes an independent contribution to policy development. Eyestone and Eulau, "City Councils and Policy Outcomes," pp. 50-53; Kramer speaks of cities in terms of their "community climate," "concentration of power," ("the extent to which power is concentrated and structured along partisan and ethnic lines"), and the "coalition capability" of local groups. Ralph M. Kramer, *Participation of the Poor: Comparative Community Case Studies in the War on Poverty* (Englewood Cliffs, N.J.: Prentice-Hall, 1969), p. 176; Williams categorizes cities by policy priorities into four major types: those geared to promoting

economic growth, those pursuing progressive standards of urban amenity, those seeking only to maintain traditional services, and those viewing their role as arbiter among local groups and interests. Oliver P. Williams and Charles R. Adrian, "City Councils and Policy Outcomes: Developmental Profiles," in *City Politics and Public Policy*, ed. James Wilson, pp. 37-66. There are, of course, many studies of city government which start with differences in political structure. For some overviews see Frank J. Sorauf, *Party Politics in America* (Boston: Little, Brown & Co., 1968), Chapter 3, "The Party Organization, State and Local," pp. 60-80; Duane Lockard, *The Politics of State and Local Government* (New York: The Macmillan Co., 1963), Chapter 6, "The Politics of Constitutionalism III: The Municipality," pp. 99-133; Samuel J. Eldersveld, *Political Parties: A Behavioral Analysis* (Chicago: Rand McNally & Co., 1964), pp. 50-62; Norton E. Long, "Local Government and Renewal Policies," in *Urban Renewal: The Record and the Controversy*, ed. James Q. Wilson, (Cambridge, Mass.: The M.I.T. Press, 1966), pp. 423-426; Daniel R. Grant and H. C. Nixon, *State and Local Government in America* (Boston: Allyn and Bacon, 1963), pp. 312-324. Others have found the city neighborhood relationship sufficiently important to base a typology of city political systems as a whole on its quality. Michael Aiken, "Community Power and Community Mobilization," special ed., Louis A. Ferman, in "Evaluating the War on Poverty," *The Annals of the American Academy of Political and Social Science* 385 (September, 1969): 88. Aiken, for example, finds support for the hypothesis that cities with low "centralization of power" have higher levels of community mobilization (measured by participation in four federal self help programs). The appropriate unit of analysis, he suggests, is not city power structures but "community decision organizations, city governments, and other organizations in a given issue arena."

11. V. O. Key, *Southern Politics* (New York: Vintage Books, 1949), pp. 298-314; Duane Lockard, *New England State Politics* (Princeton: Princeton University Press, 1959) was a major theoretical and empirical expansion of this kind of thinking based on politics in the New England states. Fred I. Greenstein, *The American Party System and the American People* (Englewood Cliffs: Prentice-Hall, 1963), Chapter 5, "State Politics and the Varieties of American Party Systems," pp. 54-75, summarizes other approaches to the categorization of political systems at the state level.

12. Thomas R. Dye and L. Harmon Ziegler, *The Irony of Democracy* Belmont: Wadsworth Publishing Co., 1970), pp. 265-267.

13. James Q. Wilson, Review of Robert R. Alford, *Bureaucracy and Participation: Political Culture in Four Wisconsin Cities* (Chicago: Rand McNally & Co., 1969); *American Politcal Science Review* 64, 1 (March, 1969): 199, argues for a class (and religion) based typology in city politics as opposed to one relying on differences in attitudes.

14. See Appendix A-2 for a discussion of the pattern analysis program. Two other typologies were tried and discarded: one emphasizing the organizational membership of residents (as revealed in the 40 interviews per city), and the other, the absolute number of leaders in each neighborhood. It could be argued that measures of militance, institutional change and political culture should have been included among the founding attributes of the typology. These are indeed key variables and will outweigh the defining attributes in analysis to follow. There were practical considerations which kept us from using them as defining characteristics. While there are enough interviews with leaders of the poor to describe the political culture of groups of communities, there are not enough to build stable measures on a community basis. On the other hand, if attributes covary with a given intensity in a cluster, causal arguments are not more, or less, strong because one or both were "defining" attributes of the group, not attributes discovered later on. Placing an attribute in "defining" status simply insures that the taxonomic program will provide relatively clear cut differentiation along that dimension. A typological analysis of the Local Change data, similar to the one presented here, has been described briefly in Bruce Jacobs, *Community Action and Urban Institutional Change*, pp. 70-75. Three types of communities are discussed (comprising one half of all communities). CAP community organization efforts and institutional change are investigated in each type with the conclusion, "Neighborhood organization efforts do seem to have an effect in the three community types (but) in summary, there is at least one community context in which the independent worth of CAA neighborhood organization activities appears to be small."

15. Communities in Rows 2, 3 and 4 all have diffuse local leadership structures but did not develop high distinctivenesses on the remaining initial characteristics.

16. The list will help readers familiar with some of the neighborhoods investigated bring their personal experience to bear on the analysis presented here. It might prove useful as well to persons investigating other hypotheses concerning poor communities on the list. The parts of the actual data which are available to the public may be obtained from Barss Reitzel and Associates, Cambridge, Mass. Several warnings are in order, however. We are analyzing communities by groups in part because the data on individual cities is too sparse to justify generalization by city. Nor is every community fully representative of its community type. Finally, events move swiftly. For some neighborhoods the period we are studying, 1964-1969, might best be viewed as one phase in a political development that has not slowed down since then.

17. See Martin Oppenheimer and George Lakey, *A Manual for Direct Action* (Chicago: Quadrangle Books, 1964); Saul D. Alinsky, *Reveille for Radicals* (New York: Random House, 1969); The O. M. Collective, *The Organizer's Manual* (New York: Bantam, 1971); Sam W. Brown, *Store-Front Organizing* (New York: Pyramid, 1972).

18. Quoted in Jerome H. Skolnick, *The Politics of Protest*, p. 128.

19. Opinion Research Corporation, p. 10. I have selected among issues cited in the poll, the five showing the greatest dissensus. V. O. Key offers an excellent introduction to the kind of analysis carried out here, V. O. Key, Jr., *Public Opinion and American Democracy* (New York: Alfred A. Knopf, 1964). In "Patterns of Distribution," pp. 27-98, Key presents some data on a question of direct relevance to our argument: Sixty-five percent of unskilled and only 38 percent of professionals agreed (in 1956) that "the government ought to help people get doctors and hospital care at low cost." Key notes that "when the issues of domestic economic policy become more abstruse—the benefits less immediate and readily perceptible—the laboring classes often cannot see their long run advantage and concur in lesser degree." (p. 150).

20. The issue is by no means solely one of race. Recently, militant blacks have begun to oppose busing in increasing numbers, leaving liberal whites the major defenders of this method for achieving racial balance.

21. Killian emphasizes the communicative aspects of confrontation politics, using Louis Coser's work on the potential of conflict as a theoretical foundation, Lewis Killian and Charles Grigg, *Racial Crisis in America: Leadership in Conflict* (Englewood Cliffs: Prentice-Hall, 1964).

22. Eldridge Cleaver's first encounter with the Panthers was in the Fillmore District of San Francisco. "I spun around in my seat and saw the most beautiful sight I had ever seen: four black men wearing black berets, powder black shirts, black leather jackets, black trousers, shining black shoes—and each with a gun!" See Ronald Steel, "Letter from Oakland: The Panthers," *The New York Review* (September 11, 1969): 20; See also Eyestone and Eulau, "City Councils and Policy Outcomes," p. 23 and Michael Lipsky, "Protest as a Political Resource," *American Political Science Review* 62, 4 (December, 1968): 1144-1158.

23. Mary Ellen Leary, "The Uproar over Cleaver," *The New Republic* (November 30, 1968): 24.

24. Killian and Grigg, *Racial Crisis in America*, p. 87.

25. Donald R. Matthews and James W. Prothro, *Negroes and the New Southern Politics* (New York: Harcourt Brace & World, Inc., 1966), pp. 186-191.

26. Saul Alinsky, *Reveille for Radicals*, pp. 132-133. Among black people generally, 33 percent feel that demonstrations "do some good—help the situation—get results." William Brink and Louis Harris, *The Negro Revolution in America* (New York: Simon & Schuster, 1963), p. 202.

27. Marvin Rich, "The Congress of Racial Equality and its Strategy," in "The Negro Protest," special ed. Arnold Rose, p. 125. An excellent discussion of the uses of protest can be found in M. Lipsky, "Protest as a Political Resource"; For further perspectives on the efficacy of

protest tactics, see Allan P. Sindler, "Protest Against the Political Status of the Negro," in "The Negro Protest," special ed. Arnold Rose, pp. 48-54, a pessimistic discussion of the potentials for progress through traditional political channels, "The experience of the Office of Juvenile Delinquency projects and more broadly the civil rights movement has indicated that (protest) techniques are highly effective as a means of mustering support, particularly broad national support . . . They can effectively bring pressure to bear on the local social system from a broader, more liberal community." See also Charles F. Grosser, *Helping Youth: A Study of Six Community Organization Programs*, U.S. Department of HEW Social and Rehabilitation Service, Office of Juvenile Delinquency and Youth Development, p. 62; Marvin Rich, "The Politics of Protest," *Trans-Action* 7, 4 (February, 1970): 115; Oppenheimer and Lakey, *A Manual for Direct Action*, pp. 73-83; and Mary Ellen Leary, "The Uproar over Cleaver," p. 24.

28. Piven's remarks are taken from a useful summary of presentations before an American Institute of Architects, Association of Collegiate Schools of Architecture seminar on community involvement, Jerry Finrow, "Community Involvement, Pros and Cons" in *Cities Fit to Live In*, ed. Walter McQuade (New York: Collier-Macmillan, 1971), p. 118. Some Marxists defend conflict because it leads to a *frustration* of progress. Milton Kotler outlines some of the implications of this approach to community organizing in Milton Kotler, *Neighborhood Government*, pp. 30-32. To the extent that the position posits a worsening of circumstances to accompany conflict based politics, it is not sustained by evidence of the Local Change Study. Kotler presents a reasoned critique of the "SDS approach" to local organizing and a viable alternative.

29. Only a third of blacks interviewed by Brink and Harris felt that demonstrations "do some good, help the situation, get results." Brink and Harris, *Revolution*, p. 202; Ladd's survey of black attitudes in the South revealed a different pattern. About half of blacks he interviewed mentioned a protest organization as the "greatest single achievement" contributing to equal treatment of the races in the last few years. Everett Carll Ladd, Jr., *Negro Political Leadership in the South* (New York: Atheneum, 1969), p. 271.

30. Ladd, *Negro Political Leadership*, p. 43, comments on this problem.

31. Too frequently this kind of reasoning ends in the dangerous misconception that political protest is a form of psychosis. "If this analogy is correct, then the Negro youth who hurls a brick or an insult at a white cop is not just reacting in anger to white society, but on another level is discharging aggression toward a father who 'let him down' and females whose hostility toward inadequate men raised doubts about his own sense of inadequacy." McCord and Howard, "Negro Opinions," in *Life Styles in the Black Ghetto*, eds. McCord et al., pp. 23-33.

32. Kenneth B. Clark, *Dark Ghetto* (New York: Harper Torchbooks,

1965), p. 227; On the imperatives of local organization see The O. M. Collective, *The Organizer's Manual*, pp. 105-138; James H. Laue, "The Changing Character of Negro Protest," in "The Negro Protest," special ed., Arnold Rose, p. 121; Matthews and Prothro, *Negroes and the New Southern Politics*, pp. 223-226.

33. Milton Kotler, Neighborhood Government, pp. 27-28.

34. This explanation prevailed among integrationist whites (37 percent), and moderates (47 percent) as well as segregationists (53 percent). Matthews and Prothro, *Negroes and the New Southern Politics*, p. 436; Oppenheimer and Lakey, *A Manual for Direct Action*, pp. 21-22, make a similar argument.

35. On the reaction of mayors to the implicit threat of disruption in the Community Action Program, see Kramer, *Participation of the Poor*, p. 235, and John Donovan, *The Politics of Poverty*, pp. 54-56; Lynn W. Eley, "Fair Housing Law—Unfair Housing Practices," *Trans-Action* (June, 1969): 56-61, discusses the reaction of realtors to threats of violence; Alan A. Altshuler, *Community Control: The Black Demand for Participation in Large American Cities* (New York: Pegasus, 1970), p. 52, discusses the case of a white neighborhood in Gary which has taken steps toward secession from the city in reaction to events there; Oppenheimer and Lakey, *A Manual of Direct Action*, pp. 115-123; Brink and Harris, *Black and White*, p. 121, note that by 1968, 85 percent of white America had come to think of demonstrations as hurting the cause. "When I see on TV those demonstrations it makes me think of them as savages." (a Joliet housewife); "Someone starts something going and then they all march," (a Rochester man); "I'd say 90 percent are a bunch of nuts—yelling because they have nothing better to do." (a mother in Garland, Texas). See also Gary Marx, *Protest and Prejudice*, p. 34.

36. Differentials are more striking considering that change was *not* one of the "defining characteristics" of the typology, i.e., one of the dimensions favored in the search for similarity.

37. The differentiation between pragmatic militants and defiant militants is based on the scores reported in the note to Table 6.2.

38. It should be remembered that our evidence concerns aggregate changes at the neighborhood level and is therefore a general test. The many aspects of the strategies outlined above (their ability to foster coalitions, or promote indirect pressures, or galvanize constituents) could be tested separately but only through a highly ramified research design. Our evaluation is in a sense quite narrow but it concerns an issue on which there has been much disagreement and very little empirical research.

39. The conclusions of this section and the data of the following two Tables are from Bruce Jacobs and John Mollenkopf, "Community Political Activity and Institutional Change," in Bruce Jacobs, *Community Action and Urban Institutional Change*, pp. 79-114.

40. *Ibid.*, p. 89. Mollenkopf highlights presentations before local agencies over other indicators of conventional activity (e.g., visits to city officials) because that measure emerged in a factor analysis of indicators as the principal component of an underlying dimension.

41. The strategy is particularly important when we note that city size, municipal expenditures and percent black, some of the defining attributes of our typology, are all related positively with change on an individual basis.

42. A *low* number of presentations before city boards and committees is actually in second place. This stigmatization of conventional political activity is puzzling. It did not emerge in our earlier analysis of types of communities.

43. It is possible to be even more specific and investigate, if, say, staffing, programming or administrative policy in schools (or private welfare agencies) was more responsive to community pressure. Both the present analysis and that carried out by Barss, Reitzel and Associates suggest, however, that this would be forcing the data beyond its limits. It is not an area with a great deal of available theory and using this data to devise explanations capable of coordinating ten types of change in three sectors for five community types would be risky in the extreme.

44. The results of Raffel's summary multiple regression, which solved for overall school change, is parent activity change, .38; CAP funds in education, .36; city population, .27; militant acts by local groups, .18; alliances between local groups, .16; PTA activity change, .15; Entered but not significant: city expenditures per person, percent black in city, community organization emphasis of CAA, service emphasis of CAA, and percent hours in community organization by CAP Neighborhood Center, Multiple r^2 = .40.

45. Sixty percent of defiant militant communities are in the upper third of all communities in overall school change, while only 46 percent of pragmatic militants and 30 percent of reformist communities are.

46. Institutional "informants" were chosen by us according to their expertise, and asked mostly questions of fact. Leaders of the poor were nominated by the poor themselves and asked predominantly questions of opinion.

47. The ordinality emerges from the data. Of six indicators of political activity derived from interviews with organization heads, ordinality is preserved on all counts between all pairs, except reformist and passive center, the latter being higher on militant acts, intergroup alliances, and turnout at presentations.

48. Both are keys to Banfield's conception of debilitating differences between lower, working, and upper classes. Edward C. Banfield, *The Unheavenly City: The Nature and Future of Our Urban Crisis* (Boston: Little, Brown & Co., 1968), pp. 48-57.

49. We investigated 18, 11, 16, 25 and 26 communities in these regions respectively.

50. It varies between 45 and 50 percent except in the South, where the figure is 72 percent.

51. "White" here means over 80 percent of the 40 persons interviewed per community were white. It seems likely that the unusually high number of mixed communities is due to our definition of neighborhoods as CAP target areas rather than locally recognized community units.

52. Banfield, *The Unheavenly City*, p. 86, has suggested that an "overemphasis on prejudice" can lead to "the adoption of futile and even destructive policies and to the nonadoption of others that might do great good."

53. The defiant militant leadership group is differentiated especially clearly from pragmatic militant leadership in this regard. About 25 percent more register alienation from national and local government.

54. On these two attributes, and especially in the extent to which local leaders say they talk about community issues, idle militant leadership is unusually high. For this group these attributes do not accompany extensive political activity, or, as Table 2.5, column B vividly suggests, involvement with local political organizations.

55. Interviewers were asked to rate the "articulateness" of each respondent. Articulateness is conditioned by personality, family environment, education, and socio-economic status. It seems a likely way in which one would change upon commitment to a political movement as well, however. Community leadership is significantly more articulate in active than inactive communities (see Table 2.5, column B). If the difference were attributable to personal characteristics one would expect concommitant differences to show up in personality, education or income levels. This is *not* the case. The suggestion that the differences are due to politicization remains live. We have already seen how political culture relates to change in local institutions; here is a glimpse of how it might bring about change in individuals as well.

NOTES TO CHAPTER 3

1. Figure adapted from Luman H. Long, *The World Almanac, 1971* (New York: Newspaper Enterprise Association, Inc., 1971), p. 172.

2. Philip Slater analyzes the problem of alienating work in America with great perceptivity. Philip Slater, *The Pursuit of Loneliness* (Boston: Beacon Press, 1970), pp. 1-28.

3. Other studies which deal with the agenda of community concerns as seen by disadvantaged groups are: Gary T. Marx, *Protest and Prejudice: A Study of Belief in the Black Community* (New York: Harper & Row, 1967), pp. 21, 221-224; Edward C. Banfield, *The Unheavenly City* (Boston: Little, Brown & Co., 1970), p. 86ff.; William Brink and

Louis Harris, *The Negro Revolution in America* (New York: Simon & Schuster, 1963), pp. 59-60; Editors, "The Politics of Protest," *Trans-Action* 7, 4 (February, 1970): 4311-4312; John F. Kraft, "Attitudes of Negroes in Various Cities", in *Federal Role in Urban Affairs*, Hearings Before the Subcommittee on Executive Reorganization of the Committee on Government Operations, U.S. Senate, 98th Congress, 2nd Session, August 31, September 1, 1966, Part 6, pp. 1408, 1420; William McCord and John Howard, "Negro Opinions" in *Life Styles in the Black Ghetto*, eds. William McCord et al. (New York: W. W. Norton & Co., Inc., 1969), p. 80; William Brink and Louis Harris, *Black and White* (New York: Simon & Schuster, 1966), pp. 224-30; Winston Prouty, *Prouty Survey Report*, Part II (mimeographed), p. 20; Donald Matthews and James W. Prothro, *Negroes and the New Southern Politics* (New York: Harcourt, Brace & World, Inc., 1966), p. 199; Opinion Research Corporation, *White and Negro Attitudes Towards Race Related Issues and Activities: A CBS News Public Opinion Survey* (Princeton: Opinion Research Corp., 1968), p. 9.

4. The nature of one's perception of problems is linked to political behavior. A closer look at persons whose problem perception is most highly politicized, those mentioning discrimination or oppression, reveals two interesting patterns. These persons have attributes which our research indicates promote political mobilization (youth, high education, politicization, disaffection from national government), and they do participate more in protest political action. Even more visible, however, is a syndrome of attributes which opens persons to the possibility of violent political responses (alienation from *local* government, experience of police harassment, a negative view of politics, cynicism concerning direct political action). These persons are accordingly much more likely than others to say they would join an urban riot or use threats of violence as a political weapon.

5. Comparisons between communities are predicated on the assumption that all communities face the same set of problems. As described in Appendix A, the Local Change Study took great care to sample neighborhoods at the same level of poverty. Although the precautions were not always successful, it is quite unlikely that sampling error was large enough to account for the differences reported here. The median incomes of the leaders in the two types mentioned here are passive center: $6,600, pragmatic militants: $5,700.

6. Perception of community problems is not universally strong in poor communities. While 83 percent of those we interviewed could describe one local problem, only a much reduced 17 percent could think of two more situations needing remedy.

7. Political information has been a popular concept among empirically oriented political scientists for bad reasons (it can be measured precisely, it correlates faithfully with political participation in the drab-

best data, it is a second cousin to cybernetic theory), as well as good. For introductions to the topic generally, see Robert E. Lane, *Political Life* (New York: The Free Press, 1959), pp. 80-86; V. O. Key, Jr., *Public Opinion and American Democracy* (New York: Alfred A. Knopf, 1964), pp. 494-95; Gabriel A. Almond and Sidney Verba, *The Civic Culture* (Boston: Little, Brown & Co., 1963), pp. 45-62; Karl W. Deutsch, *The Nerves of Government* (New York: The Free Press, 1963), pp. 145-62; Charles Lindbloom, *The Intelligence of Democracy* (New York: The Free Press, 1965), pp. 165-80; Alex Inkeles, "Participant Citizenship in Six Developing Countries," *The American Political Science Review* LXIII, 4 (December, 1969): 1128; For work much more relevant to poverty research see David K. Shipler, "Negro Legislator from South Rejects Tactics of Some Blacks," in *New York Times*, August 29, 1970, p. 11; Gary Marx, *Protest and Prejudice*, pp. 84-85; and Everett Cataldo and Lyman Kellstedt, "Conceptualizing and Measuring Political Involvement Over Time: A Study of Buffalo's Urban Poor," Paper for the Joint Statistical Meetings (August 20-23, 1968).

8. Matthews and Prothro, *Negroes and the New Southern Politics*, p. 81. Southern Whites, the authors argue, participate in politics irrespective of their information level, but for Southern blacks both interest in, and information about, politics make independent contributions to political participation. Cataldo came to a different conclusion. In a study of Buffalo's poor he found political information to be correlated with involvement in conventional but not protest activities. Cataldo and Kellstedt, "Conceptualizing and Measuring Political Involvement Over Time," p. 1.

9. Stanley B. Greenberg, *Mobilizing Poor Communities*, Prepared by Barss Reitzel and Associates, Inc., (Cambridge, Mass.: August, 1970), p. 13.

10. Brink and Harris, *Revolution*, p. 197, report that 92 percent of blacks in the South have televisions.

11. Harold Cruse, "The Fire this Time," a review of Eldridge Cleaver, *Post Prison Speeches and Writings*, ed. Robert Sheer, *New York Review* (May 9, 1969), pp. 13-34. Joyce Ladner wrote on the press, "In order to be a real militant, you have to use the (press) and that is what Malcolm did. They (the press) didn't create Malcolm . . . the Press was attuned to Malcolm." Joyce Ladner, "What 'Black Power' Means to Negroes in Mississippi," *Trans-Action* 5, 1 (November, 1967): p. 11.

12. The actual figures, taken from a 1968 Opinion Research Corporation poll commissioned by CBS, (Opinion Research Corporation, p. 12) are 72, 76 and 83 percent. The CBS poll is based on a nationwide sample of blacks, the Local Change Study on a nationwide sample of the poor.

13. Although several of the questionnaire items discussed here were drawn from other studies, there are few comparisons with findings of other studies in the analysis to follow. Three factors make a comparative

approach hazardous. Without structured time series data, differences in survey data merely add background noise to distinctions one might draw between attitude levels of different groups. Second, on issues as sensitive as these, comparability requires a consistency in item format, and interviewer approach rare in survey research. Finally, there are almost no major studies which take poor persons as a sampling universe. Brink and Harris, *Revolution* and Brink and Harris, *Black and White*, two highly comparable studies of black attitudes, offer some fascinating glimpses into changes over time. Gary Marx, *Protest and Prejudice*, pp. 215-43, has appended a postscript to his analysis of black opinions which summarizes the results of a great many studies. Most of the sources cited above contain information on topics covered in this section. Careful study of polls from Roper, Gallup and the Survey Research Center could undoubtedly contribute to historical understanding of the political movements under discussions here.

14. See Janice Perlman, *The Fate of Migrants in Rio's Pavelas: The Myth of Marginality* (Ph. D. diss. Massachusetts Institute of Technology, August, 1971), Chapter 10, "Political Marginality: Radicalism," pp. 222-41.

15. In some neighborhoods, disaffection is much more widespread than this. In Area III, a black section of Detroit, 45 percent of respondents told us they did not feel their country was worth fighting for (24 percent "no," 21 percent "depends"). On a composite measure, 37 percent of persons there scored "very high" in alienation from national government where 13 percent was the national average. (See Appendix B for scale). Two studies which report similar data on this phenomenon are Gary Marx, *Protest and Prejudice*, p. 30 and Brink and Harris, *Revolution*, pp. 60-61.

16. There is a growing literature on the nature of direct action as a political tactic. Some of it deals with the theory behind such tactics. Martin Oppenheimer and George Lakey, *A Manual for Direct Action* (Chicago: Quadrangle Books, 1964), Chapter 7 "Direct Action Tactics," pp. 73-83; Michael Lipsky, "Protest as a Political Resource," *American Political Science Review* 62, 4 (December, 1968): 1144-58; Andre Delbecq and Sidney J. Kaplan, "The Myth of the Indigenous Community Leader," Institute for Research on Poverty, Reprint #18. Preference for and participation in direct action is dealt with in Brink and Harris, *Black and White*, p. 91; John Kraft, "Attitudes of Negroes," p. 1399; Marian Lief Palley, Robert Russo and Edward Scott, "Subcommunity Leadership in a Black Ghetto: A Study of Newark, New Jersey," *Urban Affairs Quarterly* (March, 1970): 291-312; "Black America 1970," *Time* Special Issue (April 6, 1970): 13ff.; Lewis Killian and Charles Grigg, *Racial Crisis in America: Leadership in Conflict* (Englewood Cliffs, N.J.: Prentice-Hall, 1964); Gary Marx, *Protest and Prejudice*, pp. 113-14; Matthews and Prothro, *Negroes and the New Southern Politics*, pp. 38-44.

17. In this form the question is not a good one for white respondents and they have been left out of this portion of the analysis. The questionnaire was revised before data was collected from community leaders in the One Hundred City Sample.

18. Figures for the latter two activities are 11 percent and 7 percent. Participation figures in this section taken from Fred I. Greenstein, *The American Party System and The American People* (Englewood Cliffs: Prentice-Hall, 1963), p. 11.

19. The exact question was "Do you think that black people today can win their rights without violence?" The interpretation above was felt justified given the countervailing biases of having to disagree with the statement and the ambiguity in whether or not the respondent is speaking of his own preference. Our figures are similar to those of other studies. Gary Marx, *Protest and Prejudice*, pp. 32-35, summarizes some of these. For further information on contemporary theories of urban riots and further data, see Joel D. Aberbach, review of *Riots and Rebellion: Civil Violence in the Urban Community*, eds. Louis H. Masotti and D. R. Bowler (Beverly Hills: Sage Publications, 1968); J. David Greenstone and Paul E. Peterson, "Reformers, Machines and the War on Poverty," in *City Politics and Public Policy*, ed. James Q. Wilson (New York: John Wiley & Sons, Inc., 1968), p. 288; Lemberg Center for the Study of Violence, "Six City Study—A Survey of Racial Attitudes in Six Northern Cities: Preliminary Findings," Exhibit 273, Hearings Before the Subcommittee on Executive Reorganization of the Committee on Government Operations, U.S. Senate, 90th Congress, 1st Session (June 28, 1967), p. 4311; OEO, "OEO and the Riots: A Summary," Hearings Before the Subcommittee on Executive Reorganization of the Committee on Government Operations, U.S. Senate, 90th Congress, 1st Session (June 28, 1967), p. 4324; John Kraft, "Attitudes of Negroes," p. 1386; McCord and Howard, "Negro Opinions," p. 57; Jerome H. Skolnick, *The Politics of Protest*, A report submitted by Jerome H. Skolnick, Director, Task Force on Violent Aspects of Protest and Confrontation of the National Committee on the Causes and Prevention of Violence (New York: Ballantine Books, 1969), pp. 145-46.

20. For critiques of the assimilationist theory see Raymond Wolfinger, "The Development and Persistence of Ethnic Voting," *American Political Science Review* 59, 4 (December, 1965): 896-908; Michael Parenti, "Ethnic Politics and the Persistence of Ethnic Identification," *The American Political Science Review* 61, 3 (September, 1967): 717-26; Robert R. Alford and Harry M. Scoble, "Sources of Local Political Involvement," *The American Political Science Review* 62, 4 (December, 1968): 1192-1206.

21. Philip E. Converse, "The Nature of Belief Systems in Mass Publics," in *Ideology and Discontent*, ed. David E. Apter (Glencoe: The Free Press, 1964), p. 239.

22. Converse reports the following rank order correlations of a person's attitude on an issue in 1958 with the same person's attitude in 1960: party identification, .72; school desegregation, .47; F.E.P.C., .43; guaranteed employment, .49; federal aid to education, .36; foreign military aid, .31; and federal housing, .28. Philip E. Converse, p. 240.

23. Banfield, *The Unheavenly City*, Chapter 4, "Race: Thinking May Make it So," pp. 67-87.

24. Cited in Gary Marx, *Protest and Prejudice*, p. 227. In 1966, Brink and Harris found 25 percent of blacks at large supporting black power and 38 percent not sure. Among low income blacks support was *lower*, thirteen percent in favor, 47 percent not sure. See Brink and Harris, *Black and White*, p. 264. For comment on the early evolution of the term, see Joyce Ladner, "What 'Black Power' Means to Negroes in Mississippi," p. 84.

25. A 1969 Gallup poll of blacks showed only 19 percent choosing "black" and another 10 percent Afro-American. Cited in Alan A. Altschuler, *Community Control: The Black Demand for Participation in Large American Cities* (New York: Pegasus, 1970), p. 84.

26. The scale emphasizes political over cultural aspects of race identity. The mean gamma between the three items is .44 (see Appendix B). Marx summarizes several empirical studies of race identity. See Gary Marx, *Protest and Prejudice*, pp. 88-90. Several sources which help place race pride in a larger perspective are Harold Cruse, "The Fire This Time," p. 17; Gail Sheehy, "Black Against Black: The Agony of Panthermania," *New York* 3, 46 (November 16, 1970): 52; Bobby Seale, *Seize the Time: The Story of the Black Panther Party and Huey P. Newton* (New York: Random House, 1968), pp. 69-72; Robert Eyestone and Heinz Eulau, "City Councils and Policy Outcomes: Developmental Profiles," in *City Politics and Public Policy*, ed. James Q. Wilson (New York: John Wiley & Sons, Inc., 1968), p. 25; John Kraft, "Attitudes of Negroes," p. 1406.

27. Gary Marx, *Protest and Prejudice*, p. 171. The 1963 Brink and Harris poll indicated that 42 percent of blacks felt whites wanted "to keep the Negro down," 17 percent "don't care one way or the other," and 16 percent "aren't sure." Brink and Harris, *Revolution*, p. 126.

28. See John Kraft, "Attitudes of Negroes," p. 1399; and Brink and Harris, *Revolution*, p. 234.

29. Many more would undoubtedly agree if asked specifically if race was partly responsible for local problems, but the fact that race does not dominate problem-focused thought is important.

30. See Appendix B for exact scale. For further studies of black separatist sentiment, see Joyce Ladner, "What 'Black Power' Means to Negroes in Mississippi," p. 9; Bobby Seale, *Seize the Time*, p. 70; Gary Marx, *Protest and Prejudice*, pp. xvi, 28; Brink and Harris, *Revolution*, pp. 157-58; John Kraft, "Attitudes of Negroes," p. 1408; Jerome H. Skol-

nick, *The Politics of Protest*, p. 131; and Alan Altshuler, *Community Control*, pp. 85-93.

31. See Appendix B for scale.

32. Later analysis will approach these questions from a more rigorously causal perspective. For the moment, our interests are more descriptive.

33. N = 104, 14 percent of the total sample. Among persons scoring "moderately high" in race identity (N = 148, 19 percent of the sample), 6 percent show "very high" and 29 percent "some" propensity to violence.

34. Chapter 4 will indicate that absolute levels of race pride and support for race policies are not much higher among leaders than general residents. The associations of race identity and group membership are artificially low. Later analysis, which disaggregates membership by kind of group, will show stronger selective impact.

35. In the middle class control group 22 percent defined politics in negative terms, 21 percent as process. Among the poor the same percentages were 13 and 20 percent.

36. The poor cite "personal attributes" as a cause of poverty 37 percent less than the middle class control group but attention is. shifted, not to "discrimination-oppression," but to "lack of education" (9 percent more), and the "job situation" (21 percent more).

37. Seventeen percent of the middle class sample agreed "there are things around here which make a person angry," 21 percent show "high" alienation from national government.

38. In the middle class sample, 58 percent said there were no problems locally at all, 27 percent named one, 15 percent two, and no one three.

NOTES TO CHAPTER 4

1. Gary Marx summarizes many national leadership polls in Gary T. Marx, *Protest and Prejudice: A Study of Belief in the Black Community* (New York: Harper and Row, 1967), p. 217.

2. See William Brink and Louis Harris, *The Negro Revolution in America* (New York: Simon & Schuster, 1963), p. 122; William Brink and Louis Harris, *Black and White* (New York: Simon & Schuster, 1966), p. 54; James Frederick and Michael Pearson, "Black Veterans Return," *Trans-Action* 7, 5 (March, 1970): 32-37; Winston Prouty, *Prouty Survey Report*, Part II (mimeographed), p. 26; "Black America, 1970," *Time* special issue (April 6, 1970): 29; Opinion Research Corporation, *White and Negro Attitudes Towards Race Related Issues and Activities*, a CBS News Public Opinion Survey (Princeton: Opinion Research Corp., 1968), p. 12.

3. The kind of unreality that can infect studies of national elites is evidenced in Richard Bardolph's study of the "most famous Negro Americans." "For every Negro now knows in his heart," writes Bardolph, "if he considers the record of this vanguard . . . that the law and the momentum of the American tradition are on his side." Richard Bardolph, *The Negro Vanguard* (New York: Vintage Books, 1959), p. 461.

4. For several reasons, existing studies provide few precedents for our investigation. Some focus exclusively on race leadership: Everett Carll Ladd, Jr., *Negro Political Leadership in the South* (New York: Atheneum, 1969); James Q. Wilson, *Negro Politics* (New York: The Free Press, 1960), pp. 169-213; Daniel C. Thompson, *The Negro Leadership Class* (Englewood Cliffs, N.J.: Prentice-Hall, 1963); Donald R. Matthews and James W. Prothro, *Negroes and the New Southern Politics* (New York: Harcourt, Brace & World, Inc., 1956), p. 505; and Kenneth B. Clark, *Dark Ghetto* (New York: Harper Torchbooks, 1965). Many are more suited to the study of city than neighborhood power because they rely on "experts or "notables," not the poor themselves, to define leadership: Lewis Killian and Charles Grigg, *Racial Crisis in America: Leadership in Conflict* (Englewood Cliffs: Prentice-Hall, 1964); Marian Lief Palley, Robert Russo and Edward Scott, "Subcommunity Leadership in a Black Ghetto: A Study of Newark, New Jersey," *Urban Affairs Quarterly* (March, 1970), pp. 291-312; M. Elaine Burgess, *Negro Leadership in a Southern City* (1962); Ernest A. T. Barth and Baha Abu-Laban, "Power Structure and the Negro Subcommunity," *American Sociological Review* 24, 1 (1959): 69-76; Bruce P. Dohrenwend, "Urban Leadership and the Appraisal of Abnormal Behavior," in *The Urban Condition*, ed. Leonard J. Duhl (New York: Simon & Schuster, 1963), pp. 259-266. McCord et al.'s study of ghetto life has concerns similar to ours, but its ambiguous sample base and hesitant methodology keep it from conclusions of general power. William McCord and John Howard, "Negro Opinions," in *Life Styles in the Black Ghetto*, eds. McCord et al. (New York: W. W. Norton & Co., 1969), pp. 78-104.

5. The first question resulted in 1,480 attributions (77 percent of respondents gave no names, 22 percent only one), and the second in 1,137 attributions (78 percent gave no names, 17 percent only one). Names from both questions were combined. Blacks tended to give a few more names on the first question than whites, but all other characteristics of persons giving names on the questions were quite similar. In the typical community, the 40 persons gave 26 names of 12 different persons (seven on the first question, five on the second). When the list of leaders had been compiled for each community, a cross section of leaders was chosen from each of three types: those named once, those named twice, and those named three or more times.

6. Although it was project policy to destroy all lists of leaders' names before leaving a city, announcement of that fact had little influence on

suspicious respondents. Differences between interviewers in number of names elicited were found. The limiting cases were one interviewer who elicited names from 57 percent of respondents, and another who elicited names from 27 percent (the half dozen communities that each visited were probably different as well). Interviewers rate 53 percent of respondents "very co-operative," 33 percent "fairly," 130 percent "slightly" and 2 percent "not at all co-operative."

7. Data base here is the One Hundred City general residents sample. The mean number of attributions per respondent overall is .65, for persons over age 50, .51.

8. The ten percent of the sample in professional positions was more highly affiliated, mean attributions per respondent = 1.10.

9. Only limited comparisons are possible at this stage because the One Hundred City general residents were given an abbreviated questionnaire. If the difference in problem perception held only for those naming leaders on the question concerning persons active on local problems, the conclusion would be tautological. The same factors distinguish those who name leaders on the second question as well, however. The gamma between group involvement and naming problem leaders is .48, that between group involvement and naming local knowledgeables is .41.

10. The N for leaders of the poor is 630. We can now describe many more dimensions of variation, for this group was given the full questionnaire. It should be remembered, however, that the residents (N = 1114) with whom we will be comparing leaders are drawn from a subsample of five of the one hundred cities. Leaders were interviewed in the Five City portion of the study from which most of our data on general residents is drawn. It seems better to highlight the much more comprehensive One Hundred City leadership sample here, however, even at the risk of formal incomparability between resident and leader samples. The technique for sampling leaders in the One Hundred Cities was a careful miniaturization of the more elaborate, multi-stage sampling procedures of the Five City Study. The comparability of samples derived by the two techniques was the subject of Appendix B, in Barss Reitzel and Associates, *Community Action and Institutional Change*, Prepared for the Office of Economic Opportunity, Bruce Jacobs, Project Director (Cambridge, Mass., July, 1969). A comparison of the One Hundred and Five City samples indicated few differences in the samples along demographic or attitudinal lines. The conclusion can be taken as some indication that our leadership sampling technique is a good one and that comparing followers in one sample and leaders in the other is not imprecise. Except for differences in race (the Five City sample is 70 percent black, the One Hundred City sample 53 percent) differences along the 25 dimensions tested were either inconsequential or explained by the natural tendency of the much larger Five City "snowball" sample

to include a larger proportion of persons more like residents at large than like other leaders.

11. Actual figures were occasional contact (27 percent); church-social (22 percent); meetings and activities (20 percent); media (14 percent); relatives (13 percent); and friends (13 percent).

12. Actual figures are: not active on any problem (10 percent); active on jobs (7 percent); youth activities (12 percent); housing (7 percent); social services (12 percent); neighborhood conditions (6 percent); church activities (4 percent); education (4 percent); community organization (30 percent); media (4 percent); and government-politics (5 percent).

13. Multiple responses were coded in the first of the categories chosen as listed above (other and no answer = 9 percent).

14. Treating our sample of leaders as representative of leaders of the poor nationwide requires comment on a potentially serious source of data bias: the refusal of certain kinds of leaders to be interviewed. In some areas refusal rate became a serious problem. Two years before the Local Change Survey, our interviewer in Syracuse told us, a great deal of effort had gone into a local CAP project called CRUSADE. The only outcome of that effort was a survey, at the conclusion of which CRUSADE folded. People were wondering if the Local Change Survey was a plot aimed at CRUSADE's successor. "People were afraid to give any names or information about what was going on." The substitution rate across the hundred cities was high (40 percent) but its breakdown does not give cause for alarm. Fifteen percent could not be located, 10 percent were "out of town," 8 percent "too busy," and 7 percent uninterested for political reasons. The resulting biases away from cosmopolitanism and toward stable leadership elites should be kept in mind, but do not seem to prejudice major findings reported here.

15. Ralph Kramer, *Participation of the Poor: Comparative Community Case Studies in the War on Poverty* (Englewood Cliffs, N.J.: Prentice-Hall, 1969), pp. 181, 191.

16. *Federal Role in Urban Affairs*, Hearings Before the Subcommittee on Executive Reorganization of the Committee on Government Operations, U.S. Senate, 98th Congress, 2nd Session, (August 31, September 1, 1966) Part 6, p. 1366. For further comments on "creaming" of leadership in poor areas, see Herbert Gans, *The Urban Villagers: Group and Class in the Life of Italian-Americans* (New York: The Free Press, 1962), p. 277; George Brager "Organizing the Unaffiliated in a Low Income Area," in *Poverty in America*, eds. Louis A. Ferman, Joyce L. Kornbluth, Alan Haber (Ann Arbor: University of Michigan Press, 1969); M. Elaine Burgess, *Negro Leadership in a Southern City*, p. 64; and Alan Altshuler, *Community Control*, p. 120.

17. The studies are generally of city-wide not neighborhood power. Everett Ladd found 90 and 75 percent of leadership elites in Winston-Salem and Greenville to have attended college. Ladd, *Negro Political*

Leadership in the South, p. 197; Matthews and Prothro conclude, "Like most other groups, southern Negroes look to those with relatively high prestige and status for leadership. Perhaps 80 percent of the Negroes nominated as leaders by our southwide sample hold white collar jobs." Matthews and Prothro, *Negroes and the New Southern Politics,* p. 185.

18. See Kramer, *Participation of the Poor,* p. 170; Jessie Bernard, *Marriage and Family Among Negroes* (Englewood Cliffs, N.J.: Prentice-Hall, 1966), pp. 27-66; Roberta Sigel, "Citizen Committees: Advice vs. Consent," *Trans-Action* 46 (May, 1967): 51; Brink and Harris, *Black and White,* p. 17; and Joel Aberbach and Jack L. Walker, "Political Trust and Racial Ideology," *American Political Science Review* 64, 4 (December, 1970): 1212.

19. George Regan, "Harlem Clergyman Implores Black Professionals to Return from Suburbia," *New York Times,* March 26, 1970, p. 35.

20. Matthews and Prothro, *Negroes and the New Southern Politics,* pp. 184, 443-66.

21. See *Federal Role in Urban Affairs,* p. 1377.

22. Our data indicate that one effect of race consciousness has been the building of new bridges over the gulf separating blacks and the genteel black tradition. The higher a person's education, the data indicate, the more likely he is to identify strongly with his race. The percentages "moderately high" in race consciousness below high school, with high school diplomas, and any college education are: 15, 38, and 49 percent (N = 690). Other research has come to similar conclusions: Gary Marx, *Protest and Prejudice,* pp. 49-80. Aberbach's study of the interplay of race, class and alienation from government led him to the same conclusion. "It is possible . . . to speak . . . of a black political community, crossing social class lines, marked by a developing racial ideology focused on militancy and pride and connected with a strong distrust of government." Aberbach and Walker, "Political Trust and Racial Ideology," p. 1212. This development, Aberbach continues, is of "utmost importance to a minority community which needs to mobilize skills of its growing middle class."

23. Quoted in Brink and Harris, *The Negro Revolution,* p. 69.

24. See concluding "summary," Chapter 4.

25. This section will rely on comparisons between black community leaders (Row 3, Table 4.1) and black political elites (Row 5) and between white community leaders (Row 4) and white political elites (Row 7).

26. These titles will be explained in Chapter 5 devoted to organizational membership.

27. Previous work along similar lines is only tangentially relevant as precedent. Many have recognized differing roles in the political structure of poor neighborhoods. Gail Sheehy has written, ". . . the clash between middle-class values and radicalism—and even more internal and ferocious, the clash between Panthers and Black Nationalists

groups—is tearing at the black community. It is killing more poeple than the shootouts between cops and militants. The most uncomfortable spot in America 1970, may be in the black middle." Gail Sheehy, "Black Against Black," p. 38. Jessie Bernard discusses the class split in the black community at length in Jessie Bernard, *Marriage and Family*, Chapter 2, "The Two Cultures," pp. 27-66. Previous typologizing has, however, been directed almost exclusively at racial issues. Everett Ladd reviews several of these, mostly variations on divisions into racial "conservatives," "moderates," and "militants," in Ladd, Jr., *Negro Political Leadership in the South*, p. 148. William McCord, "Taking the Pulse of the Ghetto: A Note on Methods," in *Life Styles in the Black Ghetto*, eds. McCord et al., presents a typology of ghetto types ("stoic," "defeated," "rebel without a cause," etc.) but it is based on sketchy data which does not allow for precise establishment of absolute numbers and attributes of each type. For other typologies, see Matthews and Prothro, *Negroes and the New Southern Politics*, pp. 175-202; Palley, Russo and Scott, "Subcommunity Leadership in a Black Ghetto," p. 299; Killian & Grigg, *Racial Crisis in America*, p. 85; and *Time*, "Black America 1970," p. 14.

28. The technique is a refinement by Barss Reitzel and Associates of a numerical taxonomic program developed at the Massachusetts Institute of Technology. See Appendix A-2 for a review of the technique.

29. See Appendix B for scales.

30. The "defining characteristics" of each type will be given more emphasis than the larger number of other variables because empirically, these are most likely to distinguish between types. No logical difference is felt to exist between the two, however, and all attributes will be evaluated, on their own merit, for theoretical power and ability to differentiate one type from another.

31. The power of the conclusion is reduced because the propensity to violence scale scores blacks only.

32. See, for example, Robert Lane's summary, *Political Life* (New York: The Free Press, 1959), pp. 149-54; Gabriel A. Almond and Sidney Verba, *The Civic Culture* (Boston: Little, Brown & Co., 1963), pp. 186-207; "The Sense of Citizen Competence," pp. 136-67; V. O. Key, Jr., *Public Opinion and American Democracy* (New York: Alfred A. Knopf, 1964), p. 193.

NOTES FOR CHAPTER 5

1. Norman H. Nie, G. Bingham Powell, Jr., and Kenneth Prewitt, "Social Structure and Political Participation: Developmental Relation-

ships, II," *American Political Science Review* 63, 3 (September, 1969): 823-24.

2. Oscar Lewis, quoted in Charles Valentine, *Culture and Poverty* (Chicago: University of Chicago Press, 1968), p. 54.

3. George Brager, "Organizing the Unaffiliated in a Low Income Area," in *Poverty in America*, eds. Louis A. Ferman, Joyce L. Kornbluth and Alan Haber (Ann Arbor: University of Michigan Press, 1969), pp. 508-9; and Morris Axelrod, "Urban Structure and Social Participation," *American Sociological Review* 21, 1 (February, 1956): 13-18.

4. There appears to be little difference between black and white in general level of group membership. Myrdal argued the point in 1944 and, more recently, Marx has come to the same conclusion: ". . . differences in organizational membership by race are slight *when social position is controlled for* (emphasis mine)." Gary T. Marx, *Protest and Prejudice: A Study of Belief in the Black Community* (New York: Harper and Row, 1967), p. 71. Marx cites two other studies in support of his findings, N. Babchuck and R. Thompson, "Voluntary Associations Among Negroes," in *American Sociological Review* (October, 1962): 648-653 and C. Wright and H. Hyman, "Voluntary Association Memberships of American Adults: Evidence from National Sample Surveys," in *American Sociological Review* (June, 1958): 284-94. In their study of Southern politics, Matthews and Prothro discovered few disparities in general group membership by race, but some interesting differences concerning membership in political groups. "All but 9 percent of the Negroes and 15 percent of the whites belong to some kind of association, club or formal group . . . About 10.5 percent of the voting age Negroes in the South belong to political organizations and associations—most commonly the NAACP. Only 2.5 percent of the whites are similarly involved." Donald R. Matthews and James W. Prothro, *Negroes and the New Southern Politics* (New York: Harcourt, Brace and World, Inc., 1966), p. 52. These figures for group participation are extraordinarily high, probably because they count all forms of church attendance as organizational membership.

5. The question listed 13 different possible groups. It included unions and church-related organizations, but excluded church affiliation. Gabriel A. Almond and Sidney Verba, *The Civic Culture* (Boston: Little, Brown and Co., 1963), p. 247.

6. It is difficult to relate this question precisely to the membership figures. It both over- and under-estimates membership itself. One need not be a member to answer positively, yet the question, because of its brevity and emphasis on public-minded organizations, undervalues church and friendship groups.

7. This question is narrower than that used by Almond and Verba, but there is evidence that it does not underestimate the actual percentage a great deal. In the leadership sample along with this question we

asked a fuller one prompting the respondent to name up to five different "clubs, organizations, councils or committees" to which he belonged. The percentage of leaders listing any group on this question was 74, only 4 percent more than indicated any membership on the "important" group question. Inspection reveals the kinds of groups listed on the two questions to be roughly similar. The "important" group question drew somewhat more community social action, civil rights, and church affiliated mentions and somewhat fewer in the CAP and union categories.

8. Between 40 and 50 percent of blacks attend church at least once a week. Marx, *Protest and Prejudice*, p. 101, places this figure at 39 percent; William Brink and Louis Harris, *The Negro Revolution in America* (New York: Simon & Schuster, 1963), p. 100, place the figure at 49 percent. One would expect this to be reflected in membership in church affiliated groups at something approaching the 19 percent figure for Americans at large, Almond and Verba, *The Civic Culture*, p. 247.

9. Civil rights groups are older, of course. They are, however, in a process of change which later analysis will suggest places them in a borderline position between traditional and action groups.

10. See Almond and Verba, *The Civic Culture*, figures presented in Fig. 5.1. Included in the percentage are traditional and action groups.

11. In the leadership sample, in addition to the "important" group question, each respondent was asked to list up to five "clubs, organizations, councils or committees" to which he belongs and whether he has been a "leader or officer" in each. Among leaders, the "important" group question underestimates the incidence of group leadership by 24 percent. Even granting a greater disparity between "important" and total officership for general residents, the 2.8 percent figure is extremely low.

12. Almond and Verba, *The Civic Culture*, p. 259.

13. One in five mentioned leading more than one group. The figure rises to 61 percent for those with four or more mentions.

14. The actual percentages of leadership positions falling into the three group categories are 22, 28 and 49, respectively. The leadership "density" is roughly the same in each group, 49, 56 and 54, respectively.

15. The arguments of the following sections will be based on comparisons between three subgroups of our leadership sample: officers of a given kind of organization, those who do not belong to that organization, and those who belong but are not officers. We will argue that differences between these groups are caused in part by office holding. The logic is strongest when we discover "no difference" between officers and non-officers and posit no impact. It seems strong as well when we are discussing the "working values" of a given group, political attitudes in the case of action groups, for example. Impressionable persons (first-time officers, for example) would probably be more affected by the norms of organization leadership than old-line politicos. There is truth in the noncausal interpretation as well—that distinctiveness is due to

differential recruitment—but this view is not incompatible with a sensitivity to the importance of a sympathetic matrix for preexisting values.

16. The percentage of persons agreeing that they can change their life (for non-members and officers of friendship, traditional and action groups respectively) are 64, 68; 64, 63; 55, 76; N's 218, 47; 205, 62; and 129, 102.

17. See Appendix B for the occupational aspiration scale. The actual percentages with any occupational aspirations among non-members and officers in friendship, traditional and action groups, respectively, are: 33, 21; 34, 24; 25, 30; N's: 138, 28; 124, 38; and 56, 79.

18. Fifty-eight percent of those not belonging to action groups were judged "very articulate" by our interviewers, as were 81 percent of the officers of action groups.

19. It should be remembered that this is not strictly speaking a random sample of constituents. In perception of community problems, not reported in Figure 5.3, a similar pattern emerges. Three different local problems were listed by 54 percent of leaders of traditional groups, 2 percent more than non-members, but 11 percent *less* than members not in leadership positions. The figure for officers of action groups was 68 percent, about the same as that for other members but 34 percent more than non-members.

20. The friendship group pattern is not as clear cut. Officers of these groups tend to be somewhat more mobilized than constituents, but because their general membership is less politically aware than persons at large, this serves only to bring leaders back to about the neighborhood norm. Organizers might expect a mildly hostile reception to their proddings from the general membership of friendship groups but, if our evidence is any indication, they should be alert to latent sympathy among those who head-up such organizations.

21. Edward C. Banfield, *The Unheavenly City* (Boston: Little, Brown & Co., 1968), p. 86. See on this question, Bobby Seale, *Seize the Time: The Story of the Black Panther Party and Huey P. Newton* (New York: Random House, 1968), p. 68.

22. There are dangers in using this methodology. The distinct subcultures of the analyst, as Valentine suggests, usually participate in a great many attributes of the wider culture, and are often affected more by external forces than by their own internal dynamics. We hope to avoid abusing the concept here by treating it as a hypothesis to be tested in each situation. Valentine's suggestion that subcultures within a culture be compared to "dialects of a language" captures the spirit of our investigation. Valentine, *Culture and Poverty*, p. 109.

23. Both of these concerns bypass the major objection to the subculture approach, that group distinctiveness is the product of membership selectivity, not pressures generated within the organization. The objection is not a pressing issue for those sizing up forces for change, or for

those trying to allocate sympathy and support among groups intelligently.

24. Nie et al., "Social Structure and Political Parties," Developmental Relationships, II," p. 814, favor the subcultural hypothesis concerning group membership. "The self selection hypothesis is weakened since we would expect self-selective tendency to correlate with attitudes such as political efficacy and attentiveness. The absence of strong relationships between organizational involvement and these attitudes makes us suspicious of the self-selection explanation. The first explanation, that organizations are mobilizing their members, is intuitively more persuasive and has been supported by additional research."

25. Descriptions of group members based on a rank and file sample are not possible in the present data although this would give a more precise sampling of general membership. This is not only a sample of officers of these organizations, however. Typically only about half of the "leaders" who indicate they are members of a group say they are officers. Almond and Verba, The Civic Culture, p. 257, report much the same proportion, 46 percent for a completely random sample of Americans at large. The distortion involved in analyzing groups from the attributes of "notable" members seems acceptable because of the heightened importance to the subculture of the attitudes of members who have some claim to local importance at the outset.

26. The actual question was, "Which of the following do you consider your most important task as a member of this community, which second and which third: getting people angry about issues; organizing or talking before local community groups; or presenting demands of local people and groups to government officials and elected representatives."

27. The only groups showing differences from the community norm significant at the .05 level were political party groups who cited discrimination 10 percent more, and militant ethnic groups who spoke of discrimination 12 percent, and employment 17 percent more than the community average.

28. Undoubtedly a few tenant groups escaped our coding procedures. A closer analysis would require distinguishing within tenant groups between those devoted exclusively to tenant issues (rents, upkeep) and those which expand to consider wider complaints of residents living in a given area.

29. The distinction between distributive, redistributive and regulatory issues comes from Theodore Lowi, "American Business, Public Policy, Case Studies and Political Theory," World Politics 16 (July, 1964): 677-715.

30. Herbert Gans, The Urban Villagers: Group and Class in the Life of Italian-Americans (New York: The Free Press, 1962), p. 111.

31. Jack E. Weller, Yesterday's People: Life in Contemporary Appalachia (Lexington: University of Kentucky Press, 1966), p. 124.

32. William Brink and Louis Harris, Black and White (New York:

Simon & Schuster, 1966), p. 100. There is more evidence concerning
working class religious life than there is concerning religious life among
the poor. Most of the West-Enders Gans investigated were members
of the working class. The major studies of black religion, that of Gary T.
Marx, for example, are based on nation-wide samples, not only of the
poor. It seems likely that religion is somewhat less important in lower
class life than it is for the working class. Marx scored 67 percent of blacks
generally in an "extremely important" category of subjective importance
of religion (adapted from Marx, p. 100). When a sample of lower class
blacks in Houston was asked "How religious are you?" only 22 percent
answered "very" and 49 percent "some (sic)."

33. Donald R. Matthews and James W. Prothro, *Negroes and the New
Southern Politics*, p. 233.

34. Gary T. Marx, *Protest and Prejudice*, p. 96.

35. Everett Carll Ladd, Jr., *Negro Political Leadership in the South*
(New York: Atheneum, 1969), p. 237, reports that seven of the top 25
leaders in Greenville, South Carolina, and nine of 47 in Winston-Salem,
North Carolina, are clergymen. Thompson, in a somewhat earlier study
of New Orleans black leadership found similar results, reported in Marx,
Protest and Prejudice, p. 96. See also, pp. 96-7 where he reviews the many
contradictory points of view on the church and protest. Nor should a
strong rejection of religion be taken as necessary evidence of its irrelevance to personal development. The church can have a conservative influence on members generally and still give an elite leadership the skills
for commitment to action. Rejection, under some circumstances, can involve a transfer of messianic fervor from the religious to the secular
realm. This argument was made to me by Bruce Palmer who suggested
that it was central to an understanding of populist movements in American history.

36. Marx, *Protest and Prejudice*, p. 107.

37. This was the charge given black clergymen of Harlem by Bishop
William Lee Bonner. George Dugan, "Harlem Clergyman Implores
Black Professionals to Return from Suburbia," *New York Times* (March
26, 1970), p. 35. See also "Black America, 1970," *Time* special issue
(April 6, 1970): 13ff; Talcott Parsons, "Full Citizenship for the Negro
American, a Sociological Problem," in Talcott Parsons and Kenneth B.
Clark, eds. *The Negro American* (Boston: The Beacon Press, 1965),
p. 738; Daniel C. Thompson, "The Rise of Negro Protest," in "The Negro
Protest," special editor, Arnold M. Rose. *The Annals of the American
Academy of Political and Social Science* 357 (January, 1965): 26.

38. Marx, *Protest and Prejudice*, p. 103.

39. These quotes, from a housewife, salvage worker, and clergyman,
are reported in Marx, *Protest and Prejudice*, pp. 18-19.

40. *Ibid.*, p. 100. Marx related decreasing militarism to subjective importance of religion, frequency of church attendance, and denomination

(Episcopalians having the greatest proportion of militants (43 percent), Catholics a middle number (36 percent), Baptists (25 percent), and sects and cults (15 percent), pp. 96-103). See also Robert E. Lane, *Political Life* (New York: The Free Press, 1959), p. 245.

41. See Arthur J. Vidich and Joseph Bensman, *Small Town in Mass Society* (New York: Doubleday and Co., Inc., 1960), p. 237.

42. Matthews and Prothro, *Negroes and the New Southern Politics*, p. 233.

43. Gans, *The Urban Villagers*, p. 113.

44. Stan Steiner, *La Raza: The Mexican-Americans* (New York: Harper and Row, 1969), p. 343.

45. *Ibid.*, p. 343.

46. The quotes are from Jack Weller, *Yesterday's People*, pp. 125-6.

47. There are more men among social group leaders, and the category draws disproportionately from the unskilled occupations and longer term residents.

48. N = 27 for black church group members.

49. N for black party group members = 7, for non-members, 299.

50. Matthews and Prothro, *Negroes and the New Southern Politics*, pp. 10-20; John C. Donovan, *The Politics of Poverty* (New York: Western Publishing Co., Inc., 1967), pp. 106-8; Brink and Harris, *The Negro Revolution*, p. 82; James Q. Wilson, "The Negro in Politics," in *The Negro American*, eds. Parsons and Clark (Boston: The Beacon Press, 1963), pp. 423-47.

51. In a *Time* poll, 72 percent of blacks rejected party voting for "whichever man will help blacks." "Black America 1970," p. 28.

52. Fifty percent of all black leaders scored high on support for race policies; only one of seven black political party group members did.

53. The following notes on a day in the life of George Washington Plunkitt illustrate a political party serving as a people's government— a decentralized legislative, executive and judicial branch rolled into one. "Two A.M. Aroused from sleep . . . found a bartender who asked him to go to the police station and bail out a saloon-keeper . . . Returned to bed at three o'clock. Six A.M. Awakened by fire engines . . . Hastened to the scene of the fire . . . Met several of his election district captains who are always under orders to look out for fires, which are considered great vote getters. Found several tenants who had been burned out, took them to a hotel, supplied them with clothes, fed them, arranged temporary quarters . . . Eleven A.M. The District leader spent nearly three hours fixing things (for four men looking for railroad, plumbing, subway and road jobs) and succeeded in each case. Three P.M. Attended the funeral of an Italian . . . presided over meeting of election district captains . . . Went to a Church fair . . . Nine P.M. Listened to the complaints of a dozen push cart peddlers who said they were persecuted by the police and assured them he would go to Police Headquarters in the

morning to see about it." Twelve P.M. In bed." William L. Riordon, *Plunkitt of Tammany Hall* (New York: E. P. Dutton and Co., 1963), pp. 90-3. See also Edwin Harwood, "Urbanism as a Way of Negro Life," in *Life Styles in the Black Ghetto*, eds. McCord et al. (New York: W. W. Norton and Co., Inc., 1969), pp. 29-30.

54. Frank J. Sorauf, *Party Politics in America* (Boston: Little, Brown & Co., 1968), p. 78.

55. William Riordan, *Plunkitt*, p. 45.

56. This is a relatively small sample on which to base the analysis, but it compensates by being drawn uniquely from leaders as designated by the poor. Working with such a small sample necessarily places the analysis in the hypothesis creating, not testing, stage.

57. Curt Lamb, *Political Power in Poor Neighborhoods* (Ph. D. diss. Yale University, 1972). See Chapter 4-A, "Community Life in Poor Neighborhoods," pp. 29-91.

58. Forty-six percent place the cause in the former category (14 percent more than non-party group members) and 25 percent in the latter (2 percent more than non-party group members).

59. For background information on civil rights groups, see Brink and Harris, *Black and White*, pp. 246-50; John F. Kraft, "A Report on Attitudes of Negroes in Various Cities," in *Federal Role in Urban Affairs*, Hearings Before the Subcommittee on Executive Reorganization of the Committee on Government Operations, U.S. Senate, 98th Congress, 2nd Session, Part 6, pp. 1397-98; John A. Morsell, "The National Association for the Advancement of Colored People and its Strategy," *Annals* 357 "The Negro Protest," (January, 1965): 98-99; Kenneth Clark, "The Civil Rights Movement: Momentum and Organization," in Parsons and Clark, eds. *The Negro American*, pp. 608-10; Howard Zinn, *SNCC: The New Abolitionists* (Boston: The Beacon Press, 1964).

60. Ralph M. Kramer, *Participation of the Poor: Comparative Case Studies in the War on Poverty* (Englewood Cliffs: Prentice-Hall, 1969), p. 153.

61. We are unable to assess empirically the strength of pressures for decentralization of government. The support for black separatist demands among rank and file and leaders was discussed in Chapter 3, but this is a somewhat different topic.

62. Altshuler presents an excellent discussion of these issues, *Community Control*, pp. 19-61. On the question of revenues, Farrell makes the argument that ". . . in property tax states or states that depend largely on property taxes, the poor are already paying what amounts to a proportional share of the cost of their own support." Gregory R. Farrell, "Resources for Transforming the Ghetto," in *The Schoolhouse in the City*, ed. Alvin Toffler (New York: Praeger, 1968), p. 91; See also Jerome H. Skolnick, *The Politics of Protest: A Report submitted by Jerome H.*

Skolnick, Director, Task Force on Violent Aspects of Protest and Confrontation of the National Commission on the Causes and Prevention of Violence (New York: Ballantine Books, 1969).

63. Milton Kotler, "Making Local Government Truly Local," *Trans-Action* 4, 10 (October, 1967): 49-50.

64. Quoted from Patricia Cayo Sexton in Kramer, *Participation of the Poor*, p. 231. Roberta S. Sigel, "Citizen Committees: Advice vs. Consent," *Trans-Action* 4, 6 (May, 1967): 48-52, presents an excellent critique of local organization based on the experience of a Detroit Citizen's Advisory Committee which attempted to influence policy concerning a local school. See also J. David Greenstone and Paul E. Peterson, "Reformers, Machines and the War on Poverty," in *City Politics and Public Policy*, ed. James Q. Wilson (New York: John Wiley and Sons, Inc., 1968), p. 291.

65. See Curt Lamb, *Political Power*, pp. D-20-5 for further discussion of sample bias.

66. Eldridge Cleaver, *Soul on Ice* (New York: Dell Publishing Co., 1968), pp. 3-4; Malcolm X, *Autobiography*, p. 173; George Jackson, *Soledad Brother: The Prison Letters of George Jackson* (New York: Bantam Books, 1970), p. 15; and Bobby Seale, *Seize the Time: The Story of the Black Panther Party and Huey P. Newton* (New York: Random House, 1960), p. 14.

67. Seale, *Seize the Time*, p. 33.

68. Ibid., p. 4.

69. "Black America, 1970," *Time* (April 6, 1970): 13ff.

70. This does not mean that this proportion of activity was sponsored directly by these groups. Much of it is accomplished on personal initiative. It is indicative, however, of the central position action group members occupy in the nexus of local activity. The actual percentages for "political activity" and "protest activity" for action and traditional groups are 84, 81 and 37, 34. The proportions of activity carried out by members of friendship groups in the same categories are 28 and 29 (percentages do not add up to 100 because of multiple memberships).

71. On a closely related indicator of support for the political demands of income maintenance and housing for the poor, militant ethnic group members score highest of all groups—21 points above average. Community social action groups are the only other category above average on this measure, neither CAP affiliates nor civil rights group members score much above the mean.

72. Because civil rights groups are older it is possible that an initial surge of membership filled their ranks with persons who have since attained a somewhat higher class position than their neighbors. Alternatively, the class disparity could be based on the appeal of these groups to persons with some education or social status (an explanation which gains support from the fact that members are not older than other

leaders). An occupation is considered to contribute disproportionately to membership in a group if the percentage of group members in it exceeds the percentage of non-group members by 10 percent.

73. There are two minor areas of distinctiveness. Community social action group members believe somewhat more than leaders at large that outsiders are showing more interest in the fate of poor neighborhoods, and they emphasize community centered reasons for the shift (31 percent versus 19 percent for non-members). Only 8 percent of them believe poverty is rooted in personal inadequacies versus 32 percent of leaders at large, while 17 percent (versus 10 percent of leaders generally) lay the blame on discriminatory practices of the larger society.

74. Forty-one percent gave community oriented causes versus 21 percent of non-members.

75. Other community groups are not greatly differentiated from leaders at large except unions and political parties which show about half as much support for race goals as others.

76. Five City Sample, N = 1042, 1061.

77. The importance of leadership to voluntary association shows up in studies tracing political activity to group membership. Nie et al., in an extensive cross-national survey of political culture, found the correlation between group membership and participation in the United States to be .52, nine points higher than that between socio-economic status and participation. They discovered further that of this .52, only seven percent can be explained by reference to status, 20 percent by the power of membership to change values which then prompt action, and 14 percent by a combination of the two. The remaining 57 percent they argue, is attributable to the organization proper and the quality of its leadership. Nie et al., "Social Structure and Political Parties," p. 812.

NOTES TO CHAPTER 6

1. To the movement, this media smothering involves a kind of premature proselytization. People hear of women's rights not from concerned advocates who could personalize the insights of the movement, but from one-shot capsulizations in the media. Nervous dismissal is the typical reaction under such conditions. This was the overwhelming reaction of one group of Midwestern high school girls questioned about women's liberation. "The Great American Dream Machine," National Educational Television, February 10, 1971.

2. The number increased from 65 to 92 percent between May, 1970 and February, 1971. State Backs Equal Jobs, Pay for Women," *The Boston Globe*, March 20, 1971.

3. This and the following figures in this section on regional, educa-

tional, age, and urban-rural sex differences come from Angus Campbell et al., *The American Voter* (New York: John Wiley and Sons, Inc., 1964), pp. 256-59.

3. This and the following figures in this section on regional, educational, age, and urban-rural sex differences come from Angus Campbell et al., *The American Voter* (New York: John Wiley and Sons, Inc., 1964), pp. 256-59.

4. V. O. Key, Jr., *Public Opinion and American Democracy* (New York: Alfred A. Knopf, 1964), p. 331; Angus Campbell, "The Passive Citizen," in *Political Parties and Political Behavior*, eds. W. J. Crotty et al. (Boston: Allyn and Bacon, Inc., 1966), p. 400; Stanley Greenberg, Project Director, *Mobilizing Poor Communities*, Prepared for the Office of Economic Opportunity by Barss Reitzel and Associates, Inc., (Cambridge, Mass: August, 1970), pp. 11-15; Robert E. Lane, *Political Life* (New York: The Free Press, 1959), pp. 209-16. Gordon Connelly, in a 1944 study puts the overall vote disparity at 14 percent; see Gordon Connelly and Harry H. Field, "The Non-Voter: Who He Is, What He Thinks," *Public Opinion Quarterly* 8 (Summer, 1944): 175-87.

5. There is some question concerning the influence of age on voting by women. In the South, women under 35 have a vote disparity one third that among older groups. The figure probably underestimates differences in values, given the difficulty women with children face in getting to the polls. Angus Campbell et al., *The American Voter*, note that mothers of small children are somewhat less likely to vote, although they evidence no slackening of interest in politics. It would be wise not to make too much of physical impediments to action, however. In one study of non-voting women only 3 percent cited the conflicting demands of child care as a reason for not voting. Reported in Robert Lane, *Political Life*, p. 259.

6. Campbell et al. do not feel that evidence concerning age differences encourages hope of widespread change in attitudes toward voting: "If there were once strong age differentials among women in acceptance of new sex role definitions, it is likely that the resistant age cohorts have by and large passed from the population." *The American Voter*, p. 259.

7. *Ibid.*, pp. 259-69.

8. *Ibid.*, pp. 259-60.

9. Paul F. Lazarsfeld, Bernard Berelson and Hazel Gaudet, *The People's Choice* (New York: Columbia University Press, 1944), p. 141. Only one husband-wife pair in 22 indicated they had voted for different presidential candidates. Frank J. Sorauf, *Party Politics in America* (Boston: Little, Brown & Co., 1968), p. 139; and Robert E. Lane and David O. Sears, *Public Opinion*, p. 30.

10. Judith M. Bardwick, "Her Body: The Battleground," *Psychology Today* 5, 9 (February, 1972): 50 ff.; Edith De Rham, *The Love Fraud: A Direct Attack on the Staggering Waste of Education and Talent Among*

American Women (New York: Pegasus, 1965), p. 268; Robert Lane, *Political Life*, p. 213; Havelock Ellis, *Man and Woman* (Boston: Houghton Mifflin, 1929), pp. 125-27; David Riesman, "Orbits of Tolerance, Interviews and Elites," *Public Opinion Quarterly* 20 (1956): 58. In its coverage of urban riots, *Newsweek* stated that ". . . white reaction (to black militance) can be highly personal, especially among women." William Brink and Louis Harris, *Black and White* (New York: Simon & Schuster, 1966), p. 124.

11. Quoted in Milton J. Rosenberg, "Images in Relation to the Policy Process: American Public Opinion on Cold-War Issues," in *International Behavior: A Socio-Psychological Analysis*, ed. Herbert C. Kelman (New York: Holt, Rinehart and Winston, 1965), p. 306; See also Milton J. Rosenberg, "Attitude Change and Foreign Policy in the Cold-War Era," in *Domestic Sources of Foreign Policy*, ed. James N. Rosenau (New York: The Free Press, 1967), p. 156.

12. Ithiel de Sola Pool, Robert P. Abelson and Samuel Popkin, *Candidates, Issues and Strategies* (Cambridge, Mass.: M.I.T. Press, 1964), p. 85.

13. The study is based on two three month periods in 1967 and 1968, women being allowed on juries only in the latter period. With women jurors, plaintiffs' chances of winning increased from 50 to 58 percent, that of socially "inferior" litigants from 26 to 50 percent. The all male juries were more inclined to give litigants the full money settlement they sought, however (52 percent versus 20 percent). Eloise C. Snyder, "Sex Role Differentials in Juror Decisions," *Sociology and Social Research* (July, 1971).

14. Quoted in Milton Rosenberg, "Images in Relation to the Policy Process," p. 307.

15. The figures are quoted from James G. March, "Husband and Wife Interaction over Political Issues," *Public Opinion Quarterly* 17 (1953-54): 461-70. They are cited by Robert Lane, *Political Life*, p. 216. Robert Wood divides women's political movements in the suburbs into two groups: "the 'spenders' who are most conscious of unfulfilled public needs, and the 'aesthetic' who are out to preserve the charm or residential quality of the suburb." *Suburbia: Its People and Their Politics* (Boston: Houghton Mifflin Co., 1958), p. 182.

16. Frank Sorauf, *Party Politics*, p. 93, makes no mention of the role of women in the party hierarchy although hidden and unmentioned in one table is the fact that among local Pittsburgh party activists, 3/4 of the men but only 1/3 of the women were on patronage. He also mentions that women vote less frequently than men. Fred I Greenstein, *The American Party System and The American People* (Englewood Cliffs: Prentice-Hall, 1963), leaves out the topic entirely. Eldersfeld's prize-winning study of local party politics, S. J. Eldersfeld, *Political Parties: A Behavioral Analysis* (Chicago: Rand McNally and Co., 1964), is studded

with statistics on party recruitment yet nowhere does the author mention the role alloted women in the process. One of Eldersfeld's main themes is that the party is an "eclectic recruiter." Only by second guessing his presentation is it possible to see that, for example, of 12 district leaders, none are women, pp. 59-60.

17. One of the few references to the place of women in this study is an ominous quote from one respondent concerning his feelings about a certain female traffic cop he passed on his way to work: ". . . if there's anything that's not feminine, it's watching a woman doing this here (motions traffic on with his hands) you know. I can't stand that . . . That's something I can't stand . . . I could see a fat woman, maybe, in the middle of the street, doing that, but when you get a girl that's really pretty over there—it's really unfeminine—my God." Robert E. Lane, *Political Ideology: Why the American Common Man Believes What He Does* (New York: The Free Press, 1962), p. 47; Key, *Public Opinion*, a monumental survey of work by American political scientists on political attitudes, mentions women three times, once to point out that women participate in politics moderately less than men, once in reference to the reduced "issue familiarity" of women, and once to relate the peculiar statistic that in the 40's, 7 percent of women who spent over $30 for their average dress read the *Daily News* while 46 percent of those who spent less than $5 did, pp. 186, 331, 351.

18. Gabriel A. Almond and Sidney Verba, *The Civic Culture* (Boston: Little, Brown & Co., 1963), pp. 325-35.

19. Robert Lane, *Political Life*, p. 355.

20. Quoted in Edith de Rham, *The Love Fraud*, p. 76.

21. Marijean Suelzle, "Women in Labor," *Trans-Action* 8, 1 and 2 (November-December, 1970): 56.

22. It was, ironically, exactly the evidence of second class status in female political behavior that kept political scientists from investigating the topic more acutely. With their over-riding concern for elections, partisan change and the like, political analysts took the opportunity to focus on half the sample universe, men only, in the faith that their results would automatically hold for women as well.

23. Many would argue more directly that the political self-serving of male chauvinism lies directly behind these professional "oversights." This appears to be true in one sense. Most men do not feel threatened by women in their life's work because they do not think there are women capable of competing. What happens, more subtly, however, is an avoidance of issues with a potentially disruptive impact on one's private life. A man's personal reckoning with his relationships with women is a major building block of his self-image. Professionalism and common sense dictate that he not devote his purposive activity to topics potentially disruptive in this area of delicate equilibrium.

24. In searching for insight into sex roles there is no substitute for the

semi-autobiographical material now available: Betty Friedan's down-to-earth reminiscences of her encounter with the American housewife, *The Feminine Mystique* (New York: Harper Colophon Books, 1962); Sally Kempton on being intellectual and a woman, "Cutting Loose," *Esquire* (July, 1970), pp. 53-57; or Joanna Clark on the situation of black women, "Motherhood," in *The Black Woman: An Anthology*, ed. Toni Cade (New York: New American Library, Inc., 1970), pp. 63-72, to name but a few.

25. Fred I. Greenstein, "Sex-Related Political Differences in Childhood," in *Politics and Social Life* (Boston: Houghton Mifflin Co., 1963), p. 252.

26. Suelzle, "Women in Labor," p. 53; Greenstein, "Sex-Related Political Differences," p. 252.

27. Jo Freeman, "Growing up Girlish," *Trans-Action* 8, 1-2 (November, December, 1970): 40.

28. Greenstein, "Sex-Related Political Differences," p. 253.

29. These quotations are from "The Dating Game," editors, *So What Are We Complaining About*, a collection of women's articles from *The Old Mole* (Boston: The New England Free Press, 1970), p. 6. The quote "to achieve . . ." is from Jo Freeman, "Growing up Girlish," p. 39.

30. Suelzle, "Women in Labor," p. 53. Kempton, in a discussion of self-love in women suggests that ". . . since women are in a sense given their lives, since women customarily choose a life-style by choosing a man rather than a path, they do not need the self-love which is necessary to carry a man to the places he has to go. Self-love is indeed a handicap to a being whose primary function is supportive." p. 55. See also Judy Miller, "Neighborhood Organizing for Liberation," *Women: A Journal of Liberation* 1-2 (Winter, 1970): 48-49, and the regular "Movement Section" of the same periodical.

31. Unfortunately, Lazarsfeld does not give the size of the sample of which the 45 forms a part. It is probably about 190 which means that only 2 percent of husbands reported discussing the election with their wives. Lazarsfeld, Berelson and Gaudet, *The People's Choice*, p. 141.

32. Kempton, "Cutting Loose," pp. 54, 57; and Freeman, "Growing up Girlish," p. 37.

33. Margot Hentoff, "The Curse," *The New York Review of Books* XII, 1 (January 16, 1969): 3.

34. Kempton, "Cutting Loose," p. 55.

35. Freeman, "Growing up Girlish," p. 242.

36. There are technical problems in a presentation of this sort. The vertical axes of (c) and (d) are, of course, not interval scales. Difficult judgments can be involved in even an ordinal ranking of "levels of power." The device of standardizing each level to 100 percent makes absolute numbers at each level irretrievable, but underlines the phenomena of relative exclusion level-by-level.

37. Suelzle, "Women in Labor," p. 51; See Also, "For your Information:

Some Facts and Figures," *Unitarian Universalist World* (October 1, 1970): 8.

38. The figure is based on expenditures of general government, social security and public enterprise as a percentage of gross national product in 1959; see Bruce M. Russett et al., *World Handbook of Political Indicators* (New Haven: Yale University Press, 1964), p. 50. There is a prominent myth that behind the scenes, through control of the stock market, women in fact control most of the wealth of the society. By market value, 20 percent of stock is in men's names, 18 percent in women's. The remaining 62 percent is owned by corporations. For the participation of women in corporations, see Figure 6.1. See also Suelzle, "Women in Labor," p. 56.

39. Greenstein, "Sex-Related Political Differences," p. 43.

40. Donald R. Matthews, *U.S. Senators and Their World* (New York: Vintage Books, 1960), p. 13.

41. Charlotte Bunch-Weeks, "Asian Women in Revolution," *Women: A Journal of Liberation* 1, 4 (Summer, 1970): 9.

42. Traditional conceptions of family organization linger, however, and the party bureaucracy has proved resistant to full integration. Bunch-Weeks, "Asian Women in Revolution," pp. 6-8.

43. Aristide R. Zolberg, *Creating Political Order: The Party States of West Africa* (Chicago: Rand McNally and Company, 1966), "The Emergence of Dominant Parties," pp. 19-36.

44. Since independence in 1958, Guinean women have mounted successful efforts to equalize school enrollment, and get women into wage earning positions throughout the economy. Their stake in the revolution is higher than that of men, says Touré, because "it compromises their own as well as the nation's liberation." Margarita Dobert, "Liberation and the Women of Guinea," *Africa Report* (October, 1970): 26-28. Women participated actively in the struggle for Algerian independence although their support was subsequently betrayed in a series of traditionalist directives by the revolutionary government. Tunisia, since its independence 15 years ago, has banned polygamy, given women the vote and legal equality and allowed women to take the initiative in divorce. It was one of the first countries after Japan and Sweden to legalize abortion. See "In Tunisia it's Population Explosion versus Women's Liberation," *New York Times*, January 9, 1971, p. 16.

45. Whether the shift from political confrontation to communalization has speeded liberation or slowed it down for Chinese women is an open question. The communes do not seem to have been as successful in overcoming stereotyped female roles as hoped and the Women's Federation has steadily decreased in influence since affiliating itself with the party and the overall task of nation building. Bunch-Weeks, "Asian Women in Revolution," p. 6.

46. Elizabeth Racz, "The Women's Rights Movement in the French

Revolution," in *Women: A Journal of Liberation* 1, 4 (Summer, 1970): 30-31.

47. Erica Dunn and Judy Klein, "Women in the Russian Revolution," in *Women: A Journal of Liberation* 1, 4 (Summer, 1970): 25. By 1944, virtually all of these reforms had been rescinded. For some perspectives on the situation in Cuba, see Joan Berman, "Women in Cuba," and Linda Gordon, "Speculations on Women's Liberation in Cuba," in *Women: A Journal of Liberation* 1, 4 (Summer, 1970): 10-14 and 14-15.

48. Roxbury Cultural Arts Festival notes (Boston: February, 1971), unpublished.

49. A majority of this number is probably white. Office of Economic Opportunity, *Women in the War on Poverty*, U.S. Government Printing Office (1960) 0-348-671, p. 3. See also Alan A. Altshuler, *Community Control: The Black Demand for Participation in Large American Cities* (New York: Pegasus, 1970), pp. 151-73; "Black America, 1970," *Time* special issue (April 6, 1970): 13ff; Brink and Harris, *Black and White*, pp. 70-73; "The Fugitive," *Time* (August 31, 1970): 14; Joyce Ladner, "What 'Black Power' Means to Negroes in Mississippi," *Trans-Action* 5, 1 (November, 1967): 12.

50. Susan Brownmiller, "Sisterhood is Powerful," *New York Times Magazine* (March 15, 1970): 128. For further evidence of discrimination in the movement, see Nathan Hare and Julia Hare, "Black Women, 1970," *Trans-Action* 8, 1 and 2 (November-December, 1970): 65-66; Gwen Patton, "Black People and the Victorian Ethos," in *The Black Woman*, ed. Toni Cade (New York: Signet, 1970), p. 147; Eric L. Metzner, "A Convention of Panthers," *The Phoenix* (December 8, 1970), p. 39; Bobby Seale, *Seize the Time: The Story of the Black Panther Party and Huey Newton* (New York: Random House, 1968), p. 62; "SNCC Black Women's Liberation," *Women: A Journal of Liberation* 1, 2 (Winter, 1970): 76-77.

51. Two hundred and sixty-one women leaders were actually interviewed, 110 whites, 134 blacks, and 17 chicanas. Methodological prudence would dictate that chicanas, numbering only 17, be eliminated from consideration. There are many intriguing aspects to their situation, however, and it has been decided to report the data here in the hope that it will prompt others to fuller investigation. The data from the more intensive studies in five of the hundred cities uphold these general conclusions on the proportions of leadership positions held by women. The average proportion of women in a top-to-bottom cross section of 281 leaders in three black neighborhoods in Atlanta, Detroit, and Pittsburgh was 42 percent. The proportion of women leaders in a San Jose chicana community where 67 leaders were interviewed was low, 24 percent, and in one white community, Hamilton, Ohio, quite high, 58 percent.

52. This percentage is higher than that found in most empirical studies of black power. Burgess, for example, found only four of 54 individuals with over two leadership mentions in the black community

to be women. Elaine M. Burgess, *Negro Leadership in a Southern City* (Durham: University of North Carolina Press, 1962), p. 78. Matthews and Prothro, *Negroes and the New Southern Politics*, p. 180, show that of four southern counties, only nine percent of the power nominations went to women. This agrees roughly with the findings of Thompson's study of New Orleans black leadership, Daniel C. Thompson, *The Negro Leadership Class* (Englewood Cliffs: Prentice-Hall, 1963), pp. 50-83, and the findings of Hunter's seminal work on power in Atlanta, Floyd Hunter, *Community Power Structure* (Chapel Hill: University of North Carolina Press, 1953), pp. 163-92. Most of these studies, however, were carried out before recent increases in political activity in poor areas, at a city-wide, not a nighborhood level and, importantly, used a top-down system of leadership attribution. The only study that agrees generally with the present one is Ernest A. T. Barth and Baha Abu-Laban, "Power Structure and the Negro Sub-Community," *American Sociological Review* 24 (1959): 69-76, which found 44 percent of the top leadership strata in a black community to be women.

53. Average network size = eight leaders. The figures which follow are based on the analysis of this data by Staﬁley Greenberg, *Mobilizing Poor Communities*, a Barss Reitzel and Associates report to the Office of Economic Opportunity (August, 1970).

54. Actual figures are: pragmatic militant: 47 percent of leaders of the poor are women; defiant militant: 38 percent; reformist: 36 percent; passive center: 48 percent; and idle radicals: 38 percent.

55. Kempton, "Cutting Loose," pp. 54, 57; Freeman, "Growing up Girlish," p. 37.

56. The quotation is from Bernard, *Marriage and Family Among Negroes* (Englewood Cliffs: Prentice-Hall, 1966), p. 73. The phrase "unnatural superiority" is also hers. See also Pat Robinson and group, "A Historical and Critical Essay for Black Women in the Cities," in *The Black Woman*, ed. Toni Cade (New York: Signet, 1970), pp. 198-210; Linda J. M. La Rue, "Black Liberation and Women's Lib," *Trans-Action* 8, 1-2 (November-December, 1970): 59-64; Charles E. Silberman, *Crisis in Black and White* (New York: Vintage Books, 1964), pp. 90-1; E. Franklin Frazer, *The Negro Family in the United States* (Chicago: University of Chicago Press, 1939), "In the House of the Master," pp. 3-73.

57. Bernard, *Marriage and Family*, pp. 69-70.

58. The figure is based on the one hundred city sample, N = 3,710. Matthews and Prothro report that among southern women, 68 percent of blacks and 45 percent of whites report some occupation beside housewife. See Matthews and Prothro, *Negroes in the New Southern Politics*, p. 66.

59. Reported in Bernard, *Marriage and Family*, p. 42.

60. *Ibid.*, p. 14. In assuming the double role of mother and father, the

one out of four black women who heads her household escapes the pervasive depoliticization of the traditional conception of a wife's place.

61. *Ibid.*, pp. 91, 95.

62. On this topic see "A Mother Can't Do a Man's Job," *Newsweek* (August 22, 1966): 41; Bernard, *Marriage and Family*, pp. 4-23; Charles Silberman, *Crisis in Black and White* (New York: Vintage, 1964), pp. 308-55; Abbey Lincoln, "Who Will Revere the Black Woman," in *The Black Woman*, ed. Toni Cade, pp. 80-84; Thomas F. Pettigrew, *A Profile of the Negro American* (New York: Van Nostrand Co., Inc., 1964), pp. 17-24. A most cogent statement of the problem comes from Elliot Liebow's study of black men and women in a Washington, D.C. ghetto, *Tally's Corner* (Boston: Little, Brown & Co., 1967), Chapter IV, "Husbands and Wives," pp. 103-36, and Chapter V, "Lovers and Exploiters," pp. 137-60.

63. Pat Robinson and Group, "A Historical and Critical Essay for Black Women in the Cities," in *The Black Woman*, ed. Toni Cade, p. 194.

64. Nathan and Julia Hare, "Black Women, 1970," pp. 65-68.

65. See Gwen Patton, "Black People and the Victorian Ethos," in *The Black Woman*, ed. Toni Cade, p. 147.

66. Gail Sheehy, "The Consequences of Panthermania," *New York* 3, 47 (November 23, 1970): 45ff.

67. Our results thus coincide with those of other major surveys of black political attitudes. Matthews and Prothro, *Negroes in the New Southern Politics*, found, for example, that in the South, black women are less politically active than men, especially at lower levels of education. In their subsample of southern blacks with grade school education, 37 percent of the women and 56 percent of the men participated in politics beyond just talking. William McCord and John Howard, "Negro Opinion," in *Life Styles in the Black Ghetto*, eds. McCord et al. (New York: W. W. Norton and Co., Inc., 1969), report "our results are confusing but lead, generally, to the conclusion that males and females in the Negro urban ghetto had about the same feelings," p. 91. The former study included 300 black respondents from four Southern counties. The latter is based on 144 questionnaires collected in 1967-68 among Houston blacks. Gary Marx's nationwide sample of 1,095 black men and women indicated the same general pattern of less militancy among black women than men; *Protest and Prejudice: A Study of Belief in the Black Community* (New York: Harper and Row, 1967), p. 54. The *Newsweek* studies, Brink and Harris, *Black and White* and Brink and Harris, *The Negro Revolution in America* (New York: Simon & Schuster, 1963) do not deal with the role of women in black politics.

68. The sample is nationwide and consists of 110 whites, 134 blacks, and 17 chicanas. See Note 51 for more details.

69. Perhaps some of these differences emerge from the differing socioeconomic situations of women leaders. More black women leaders than white have jobs (later analysis will show how important job holding is to

the political involvement of women), but they actually report somewhat *less* income. Employment is distinctly more tenuous for black than white women leaders. Over half experience "some" job insecurity compared to a third of whites. It seems natural that more white women than black feel they can change their lives if they want to (See Figure 6.8). Interestingly, however, black women have much higher aspirations for their own development—twice as many told us they were hoping to get more education or improve their job situations.

70. Five out of 11 persons.

71. For an excellent discussion of the evidence concerning these myths, see Suelzle, "Women in Labor," pp. 52-56.

72. Quoted in Sherrill, "That Equal Rights Amendment," p. 27. Most states, prodded by the Federal Equal Employment Opportunities Commission have already eliminated laws inconsistent with the anti-sex discrimination provisions of the Civil Rights Act.

73. *Ibid.*, p. 98.

74. Kempton, "Cutting Loose," p. 57.

75. The first quotation is from Brownmiller, "Sisterhood is powerful," p. 134; the second from Annie Gottlieb, "Female Human Beings," *The New York Times Book Review* (February 21, 1971): 27. The personal reminiscences are from Anita Lynn Micossi, "Conversion to Women's Lib," *Trans-Action* 8, 1-2 (November-December, 1970): 82-90. Other sources on the strategies of women's liberation are Miller, "Neighborhood Organizing for Liberation," Kempton, "Cutting Loose," and Hentoff, "The Curse." For one insightful study of small group political strategies, see Robert Jay Lifton, *Thought Reform and the Psychology of Totalism* (New York: W. W. Norton and Co., 1963).

76. Miller, "Neighborhood Organizing for Liberation," is an optimistic report on the utility of "consciousness raising" in the mobilization of lower class women.

77. The three quotations are from Thomas A. Johnson, "Yale Conference Studies Role of Black Women," *New York Times* (December 14, 1970); Linda J. H. LaRue, "Black Women and Women's Liberation" in *Trans-Action* 8, 1 and 2: 60; Juli Malveaux and Joyce Bulgar, "The Black Woman and Women's Liberation," notes from pamphlet commemorating the first annual Roxbury Black Cultural Festival, Boston, Mass. (February, 1971), p. 8.

78. Nathan Hare and Julia Hare, "Black Women, 1970;" see also Pat Robinson and group, "A Historical and Critical Essay," p. 194; Francis M. Beal, "Double Jeopardy: To Be Black and Female," *New Generation* 51, 4 (Fall, 1969): 23-28; "Who's Come a Long Way, Baby," *Time* (August 31, 1970): 21.

79. Each column of titles represents one multiple regression. "Level of importance," the vertical axis, is the β weight, indicating "how much change in the dependent variable is produced by a standardized change

in one of the independent variables when the others are controlled for." Hubert Blalock, *Social Statistics* (New York: McGraw Hill Co., 1960), p. 345. Factors having β weights of .10 and above are reported for the black samples. The sample is large enough so that all but one of these factors in the four regressions is significant at .05. In any case, the precise value of the β weight and its significance are reported in the Appendix for the table. The table also reports N's and the multiple correlation coefficients.

80. Variables included are: (A) Life Situation variables: *Age; Education; Income;* Length of *Residence* in the neighborhood; whether or not respondent has a *Job*, is *Married*, or is on *Welfare*; and the amount of *Job Insecurity* he experiences; (B) Personal attitudes and social involvement: Level of *Anger* at "things around here;" *Belief in Self* (whether respondent feels he could "change his life"); *Group Membership* (participation in "important community groups"); *Race Identity*; and (C) Political Attitudes: *Alienation from National Government; Alienation from Local Government; Problem Perception* (number of community problems respondent describes); Politicization (number of areas, "courts," "movies," etc. respondents believe are political); level of *Political Information.* Including many variables tends to dilute the relative impact of those variables whose hypothesized influence are the strongest, education and political information, for example, but it compensates for this loss by allowing many intriguing establishments of "no effect." Robert A. Gordon, "Issues in Multiple Regression," *The American Journal of Sociology* 73.5 (March, 1968): 592-616.

81. The syndrome of high education and low income has recurred at several points in our analysis. It characterized black as opposed to white political elites and militant ethnic group members, for example. It appears here for both black men and black women leaders, but we have emphasized the fact that for men, high education is highest on the list, and low income in the middle range, while for women the order is reversed. Having a job, level of job insecurity, and income are not highly intercorrelated in the lower class context. In this sample, the largest pairwise correlation of the three is .18.

82. See Appendix A-2 for a description of the statistical technique.

83. Gloria Steinem, "What it Would Be Like if Women Win," *Time* (August 31, 1970): 22.

84. Previous figures, similar to this one, have had ordinally ranked vertical axes. A typology is not an ordinal series, of course, but as Figure 6.11 indicates, enough attributes do show similar rankings to justify this ordering of types.

85. The average income of the middle class sample was $7,100 compared to $5,300 for the rank and file Five City sample. It was 98 percent white. Twenty-eight percent of its members had been to college compared to 7 percent of the five city sample.

86. Kay Lindsey, "Poem," in *The Black Woman*, ed. Toni Cade, p. 17.

87. Pat Robinson and Group, "A Historical and Critical Essay," p. 209.

88. Linda La Rue, "Black Liberation and Women's Lib," p. 63; see also Johnson, "Yale Conference . . ." and Eve, "Women's Liberation," *The Black Panther* (July 11, 1970): 18-19.

Bibliography

Aberbach, Joel D. Review of *Riots and Rebellion: Civil Violence in the Urban Community*. Edited by Louis H. Masotti and Don R. Bowen. Beverly Hills: Sage Publications, 1968. *American Political Science Review* 64, 1 (March, 1970): 219-20.

Aberbach, Joel D. and Walker, Jack L. "Political Trust and Racial Ideology." *American Political Science Review* 64, 4 (Dec. 1970): 1199-219.

Aiken, Michael. "Community Power and Community Mobilization." *The Annals of the American Academy of Political and Social Science* 385 (September, 1969): 76-88.

Alford, Robert R. and Scoble, Harry M. "Sources of Local Political Involvement." *American Political Science Review* 62, 4 (December, 1968): 1192-1206.

Alinsky, Saul D. *Reveille for Radicals*. New York: Random House, 1969.

Almond, Gabriel A. and Verba, Sidney. *The Civic Culture*. Boston: Little, Brown & Co., 1963.

Altshuler, Alan A. *Community Control: The Black Demand for Participation in Large American Cities*. New York: Pegasus, 1970.

Axelrod, Morris. "Urban Structure and Social Participation." *American Sociological Review* 21, 1 (February, 1956): 13-18.

Babchuk, N. and Thompson, R. "Voluntary Association Among Negroes." *American Sociological Review* 27, 5 (October, 1962): 647-655.

Banfield, Edward C. *Political Influence*. New York: The Free Press, 1961.

———. *The Unheavenly City, The Nature and Future of Our Urban Crisis*. Boston: Little, Brown & Co., 1968.

Bardolph, Richard. *The Negro Vanguard*. New York: Vintage Books, 1959.

Bardwick, Judith M. "Her Body the Battleground." *Psychology Today* 5, 9 (February, 1972): 50 ff.

Barss Reitzel & Associates. *Community Action and Institutional Change.* Prepared for the Office of Economic Opportunity (July, 1969) Bruce Jacobs, Project Director, Cambridge, Mass.

————— . *A Final Report on Phase I Data Analysis* for the Office of Economic Opportunity Contract B-99-4730 (February 3, 1969).

Barth, Ernest A. T. and Abu-Laban, Baha. "Power Structure and the Negro Sub-Community." *American Sociological Review* 24 (1959): 69-76.

Beal, Francis M. "Double Jeopardy: To Be Black and Female." *New Generation* 51, 4 (Fall, 1969): 23-28.

Berman, Joan. "Women in Cuba." In *Women, A Journal of Liberation.* Issue on Women in Revolution, 1, 4 (Summer, 1970): 10-14.

Bernard, Jessie. *Marriage and Family Among Negroes.* Englewood Cliffs: Prentice-Hall, Inc., 1966.

"Black America 1970," *Time.* Special Issue (April 6, 1970): 13ff.

Blalock, Hubert M. Jr. *Social Statistics.* New York: McGraw Hill Co., 1960.

Boesel, David; Berk, Richard; Graves, W. Eugene; Edison, B; and Rossi, Peter H. "White Institutions and Black Rage." *Trans-Action* 6, 5 (March, 1969): 24-31.

Bogue, Donald J.; Misra, Bhaskar D.; and Dandekar, D. P., "A New Estimate of the Negro Population and Negro Vital Rates in the United States, 1930-1960," *Demography* 1, 1 (1964).

Brager, George. *Organizing the Unaffiliated in a Low Income Area.* New York: The Free Press, 1962.

Brink Wm. and Harris, Louis. *Black and White.* New York: Simon & Schuster, 1963.

————— . *The Negro Revolution in America.* New York: Simon & Schuster, 1963.

Brown, Claude. *Manchild in the Promised Land.* New York: Signet Books, 1965.

Brown, Sam W. *Store-Front Organizing.* New York: Pyramid, 1972.

Brownmiller, Susan. "Sisterhood is Powerful." *New York Times Sunday Magazine* (March 15, 1970): 27ff.

Bunch-Weeks, Charlotte. "Asian Women in Revolution." In *Women, a Journal of Liberation.* Issue on Women in Revolution, 1, 4 (Summer, 1970): 2-9.

Burgess, M. Elaine. *Negro Leadership in a Southern City.* Durham: University of North Carolina Press, 1962.

Campbell, Angus; Converse, Philip E; Miller, Warren E; and Stokes, Donald E., *The American Voter.* New York: John Wiley and Sons, Inc., 1964.

Campbell, Angus. *The Passive Citizen.* Boston: Allyn & Bacon, Inc., 1966, pp. 400-13.

Campbell, Angus and Schuman, Howard. *Racial Attitudes in 15 American Cities.* Ann Arbor, Michigan: The Survey Research Center, the University of Michigan, 1968.

Cataldo, Everett and Kellstedt, Lyman. "Conceptualizing and Measuring Political Involvement over Time: A Study of Buffalo's Urban Poor." Paper for the Joint Statistical Meetings, August 20, 1968.

Cater, Douglas. *The Fourth Branch of Government.* New York: Vintage Books, 1959.

Clark, Joanna. *Motherhood.* New York: New American Library Inc., 1970, pp. 63-72.

Clark, Kenneth. "Alternatives to Urban Public Schools." In *The Schoolhouse in the City,* edited by Alvin Toffler, pp. 136-42. New York: Praeger, 1968, pp. 136-42.

————. *Dark Ghetto.* New York: Harper Torchbooks, 1965.

Cleaver, Eldridge. *Soul on Ice.* New York: Dell Publishing Co., 1968.

Cobb, Nathan. "How Boston's Spanish Speaking Hope to Emerge." *The Boston Sunday Globe* (December 20, 1970): A-3.

Cohen, David. "The Price of Community Control." *Commentary* (July, 1969): 23-30.

Coleman, James S. et al. "Equality in Educational Opportunity." U.S. Office of Education, 1966.

Connelly, Gordon M. and Field, Harry H. "The Non-Voter—Who He Is, What He Thinks." *Public Opinion Quarterly* 8 (Summer, 1944): 175-87.

Converse, Philip E. "The Nature of Belief Systems in Mass Publics." In *Ideology and Discontent,* edited by David E. Apter. Glencoe: The Free Press, 1964.

Crain, Robert C. *The Politics of School Desegregation: Comparative Case Studies of Community Structure and Policy Making.* Chicago: Aldine, 1968.

Cruse, Harold. *"The Fire This Time."* A review of Eldridge Cleaver *Post Prison Speeches and Writings.* Edited by Robert Sheer. *New York Review* (May 8, 1969): 13-18.

Dahl, Robert A. "The City in the Future of Democracy." *American Political Science Review* 61 (December, 1967): 953-70.

Dahl, Robert. *Who Governs: Democracy and Power in an American City.* New Haven: Yale University Press, 1961.

Dennison, George. *The Lives of Children.* Westminster, Maryland: Random House, 1969.

Delbecq, Andre L. and Kaplan, Sydney J. *The Myth of the Indigenous Community Leader.* Institute for Research on Poverty, reprint #18, pp. 25.

deRham, Edith. *The Love Fraud, A Direct Attack on the Staggering Waste of Education and Talent Among American Women.* New York: Pegasus, 1965.

Deutsch, Karl W. *Nationalism and Social Communication.* Cambridge, Mass.: The M.I.T. Press, 1953.

————. *The Nerves of Government.* New York: The Free Press, 1963.

Dobert, Margarita. "Liberation and the Women of Guinea." From *Africa Report* (October, 1970): 26-28.

Dohrenwend, Bruce P. *Urban Leadership and the Appraisal of Abnormal Behavior.* New York: Simon & Schuster, 1963, pp. 259-66.

Donovan, John C. *The Politics of Poverty.* New York: Western Publishing Co., Inc., 1967.

Duhl, Leonard J., ed. *The Urban Condition.* New York: Simon & Schuster, 1963.

Dunbar, Leslie W. The Southern Regional Council. *The Annals of the American Academy of Political and Social Science* 357 (January, 1965): 108-112.

Dunn, Erica and Klein, Judy. "Women in the Russian Revolution." *Women, A Journal of Liberation* 1, 4 (Summer, 1970): 22-26.

Dye, Thomas R. and Ziegler, L. Harmon. *The Irony of Democracy.* Belmont, California: Wadsworth Publishing Co., 1970.

Eldersveld, Samuel J. *Political Parties: A Behavioral Analysis.* Chicago: Rand McNally & Co., 1964.

Eley, Lynn W. "Fair Housing Laws—Unfair Housing Practices." *Trans-Action* (June, 1969): 56-61.

Ellis, Havelock. *Man and Woman.* Boston: Houghton Mifflin, 1929.

Essien-Udom, E. U. *Black Nationalism, A Search For Identity in America.* New York: Dell, 1964.

Eve. "Women's Liberation." *The Black Panther,* Sat., July 11, 1970, pp. 18-19.

Eyestone, Robert and Eulau, Heinz. "City Councils and Policy Outcomes: Developmental Profiles." In James Q. Wilson ed. *City Politics and Public Policy.* New York: John Wiley & Sons, Inc., 1968, pp. 37-65.

Farrell, Gregory R. "Resources for Transforming the Ghetto." In *The Schoolhouse in the City,* edited by Alvin Toffler, pp. 86-96. New York: Praeger, 1968.

Featherstone, Joseph. "The Primary School Revolution in Britain." Pitman/New Republic Reprint, Pitman Publishing Corp., 6 East 43rd St., N.Y., N.Y. 10017. Reprinted from *New Republic,* (August 10, Sept. 2 and Sept. 9, 1967).

Federal Role in Urban Affairs. Hearings before the Subcommittee on Executive Reorganization of the Committee on Government Operations. U.S. Senate, 89th Congress 2nd Session, August 31-Sept. 1, 1966, Part 6.

Fendrich, James and Pearson, Michael. "Black Veterans Return." *Trans-Action,* 7, 5 (March, 1970): 32-37.

Ferman, Louis A., special editor "Evaluating The War on Poverty." *The Annals of the American Academy of Political & Social Science* 385 (September, 1969).

Finrow, Jerry. "Community Involvement, Pros and Cons." In *Cities Fit To Live In,* edited by Walter McQuade, pp. 117-22. New York: Collier-Macmillan, 1971.

Frazier, E. Franklin. *The Negro Family in the United States.* Chicago: University of Chicago Press, 1939.

Freeman, Jo. "Growing Up Girlish." *Trans-Action,* 8, 1 & 2 (Nov.-Dec., 1970): 36-43.

Friedan, Betty. *The Feminine Mystique.* New York: Harper Colophon Books, 1962.

Friedberg, Bernard. "Houston and the TSO Riot." In *Life Styles in the Black Ghetto,* edited by William McCord, John Howard, Bernard Friedberg and Edwin Marwood, pp. 36-51. New York: W. W. Norton and Co., Inc., 1969.

"The Fugitive," *Time.* (August 31, 1970) pp. 14.

Gans, Herbert. *The Urban Villagers, Group and Class in the Life of Italian-Americans.* New York: The Free Press, 1962.

Globe Newspaper Co. "80 Percent in State Back Equal Jobs, Pay for Women." *The Boston Sunday Globe* (Sun., March 20, 1971).

Gordon, Linda. "Speculation on Women's Liberation in Cuba." *Women, A Journal of Liberation* 1, 4 (Summer, 1970): 14-15.

Gordon, Robert A. "Issues in Multiple Regression." *The American Journal of Sociology* 73, 5 (March, 1968): 592-616.

Gottlieb, Annie. "Female Human Beings." *The New York Times Book Review* (February 21, 1971): 23 ff.

Grant, Daniel R. and Nixon, H. C. *State and Local Government in America.* Boston: Allyn and Bacon, 1963.

Graves, Ben E. "The Decaying Schoolhouse." In *The Schoolhouse in the City,* edited by Alvin Toffler, pp. 61-66. New York: Praeger, 1968.

Greenberg, Stanley B., Project Director *Mobilizing Poor Communities.* Prepared for the Office of Economic Opportunity by Barss Reitzel & Associates, Inc., Cambridge, Mass. (August, 1970).

Greenstein, Fred I. *The American Party System and The American People.* Englewood Cliffs: Prentice-Hall, 1963.

————— . *Sex-Related Political Differences in Childhood.* Boston: Houghton Mifflin Co., 1963, pp. 244-54.

Greenstone, J. David and Peterson, Paul E. "Reformers, Machines and the War on Poverty." In *City Politics and Public Policy,* edited by James Q. Wilson, pp. 267-292. New York: John Wiley and Sons, Inc., 1968.

Grosser, Charles F. *Helping Youth: A Study of Six Community Organization Programs.* U.S. Dept. of H.E.W. Social and Rehabilitation Service, Office of Juvenile Delinquency and Youth Development.

Havighurst, Robert J. "Differing Needs for Social Renewal." In *The Schoolhouse in the City,* edited by Alvin Toffler, pp. 47-60. New York: Praeger, 1968.

Hare, Nathan and Hare, Julia. "Black Women, 1970" *Trans-Action,* 8. 1 & 2 (Nov.-Dec., 1970): 65-68.

Hartman, Elizabeth L.; Issacson, H. Lawrence; and Turgell, Cynthia M. "Public Reaction to Public Opinion Surveying." *Public Opinion Quarterly* 32, 2 (Summer, 1968).

Hentoff, Margot. "The Curse." *The New York Review of Books* 12, 1 (January 16, 1969): 3.

"Here Come the Ethnics," *Newsweek,* (April 3, 1972): 86.

Hill, Herbert. "Racial Inequality in Employment: The Patterns of Discrimination," in "The Negro Protest," Arnold H. Rose, Special Editor, *The Annals of the American Academy of Political and Social Science* 357 (January, 1965): 30-47.

Hill, Richard J. and Hall, Nason E. "A Note on Rapport and the Quality of Interview Data," *Southwest Social Science Quarterly* 44, 3 (December, 1963): 32-35.

Holt, John. *How Children Learn.* New York: Pitman, 1967.

Howard, John and McCord, William. "Watts: the Revolt and After." In *Life Styles in the Black Ghetto,* edited by William McCord, John Howard, Bernard Friedberg and Edwin Hardwood, pp. 52-72. New York: W. W. Norton and Co., Inc., 1969.

Howe, Harold II. "The City as Teacher," In *The Schoolhouse in the City,* edited by Alvin Toffler, pp. 9-25. New York: Praeger, 1968.

Hunter, Floyd. *Community Power Structure.* Chapel Hill: University of North Carolina Press, 1953.

Hunt, J. McVicker. "Black Genes—White Environment," *Trans-Action* 6, 7 (June, 1969): 12-22.

Inkeles, Alex. "Participant Citizenship in Six Developing Countries." *The American Political Science Review* 63, 4 (December, 1969): 1120-1141.

Institute of Public Administration, Study Group on Housing and Neighborhood Improvement, City of New York, Edward J. Logue, Chrm. "Harlem Attitude Survey" *Federal Role in Urban Affairs.* Hearings Before the Subcommittee on Executive Reorganization of the Committee on Government Operations, U.S. Senate, 89th Congress, 2nd Session, Aug. 31, Sept. 1, 1966 Part 6. Exhibit 125, pp. 1409-23.

Interview with ACLU lawyer involved as advocate lawyer in Newark, New Jersey, Central Ward ghetto politics. April, 1968.

"In Tunisia, It's Population Explosion vs. Women's Lib." *New York Times,* (Jan. 9, 1971).

Jackson, George. *Soledad Brother, The Prison Letters of George Jackson.* New York: Bantam Books, 1970.

Jacobs, Bruce. Project Director *Community Action and Urban Institutional Change.* A National Evaluation of the Community Action Program Prepared for the Office of Economic Opportunity by Barss, Reitzel and Associates, Inc., Cambridge, Mass. (Aug., 1970).

——— . "The Poverty Program and Institutional Change: Opinions of Leaders of the Poor." In *Community Action and Urban Institutional Change.* A National Evaluation of the Community Action Program. Prepared for the Office of Economic

Opportunity by Barss Reitzel and Associates, Cambridge, Mass. (August, 1970) pp. 231-278.

Jencks, Christopher. "Private Schools for Black Children." *New York Times Magazine* (Nov. 3, 1968): 29ff.

Jennings, Kent. *Community Influentials*. New York: The Free Press of Glencoe, 1964.

Johnson, Thomas A. "Yale Conference Studies Role of Black Women." *New York Times* (Mon., Dec. 14, 1970).

Joseph, Stephen M. *The Me Nobody Knows*. New York: Avon, 1969.

Kempton, Sally. "Cutting Loose." *Esquire* (July, 1970): 53-57.

Key, V. O. Jr. *Public Opinion and American Democracy*. New York: Alfred A. Knopf, 1964.

_____. *Southern Politics*. New York: Vintage Books, 1949.

Killian, Lewis. *The Impossible Revolution? Black Power and the American Dream*. New York: Random House, 1968.

_____. and Grigg, Charles. *Racial Crisis in America, Leadership in Conflict*. Englewood Cliffs: Prentice-Hall, 1964.

Kohl, Herbert R. *The Open Classroom*. Westminister, Maryland: Random House, 1969.

Kotler, Milton. "Making Local Government Truly Local." *Trans-Action* 4, 10 (Oct., 1967): 49-50.

_____. *Neighborhood Government: The Local Foundations of Political Life*. Indianapolis: The Bobbs-Merrill Co., 1969.

Kraft, John F. "Attitudes of Negroes in Various Cities," in *Federal Role in Urban Affairs*. Hearings Before the Subcommittee on Executive Reorganization of the Committee on Government Operations, U.S. Senate, 89th Congress, 2nd Session Aug. 31, Sept. 1, 1966, Part 6, pp. 1383-1408.

Kramer, Ralph M. *Participation of the Poor: Comparative Community Case Studies in the War on Poverty*. Englewood Cliffs, N.J.: Prentice-Hall, 1969.

Ladd, Everett Carll Jr. *Negro Political Leadership in the South*. New York: Atheneum, 1969.

Ladner, Joyce. "What'Black Power' Means to Negroes in Mississippi." *Trans-Action* 5, 1 (Nov., 1967): 7-15.

Lane, Robert E. *Political Ideology: Why the American Common Man Believes What He Does.* New York: The Free Press of Glencoe, 1962.

———. *Political Life.* New York: The Free Press, 1959.

Lane, Robert E. and Sears, David O. *Public Opinion.* Englewood Cliffs: Prentice-Hall, Inc., 1964.

LaRue, Linda J. M. "Black Liberation and Women's Lib." *Trans-Action* 8, 1 & 2 (Nov., Dec., 1970): 59-64.

Laue, James H. "The Changing Character of Negro Protest." In "The Negro Protest," special editor, Arnold M. Rose, *The Annals of the American Academy of Political and Social Science* 357 (Jan., 1965): 119-26.

Lazarsfeld, Paul F.; Berelson, Bernard; and Gaudet, Hazel. *The People's Choice.* New York: Columbia University Press, 1944.

Leary, Mary Ellen. "The Uproar over Cleaver." *The New Republic* (Nov. 30, 1968): 21-24.

Levitan, Sar. *The Great Society's Poor Law.* Baltimore: The Johns Hopkins Press.

Lemberg Center for the Study of Violence. "Six City Study—A Survey of Racial Attitudes in Six Northern Cities—Preliminary Findings." Exhibit 273 Hearings Before the Subcommittee on Executive Reorganization of the Committee on Government Operations U.S. Senate, 90th Congress 1st Session (June 28, 1967): 4309-17.

Lerner, Daniel. *The Passing of Traditional Society.* Glencoe: The Free Press, 1958.

Lichtenstein, Grace. "Farbstein Faces a Strong Challenge by Bella Abzug." *New York Times* (June 9, 1970), p. 2.

Liebow, Elliot. "No Man can Live with the Terrible Knowledge That he is not Needed." *New York Times Magazine* (April 5, 1970): 28ff.

———. *Tally's Corner.* Boston: Little, Brown & Co., 1967.

Lifton, Robert Jay. *Thought Reform and the Psychology of Totalism.* New York: W. W. Norton & Co., 1963.

Lincoln, Abbey. "Who Will Revere the Black Woman." In *The Black Woman: An Anthology,* edited by Toni Cade, New York: New American Library, Inc., 1970, pp. 80-84.

Lindbloom, Charles. *The Intelligence of Democracy.* New York: The Free Press, 1965.

Lindsey, Kay. "Poem." In *The Black Woman,* edited by Toni Cade. New York: Signet, 1970.

Lipset, Seymour Martin. *Political Man: The Social Bases of Politics.* New York: Anchor Books, 1963.

Lipsky, Michael. "Protest as a Political Resource." *American Political Science Review* (Dec., 1968): 1144-58.

Lockard, Duane. *New England State Politics.* Princeton: Princeton University Press, 1959.

———. *The Politics of State and Local Government.* New York: The Macmillan Co., 1963.

Long, Luman H., ed. *The World Almanac.* New York: Newspaper Enterprise Associates, Inc., 1971.

Long, Norton E. "Local Government and Renewal Politics." In *Urban Renewal: The Record and the Controversy,* edited by James Q. Wilson, pp. 422-34. Cambridge: The M.I.T. Press, 1966.

Lowi, Theodore. "American Business, Public Policy, Case Studies and Political Theory." *World Politics* 16, (July, 1964): 677-715.

Lurie, Ellen. *How to Change the Schools.* Westminster, Maryland: Random House, 1970.

Magnum, Garth. "The Why, How and Whence of Manpower Programs," *The Annals of the American Academy of Political and Social Science* 385 (Sept., 1969): 52-60.

Malcom X. *The Autobiography of Malcom X.* New York: Grove Press, 1964.

Malveaux, Juli and Bulgar, Joyce. "The Black Woman and Women's Liberation." Notes from pamphlet on the First Roxbury Black Cultural Festival, Boston, Mass. (Feb., 1971), p. 8ff.

March, James G. "Husband-Wife Interaction Over Political Issues." *Public Opinion Quarterly* 17 (1953-54): 461-70.

Marx, Gary T. *Protest and Prejudice: A Study of Belief in the Black Community.* New York: Harper & Row, 1967.

Matthews, Donald R. and Prothro, James W. *Negroes and the New Southern Politics.* New York: Harcourt, Brace and World, Inc., 1966.

Matthews, Donald R. *U.S. Senators and Their World.* New York: Vintage Books, 1960.

McCord, William and Howard, John. "Negro Opinions." In *Life Styles in the Black Ghetto,* edited by William McCord, John Howard, Bernard Friedberg and Edwin Harwood, pp. 78-104. New York: W. W. Norton and Co., Inc., 1969.

McCord, William. "Taking the Pulse of the Ghetto: A Note on Methods." In *Life Styles in the Black Ghetto,* edited by William McCord, John Howard, Bernard Friedberg and Edwin Harwood, pp. 73-77. New York: W. W. Norton and Co., Inc., 1969.

Metzner, Eric L. "A Convention of Panthers." *The Phoenix* (Dec. 8, 1970): 1ff.

Micossi, Anita Lynn. "Conversion to Women's Lib." *Trans-Action* 8, 1 & 2 (Nov., Dec., 1970): 82-90.

Miller, Judy. "Neighborhood Organizing for Liberation." *Women: A Journal of Liberation* 1, 2 (Winter, 1970): 48-49.

Mollenkopf, John. "Community Political Activity and Institutional Change," in *Community Action and Urban Institutional Change,* Bruce Jacobs, Project Director, Prepared for the Office of Economic Opportunity by Barss Reitzel & Associates, Cambridge, Mass., 1970, pp. 79-114.

Moore, Alexander. *Realities of the Urban Classroom.* New York: Doubleday & Co., 1967.

Morsell, John A. "The National Association for the Advancement of Colored People and Its Strategy." In "The Negro Protest," Arnold M. Rose, special editor, *The Annals of the American Academy of Political and Social Science* 357 (Jan., 1965): 97-101.

"A Mother Can't Do a Man's Job." *Newsweek* (August 22, 1966): 41-4.

Moynihan, Daniel P. "The Professors and the Poor." In *On Understanding Poverty*, edited by Daniel P. Moynihan, pp. 3-35. New York: Basic Books, 1968.

National Opinion Research Center. "Community Political Leader, Parent Teacher Association, Employer, and Social Service Agency Director Assignment" Survey 5026 (January, 1969) 9pp.

Nie, Norman H.; Powell, G. Bingham Jr.; and Prewitt, Kenneth. "Social Structure and Political Parties: Developmental Relationships, II." *American Political Science Review* 63, 3 (September, 1969): 808-832.

"OEO and the Riots—A Summary." Hearings Before the Subcommittee on Executive Reorganization of the Committee on Government Operations, U.S. Senate, 90th Congress, 1st Session (June 28, 1967): 4320-27.

Office of Economic Opportunity, *Women in the War on Poverty.* U.S. Government Printing Office 0-348-671, 1969.

Opinion Research Corporation, *White and Negro Attitudes Towards Race Related Issues and Activities.* A CBS News Public Opinion Survey, Princeton, 1968.

Oppenheimer, Martin and Lakey, George. *A Manual for Direct Action.* Chicago: Quadrangle Books, 1964.

Palley, Marian Lief; Russo, Robert; and Scott, Edward. "Subcommunity Leadership in a Black Ghetto, a Study of Newark, New Jersey." *Urban Affairs Quarterly* (March, 1970): 291-312.

Parenti, Michael. "Ethnic Politics and the Persistence of Ethnic Identification." *The American Political Science Review* 61, 3 (September, 1967): 716-26.

Parsons, Talcott. "Full Citizenship for the Negro American: A Sociological Problem." In *The Negro American*, edited by Talcott Parsons and Kenneth B. Clark. Boston: The Beacon Press, 1965.

Patton, Gwen. "Black People and the Victorian Ethos." In *The Black Woman*, edited by Toni Cade, pp. 143-148. New York: Signet, 1970.

Perlman, Janice. *The Fate of Migrants in Rio's Favelas, The Myth of Marginality.* Ph.D. Thesis, Massachusetts Institute of Technology, August, 1971.

Pettigrew, Thomas F. *A Profile of the Negro American.* New York: D. Van Nostrand Co., Inc., 1964.

"The Politics of Protest." *Trans-Action* editors, 7, 4 (Feb. 1970):11.

Polsby, Nelson. *Community Power and Political Theory.* New Haven: Yale University Press, 1963.

Pool, Ithiel de Sola; Abelson, Robert P.; and Popkin, Samuel. *Candidates, Issues and Strategies.* Cambridge, Mass.: M.I.T. Press, 1964.

Portola Institute. *The Last Whole Earth Catalogue.* New York: Random House, 1971.

Postman, Neil and Weingartner, Charles. *Teaching as a Subversive Activity.* New York: Delta Books, 1969.

Poston, Richard W. "Comparative Community Organization." In *The Urban Condition,* edited by Leonard Duhl, pp. 311-18. New York: Simon & Schuster, 1969.

Prouty, Winston. *Prouty Survey Report,* Part II, (Unpublished mimeo).

Pye, Lucian W. and Verba, Sidney. *Political Culture and Political Development.* Princeton: Princeton University Press, 1965.

Racz, Elizabeth. "The Women's Rights Movement in the French Revolution." In *Women a Journal of Liberation.* Issue on Women in Revolution. 1:4 (Summer, 1970): 28ff.

Rich, Marvin. "The Congress of Racial Equality and Its Strategy." In "The Negro Protest." Arnold Rose, special editor, *The Annals of the American Academy of Political and Social Science* 357 (Jan., 1965): 113-118.

Riesman, David. "Orbits of Tolerance, Interviews, and Elites." *Public Opinion Quarterly* 20 (1956): 49-73.

Riordon, William L. *Plunkitt of Tammany Hall.* New York: E. P. Dutton & Co., 1963.

Robins, Lee N. "The Reluctant Respondent." *Public Opinion Quarterly* 27, 2 (Summer, 1963): 276-86.

Robinson, Pat and Group. "A Historical and Critical Essay for Black Women in the Cities." In *The Black Woman*, edited by Toni Cade, pp. 198-210. New York: Signet, 1970.

_____ . "On the Position of Poor Black Women in this Country." From *Poor Black Women's Study Papers* by Poor Black Women of Mount Vernon, New York. In *The Black Woman*, edited by Toni Cade, pp. 194-197. New York: Signet, 1970.

Rogers, David. *110 Livingston Street, Politics and Bureaucracy in the New York City School System*. New York: Vintage Books, 1969.

Rose, Arnold M. Special editor. "The Negro Protest." *The Annals of the American Academy of Political and Social Science* 357 (Jan., 1965).

Rosenberg, Milton J. "Attitude Change and Foreign Policy in the Cold War Era." In *Domestic Sources of Foreign Policy*, edited by James N. Rosenau. New York: The Free Press, 1967.

Rosenberg, Milton J. "Images in Relation to the Policy Process, American Public Opinions on Cold War Issues." In *International Behavior: A Socio-Psychological Analysis*, edited by Herbert C. Kehnan. New York: Holt, Rinehart and Winston, 1965.

Rossi, Peter H. and Crain, Robert. "The NORC Permanent Community Sample." *Public Opinion Quarterly* 32, 2 (Summer, 1968): 261-72.

Roxbury Black Cultural Festival. "Notes" Boston, Mass., Feb., 1971.

Royal Institute of British Architects. "Building for Education." *Royal Institute of British Architects Journal* (August, 1968): 349-381.

Russett, Bruce M.; Alker, Hayward R. Jr.; Deutsch, Karl W.; and Lasswell, Harold D. *World Handbook of Political and Social Indicators*. New Haven, Conn.: Yale University Press, 1964.

Ryan, Edward J. "Personal Identity in an Urban Slum." In *The Urban Condition*, edited by Leonard J. Duhl, pp. 135-149. New York: Simon & Schuster, 1963.

Seale, Bobby. *Seize the Time: The Story of the Black Panther Party and Huey P. Newton*. New York: Random House, 1968.

Sheehy, Gail. "Black Against Black: The Agony of Panthermania." *New York,* 3, 46 (Nov., 1970): 38ff.

——. "The Consequences of Panthermania." *New York* 3, 47 (Nov. 23, 1970): 45ff.

Shepard, Samuel Jr. "The Disadvantaged Child." In *The School-house in the City,* edited by Alvin Toffler, pp. 77-85. New York: Praeger, 1968.

Sherrill, Robert. "That Equal Rights Amendment—What, Exactly, Does it Mean." *New York Times Magazine* (September 20, 1970): 25ff.

Shibutani, Tamotsu. *Society and Personality.* Englewood Cliffs: Prentice-Hall, 1961.

Shipler, David K. "Negro Legislator from South Rejects Tactics of Some Blacks." *New York Times* (Aug. 29, 1970): 11.

Sigel, Roberta S. "Citizen Committees—Advice vs. Consent." *Trans-Action* 4, 6 (May, 1967): 47-52.

Silberman, Charles E. *Crisis in Black and White.* New York: Vintage Books, 1964.

Sindler, Allan P. "Protest Against the Political Status of the Negro." In "The Negro Protest," Arnold Rose, special editor. *The Annals of the American Academy of Political and Social Science* Vol. 357, (Jan., 1965), pp. 48-54.

Skolnick, Jerome H. *The Politics of Protest.* A Report Submitted to Jerome H. Skolnick, Director Task Force on Violent Aspects of Protest and Confrontation of the National Commission on the Causes and Prevention of Violence. New York: Ballantine Books, 1969.

"SNCC-Black Women's Liberation." In *Women: A Journal of Liberation* 1, 2 (Winter 1970): 76-77.

Snyder, Eloise C. "Sex Role Differentials and Juror Decisions." *Sociology and Social Research* (July, 1971): 85-93.

Sorauf, Frank J. *Party Politics in America.* Boston: Little, Brown & Co., 1968.

Spence, John D. "Phase I vs. Phase II: A Comparison of Survey Methodologies Utilized in the 50 City CAP Evaluation." In

National Evaluation of Community Action Programs, Report No. 2. Barss Reitzel and Associates, (May, 1970).

Starr, Emily S. "CAP Impact on Institutions: Reports from Institutional Leaders." In *National Evaluation of Community Action Programs,* Barss Reitzel and Associaties, Inc., Report No. 2 Cambridge, Mass. (May, 1970), pp. 1-36.

Steel, Ronald. "Letter from Oakland: The Panthers." *The New York Review* (September 11, 1969): 14-24.

Steinem, Gloria. "What it Would be Like if Women Win." *Time* (August 31, 1970): 22-23.

Steiner, Stan. *La Raza, The Mexican Americans.* New York: Harper & Row, 1969.

Suelzle, Marijean. "Women in Labor." *Trans-Actions* 8, 1 & 2 (Nov.-Dec., 1970): 50-58.

Summers, Gene F. and Hammonds, Andre D. "Effects of Racial Characteristics of Investigator on Self Enumeration Responses to Negro Prejudice Scale." *Social Forces* 44, 4 (June, 1966): 515-18.

The National Advisory Commission on Civil Disorders, Otto Kerner, Chairman, *Supplemental Studies for the National Advisory Commission on Civil Disorders.* Washington: U.S. Government Printing Office, 1968.

The O.M. Collective. *The Organizer's Manual.* New York: Bantam, 1971.

Thompson, Daniel C. *The Negro Leadership Class.* (Englewood Cliffs, N.J.: Prentice-Hall, 1963).

———. "The Rise of Negro Protest." In "The Negro Protest," edited by Arnold M. Rose, special editor. *The Annals of the American Academy of Political and Social Science* 357 (January, 1965): 18-29.

Thomas, Piri. *Down These Mean Streets.* New York: Signet Books, 1968.

Tomlinson, T. M. and Tenhouten, Diana L. *Los Angeles Riot Study Method: Negro Reaction Survey.* Los Angeles: Institute of Government and Public Affairs, 1967.

Valentine, Charles A. *Culture and Poverty.* Chicago: University of Chicago Press, 1968.

Vidich, Arthur J. and Bensman, Joseph. *Small Town in Mass Society.* New York: Doubleday & Co., Inc., 1960.

Ward, Robert E. "Japan, The Continuity of Modernization," In *Political Culture and Political Development,* edited by Lucian Pye and Sidney Verba, pp. 27-83. Princeton: Princeton University Press, 1965.

Weiner, Myron. "India: Two Political Cultures." In *Political Culture and Political Development,* edited by Lucian Pye and Sidney Verba, pp. 119-244. Princeton: Princeton University Press, 1965.

Weller, Jack E. *Yesterday's People: Life in Contemporary Appalachia.* Lexington: University of Kentucky Press, 1966.

White, Jean M. "Census Missed One in Ten Negroes: Federal Planning Seen Periled." *Washington Post* (June 23, 1967): 7.

"Who's Come A Long Way, Baby." *Time* (Aug. 31, 1970): 16-23.

Wilcox, Preston R. "The Community Centered School." In *The Schoolhouse in the City,* edited by Alvin Toffler, pp. 97-109. New York: Praeger, 1968.

Williams, Oliver P. and Adrian, Charles R. "City Councils and Policy Outcomes: Developmental Profiles." In *City Politics and Public Policy,* edited by James Q. Wilson, pp. 37-66. New York: John Wiley and Sons, Inc., 1968.

Williams, J. Allen Jr. "Interviewer Role Performance: A Further Note on Bias in the Information Interview." *Public Opinion Quarterly* 32, 2 (Summer, 1968): 287-94.

Wilson, James Q. Review of *Bureaucracy and Participation: Political Culture in Four Wisconsin Cities,* Robert R. Alford. Chicago: Rand McNally & Co., 1969, *American Political Science Review* 64, 1 (March, 1969): 198-200.

———. *City Politics and Public Policy.* New York: John Wiley and Sons, Inc., 1968.

———. "The Negro in Politics." In *The Negro American,* edited by Talcott Parsons and Kenneth B. Clark, pp. 423-447. Boston: The Beacon Press, 1965.

————. *Negro Politics.* New York: The Free Press, 1960.

————. ed. *Urban Renewal: The Record and the Controversy.* Cambridge: The M.I.T. Press, 1966.

Wolfinger, Raymond. "The Development and Persistence of Ethnic Voting." *American Political Science Review* 59, 4 (December, 1965): 896-908.

Wood, Robert C. *Suburbia: Its People and Their Politics.* Boston: Houghton Mifflin Co., 1958.

Wright, C. and Hyman, H. "Voluntary Association Memberships of American Adults: Evidence from National Sample Surveys." *American Sociological Review* 23, 3 (June, 1958): 284-94.

Zinn, Howard. *SNCC, The New Abolitionist.* Boston: Beacon Press, 1964.

Zolberg, Aristide R. *Creating Political Order, The Party-States of West Africa.* Chicago: Rand McNally & Co., 1966.